Teachers and Politics in France

✠ ✠

Teachers and Politics in France

A PRESSURE GROUP STUDY
OF THE FEDERATION
DE L'EDUCATION NATIONALE

JAMES M. CLARK

SYRACUSE UNIVERSITY PRESS

✠ ✠

Aw

Manufactured in the
United States of America

For My Mother and Father

Preface

In France public school teachers are held in high esteem. Not only are they respected as guardians of the rich cultural heritage that is the pride of France, but they are also regarded as notables in the village and worthy citizens in the city. As missionaries for reason, progress, and democracy, they have traditionally been sturdy pillars of the Republic.

Moreover, since the earliest days of the Third Republic and even before, teachers in France have been drawn to politics. Their high prestige, their education, their knowledge of the past, and their responsibility for teaching the civic virtues all dispose them to political participation. Teachers in provincial France become town clerks. Teachers throughout the country join and contribute to the support of political parties. Many have run for Parliament, and some have been elected. A few have attained the office of Prime Minister. Teachers as individuals have played no small part in French politics.

More important, however, is the roll that teachers as an organized body play in the political process. United in a nation-wide federation, the teachers bring their weight to bear on issues requiring government decisions. In a field of giant interest groups seeking to influence policy, the organized teachers stand out as a political force wielding influence out of all proportion to their relatively small numbers.

In this study the concepts and methods of pressure group analysis have been applied to the principal teachers' organization in France, the Fédération de l'Education Nationale (FEN). The history, aims, structure, cohesion, and methods of the Federation have been described, and FEN action is illustrated and interpreted in two case studies—Chapters VI and VII. Certain conclusions have been drawn about the political importance and effectiveness of the organized teachers.

The author is indebted to many persons, both here and abroad, who gave generously of their time and knowledge to lead him safely (it is hoped) around the pitfalls and through the intricacies of French politics. The assistance of the FEN leaders and their staff was particularly important and gratifying. Others whom the author would like to cite in particular are: M. Jean Touchard, secretary general, and M. René Rémond, director of studies and research, both of the Fondation Nationale des Sciences Politiques; Senator Jean Berthoin, former Minister of Education; M. François Goguel, secretary general of the French Senate; and M. André Bianconi of the Centre National de la Recherche Scientifique. Valuable suggestions were made by Professors Samuel J. Eldersveld, Robert E. Ward, Samuel H. Barnes, and Alfred C. Jefferson, all of the faculty of the University of Michigan. A special expression of gratitude goes to Professor Roy Pierce of the Department of Political Science in the University of Michigan for the assistance, encouragement, and advice which he generously supplied at all stages of the task. (Naturally I bear full responsibility for any errors of fact or judgment which this work may contain.) My wife who patiently typed several revisions of the manuscript and who shared my joys and frustrations throughout deserves a public acknowledgment of gratitude greater than can be expressed by words at my command; this statement will therefore have to do.

Documentary research and interviews in France for this study were made possible by a University of Michigan Rackham pre-doctoral fellowship for the academic year 1959–60. Of great assistance were the staffs of the Centre de Documentation de la Fondation Nationale des Sciences Politiques; the Centre de Documentation de l'Institut Pédagogique National; the Bibliothèque Nationale; the General Library of the University of Michigan; and the Raymond H. Fogler Library of the University of Maine. The names of some persons interviewed have been omitted to protect their anonymity.

JAMES M. CLARK

Orono, Maine
September 27, 1966

Contents

TABLES

FIGURES

List of Abbreviations

APEL	Association des Parents d'Elèves de l'Enseignement Libre
APLE	Association Parlementaire pour la Liberté de l'Enseignement
CFTC	Confédération Française des Travailleurs Chrétiens
CGT	Confédération Générale du Travail
CGT-FO	Confédération Générale du Travail—Force Ouvrière
CGTU	Confédération Générale du Travail Unitaire
CNAL	Comité National d'Action Laïque
CNDL	Comité National de Défense Laïque
E.L.	*L'Ecole Libératrice*
E.P.	*L'Enseignement Public*
FEN	Fédération de l'Education Nationale
FGAF	Fédération Générale Autonome des Fonctionnaires
FGE	Fédération Générale de l'Enseignement
FGF-FO	Fédération Générale des Fonctionnaires—Force Ouvrière
FMEL	Fédération des Syndicats des Membres de l'Enseignement Laïque
FNSI	Fédération Nationale des Syndicats d'Instituteurs
J.O.	*Journal Officiel*
MRP	Mouvement Républicain Populaire
OAS	Organisation Armée Secrète
RGR	Rassemblement des Gauches Républicaines
RPF	Rassemblement du Peuple Français
SFIO	Section Française de l'Internationale Ouvrière (Socialist Party)
SGEN	Syndicat Général de l'Education Nationale
SNES	Syndicat National de l'Enseignement Secondaire
SNET	Syndicat National de l'Enseignement Technique

SNI	Syndicat National des Instituteurs
UDSR	Union Démocratique et Socialiste de la Résistance
UFD	Union des Forces Démocratiques
UGTA	Union Générales des Travailleurs Algériens
UGFF	Union Générale des Fédérations de Fonctionnaires
UNR	Union pour la Nouvelle République
U.S.	*L'Université Syndicaliste*

Introduction

Only in the past twelve years or so have American students of comparative politics begun to focus their attention on pressure groups abroad. Drawing on the store of concepts and techniques accumulated over several decades of research in American politics,[1] a number of Americans have applied themselves to the study of foreign pressure groups. Val R. Lorwin and Henry W. Ehrmann in France, Harry Eckstein and Samuel H. Beer in Great Britain, and Joseph LaPalombara in Italy are some of the best known of these traveling American scholars.[2] They have been joined by Europeans seeking to apply the same methods and techniques to pressure group studies in their own countries. Books describing the panorama of pressure groups in separate countries have been published by European scholars. Rupert Breitling in Germany, John D. Stewart in Great Britain, and Jean Meynaud in France are in the vanguard of this movement.[3] The Fifth

---

[1] Existing knowledge about pressure groups was summarized and a theoretical framework for new research provided by David B. Truman in *The Governmental Process* (New York: Knopf, 1951). Truman, considering the term "pressure group" emotionally loaded and associated with certain limited methods of action, prefers the designation "interest group." In this study, the terms are used interchangeably and without evaluative intent. Another recent contribution to the literature of pressure groups is Donald C. Blaisdell (ed.), "Unofficial Government: Pressure Groups and Lobbies," *The Annals of the American Academy of Political and Social Science*, Vol. CCCXIX (September, 1958).

[2] Lorwin, *The French Labor Movement* (Cambridge: Harvard University Press, 1954); Ehrmann, *Organized Business in France* (Princeton: Princeton University Press, 1957); Beer, "Pressure Groups and Parties in Britain," *American Political Science Review*, Vol. L (March, 1956), 1–23; Eckstein, *Pressure Group Politics* (Stanford: Stanford University Press, 1960); LaPalombara, *The Italian Labor Movement: Problems and Prospects* (Ithaca: Cornell University Press, 1957); and LaPalombara's excellent recent work, *Interest Groups in Italian Politics* (Princeton: Princeton University Press, 1964).

[3] Breitling, *Die Verbände in der Bundesrepublik: Ihre Arten und Ihre Politische Wirkungsweise* (Meisenheim am Glan: Verlag Anton Hein, 1955); Stewart, *British Pressure Groups: Their Role in the House of Commons* (Oxford: Clarendon, 1958); and Meynaud, *Les Groupes de Pression en France* (Paris: Colin, 1958). An article on British pressure groups that antedated that of Professor Beer by a few months was published by W. J. M. Mackenzie, "Pressure Groups in British

Round Table of the International Political Science Association in 1957 brought together a number of these American and European students of pressure groups. In discussions there the view was expressed that before existing pressure group theory could be further elaborated and confirmed, more empirical data and straightforward descriptive material would have to be gathered.[4] Gabriel A. Almond's report of the Committee on Comparative Politics of the Social Science Research Council similarly called for "intensive analysis of the characteristics of specific, selected interest groups."[5]

Hopefully, the present work will be a contribution to the growing body of literature on selected foreign interest groups, and on French groups in particular. It seeks to add further detail to the general picture of French pressure groups already furnished by Meynaud. It complements published works which describe and analyze the pressure groups in single sectors of French society. Henry W. Ehrmann's book on French business organizations is an excellent pressure-group study of employers' lobbies. Val Lorwin devoted a chapter of his book on French labor to the relationships between trade unions and politics. Bernard E. Brown has published articles dealing with the alcohol lobby, church schools, and the French army; and Gordon Wright has written on Roman Catholic farm organizations.[6] But the organized teachers have until recently been practically ignored.[7]

The Fédération de l'Education Nationale (FEN) is the largest and most powerful union of educators in France. It organizes practically all elementary teachers, most of the secondary teachers, and

Government," *British Journal of Sociology*, Vol. VI (June, 1955), 133–48. A thorough revision of Meynaud's book has appeared under the title *Nouvelles Etudes sur les Groupes de Pression en France* (Paris: Colin, 1962).

[4] Henry W. Ehrmann (ed.), *Pressure Groups on Four Continents* (Pittsburgh: University of Pittsburgh Press, 1958), p. 299. In September, 1964, European and American students of pressure groups met once again at special sessions in Geneva sponsored by the International Political Science Association.

[5] Almond, "A Comparative Study of Interest Groups and the Political Process," *American Political Science Review*, Vol. LII (March, 1958), 270–82.

[6] Brown, "Alcohol and Politics in France," *American Political Science Review*, Vol. LI (December, 1957), 976–94; "Religious Schools and Politics in France," *Midwest Journal of Political Science*, Vol. II (May, 1958), 160–78; "The Army and Politics in France," *Journal of Politics*, Vol. XXIII (May, 1961), 262–78; and Wright, "Catholics and Peasantry in France," *Political Science Quarterly*, Vol. LXVIII (December, 1953), 526–51.

[7] Two case studies by French authors appeared recently: Aline Coutrot, "La Loi Scolaire de Décembre 1959," *Revue Française de Science Politique*, Vol. XIII (June, 1963); and F.-G. Dreyfus, "Un Groupe de Pression en Action: Les Syndicats Universitaires devant le Projet Billères de Réforme de l'Enseignement (1955–1959)," *Revue Française de Science Politique*, Vol. XV (April, 1965), 213–50.

many professors and instructors in higher education and special fields. Heir to a long and colorful history of militant unionism and ideological diversity, the unified Federation resolutely seeks the improvement of teachers' salaries and the betterment of education in general. Loyal to its traditions and to what it considers to be its moral responsibilities, the Federation advocates its own solutions to political problems which face the nation as a whole.

Partly because its members are government employees and partly by choice, the FEN deploys all the means at its disposal to influence the political process. No legitimate targets or techniques are unknown to it. It aims at the government, the administration, the parties, Parliament, and public opinion. It uses negotiations, delegations, press conferences, petitions, letters, rallies, and strikes. It is evident that the Federation is an active political organization which is well suited to pressure group analysis.

Since the Federation is made up of disparate categories of educational employees organized into national unions, and since the conflicting ideological loyalties so characteristic of France's fragmented political culture are officially recognized within the organization, the problem of organizational cohesion and its impact on the political effectiveness of the group may be studied with unusual facility. Furthermore, the study of an organization which takes action on behalf of a politically sophisticated membership adds greatly to our understanding of French politics. Without comprehension of the Federation's history, ideological outlook, and political leanings, for example, it would be impossible to explain the 1958 teachers' strike against de Gaulle's assumption of power. In addition, the collapse of the Fourth Republic and the establishment of the Fifth have provided an opportunity for observing changes in pressure group behavior under different regimes. While the patterns of the new constitutional system have not yet become sufficiently fixed to permit sure generalizations, it is possible to make some preliminary observations and statements.

But most important, the activities of the FEN not only confirm much of what is known about pressure group behavior but also throw light on questions raised about pressure group theory. The theoretical implications of the significant findings are noted in the course of this work; they are then consolidated and given full treatment in the concluding chapter. Although the field research for this study was completed prior to the publication of Eckstein's *Pressure Group Politics* in 1960, his comprehensive scheme of analysis is used in the last chapter to report the findings. It is hoped that in this way the cause of a genuinely comparative and cumulative political science may be served.

Teachers and Politics in France

Origins and Development

The origins, development, and contemporary operations of the FEN cannot be fully understood without some knowledge of the French educational system. And in order to appreciate the motives which impelled the teachers in this system to organize originally, it is also necessary to understand the social and administrative milieu which existed during the "heroic times"[1] of French unionism. Both the enduring characteristics of the educational system and the conditions surrounding the birth of the unions influenced the development of the teachers' unions between the two world wars and throughout the postwar period.

CHARACTERISTICS OF THE FRENCH SCHOOL SYSTEM

While it is difficult to describe a whole school system in brief terms, certain essential characteristics can be cited. Four characteristics regularly noted by observers of the French system are: centralized administration, free and compulsory attendance, religiously neutral instruction, and freedom of operation for private schools.

The single feature of the French educational system which most strikes the Anglo-Saxon observer is its high degree of administrative centralization. French government administration in general "is a tightly centralized system, based on a uniform pattern and closely controlled from Paris. . . . Its . . . structure has stood without fundamental alteration since the reforms of Napoleon."[2] Alfred Diamant attributes this centralization to "the mystique of the indivisible nation created by the Revolution."[3] For many years after the rule of Napoleon,

---

[1] A phrase used by M. Edouard Dolléans to describe the decade of 1899–1909 in his *Histoire du Mouvement Ouvrier*. 3 vols.; 3d ed. (Paris: Colin, 1947–53), II, 87.

[2] Philip M. Williams, *Politics in Post-War France*. 2d ed. (London: Longmans, Green, 1958), p. 2.

[3] Diamant, "The French Administrative System—The Republic Passes but the Administration Remains," *Toward the Comparative Study of Public Administration*, ed. William J. Siffin (Bloomington: Indiana University Press, 1959), p. 186.

1

the Minister of Education in Paris was able to boast that he could tell at any particular moment what every pupil in France was doing.[4] While today's system is less centralized than formerly, the Minister of Education still finds himself at the apex of an organizational pyramid which encompasses the entire educational system.

The Minister of Education, responsible to the Prime Minister and through him to the Parliament, ultimately answers for the administration of all the public schools of France, from the communal school to the University of Paris.[5] Except for limited controls, private schools lie outside the jurisdiction of the Minister of Education. The only other exceptions are those institutions which come under the jurisdiction of some other ministry because of the specialized nature of the preparation they offer (such as agricultural institutes under the Minister of Agriculture and military academies under the Minister of the Armed Forces). He is, of course, aided by a multiplicity of bureaus, commissions, and councils. As in most French ministries, the Minister's immediate collaborators, including personal and political friends, constitute his cabinet and insure that the Ministry is responsive to his political orientations and policy orders.

In recent years the Ministry of Education has undergone a series of reorganizations designed to improve administration and to facilitate the application of important educational reforms. Under the Minister and his cabinet a Secretary General now supervises all the activities of the Ministry and coordinates the different bureaus; formerly the highest-ranking civil servants heading the various bureaus and services reported directly to the Minister and his cabinet. A major reorganization in 1961, which followed some smaller changes in 1960, ended the pronounced administrative isolation of elementary and secondary education by organizing bureaus along functional lines, with responsibilities such as personnel, school programs, and so forth. This change was intended to diminish the rivalry between levels and kinds of

---

[4] For an outline of Napoleon's educational reforms, see J. M. Thompson, *Napoleon Bonaparte: His Rise and Fall* (Oxford: Blackwell, 1958), pp. 203–208.

[5] For a complete if somewhat dated description of the organization of French public education, see France, Ministère de l'Éducation Nationale, de la Jeunesse et des Sports, Institut Pédagogique National, *L'Organisation de l'Enseignement en France* (Paris: La Documentation Française, 1957). For a briefer account see the publication of the Ministry of Education's Bureau Universitaire de Statistique et de Documentation Scolaires et Professionnelles, *Avenirs*, No. 103–104 (May-June, 1959), pp. 12–21, hereafter referred to as *Avenirs*. A recent description in English entitled *The French System of Education* has been published by the Cultural Services of the French Embassy, 972 Fifth Avenue, New York. This agency summarizes current developments in the quarterly publication *Education in France*.

education which had plagued sponsors of educational reform. Other recent changes in administrative organization have been similarly inspired.[6]

The Minister of Education is aided in his task of controlling the vast establishment which he heads by a corps of Inspectors General. These inspectors circulate in the field, checking on the schools, their teachers, and the performance of the specialized services of the Ministry and make their reports directly to the Minister and the Secretary General. As the roaming representatives of the Minister, the Inspectors make it possible for him to bridge the bureaucratic gap between himself and the classroom teachers. The functions of control and communication which the Inspectors General perform are necessary for the efficient administration of a highly centralized bureaucracy.

The Minister is represented regionally by a rector in each of the twenty-three academic regions or *académies* into which France is divided. Normally a university professor, the rector is aided in his work of coordinating and overseeing the branches and services of the Ministry for his academic region by a number of specialized inspectors.

In each department of France, an academy inspector represents the rector and the Minister and oversees the operation of all the services of the Ministry of Education in that department. At the local level, administrative authority is vested in the chief of establishment, i.e., the *proviseur*, principal, or director of each school.

While the administration of education in France is highly centralized, it cannot be accurately described as authoritarian. On each of the administrative levels cited above there are councils and committees in which teachers' representatives are consulted on such matters as pedagogical policy, educational reform, and personnel administration. Informal organization and the interplay of personalities of course also have a tempering effect on the downflow of authority. Nevertheless, despite these factors and a conscious attempt to decentralize, French education remains relatively centralized.

However, a high degree of centralization does not necessarily end problems of coordination. The various branches of education grew up side by side and remained in many ways separate from each other. For example, while the primary schools extended their offerings upward through the higher primary education (*enseignement primaire supé-*

---

[6] *Le Monde*, May 25, 1960, and October 12, 1961; and *Education in France*, No. 26 (December, 1964), pp. 8–9. Reactions of the FEN to the reforms of 1960 and 1961 may be found in the organization's monthly bulletin, *L'Enseignement Public*. See *E.P.*, 15e année, No. 9 (June-July, 1960), pp. 19–20; 16e année, No. 1 (October, 1960), pp. 9–10; and 17e année, No. 2 (November, 1961), p. 20.

rieur) and complementary courses (*cours complémentaires*) which paralleled the secondary schools, the *lycées* and *collèges*[7] operated elementary-level preparatory classes which duplicated those offered in the primary schools. In actual practice, there was little crossing over between these two uncoordinated parallel tracks. An example makes this clear: a five-year-old child could enter either the regular primary school or the preparatory classes of the *lycée* or *collège*. If he was enrolled in the latter, he would normally continue on to higher education; if, however, he was entered on the other track, he was likely to continue through the complementary courses which led not to higher education but to a trade. The selection of students for educational differentiation, therefore, not only took place much too early but was also largely determined by residence and family background instead of intellectual or personal qualifications. In the 1920's the Minister of Education, Jean Zay, removed some of these artificial divisions by placing all primary courses under the Director of First Degree Education and most of the secondary courses taught by primary teachers under the Director of Second Degree Education. This facilitated the transfer of capable pupils from the primary schools to the *lycée* at about the age of eleven. But later transfers remained difficult. One member of the National Assembly complained in 1959 that despite the strongly centralized organization of the Ministry there reigned a "profound anarchy which is translated on the practical level by the impermeability of the partitions separating the various branches and by the total absence of liaison."[8]

In his study of the British Medical Association, Harry Eckstein observed that pressure groups tend to resemble the organizations they seek to influence.[9] Centralized agencies spawn centralized interest groups; agency reorganization promotes interest group reorganization. The centralization of the Ministry of Education is reflected in the

---

[7] *Lycées* were high-quality schools maintained and controlled by the state; *collèges* were supported partly by the state and partly by the municipality and were considered to be slightly inferior academically. According to the terminology instituted by the reform of January, 1959, *lycée* refers to secondary schools preparing students for the secondary school diploma (*baccalauréat*) and higher education (formerly *lycées* and *collèges modernes*). Former *collèges techniques* and *ecoles nationales professionnelles* are now called *lycées techniques*. The word *collège* has retained its less prestigious connotation in the titles *collèges d'enseignement technique* (former *centres d'apprentissage*) and *collèges d'enseignement général* (former *cours complémentaires*). *Avenirs*, p. 21.

[8] France, *J.O., Débats Parlementaires, Assemblée Nationale*, November 23, 1959, p. 2798. (All quotations in this study which cite sources in French are translations by the author.)

[9] Eckstein, *Pressure Group Politics*, p. 21.

teachers' unions which are themselves highly centralized. Key decisions on policy and tactics are made by their national leaders in the top organs of the FEN. It is quite natural that the power of the FEN should be focused at its top for it is at the corresponding pinnacle of the Ministry that the decisions to be influenced are made. Local units of the Federation cannot function as negotiating bodies since the governmental agent on their level does not have sufficient authority to handle their most important demands. Furthermore, the horizontal organization of the Ministry has also been reflected in the FEN. The Federation is composed of national unions representing the employees of one branch or service in the Ministry. The teachers in primary, secondary, technical, and higher education were, until the reforms of 1961, under separate offices ("Directions") of the Ministry and belonged to correspondingly separate national unions. The technical school teachers' union did not fuse with the enlarged secondary teachers' union in 1949 because they were under a separate office in the Ministry. The unification of the secondary and technical teachers under a single office in 1961 led union leaders to discuss the question of joining together the corresponding national unions.[10]

Significantly, the FEN does not oppose this centralization but, on the contrary, has demanded that *all* educational services be brought under the control of the Ministry of Education (where it enjoys considerable influence). The FEN has also fought the poor coordination between the levels and branches of the educational system in numerous proposals for educational reform.

The Third Republic established compulsory education to the age of twelve, and to transform this principle into reality it set out to provide a public elementary school in every commune. The period of required school attendance was lengthened in 1936 to the age of fourteen and in 1959 to the age of sixteen.[11] The corollary of compulsory education, that it be free of charge, was also established for primary education

[10] The SNES (Syndicat National de l'Enseignement Secondaire), an important member union of the FEN representing the secondary school teachers, has told the story of the reorganization of the SNES after the war in its publication *Vade Mécum: Textes Généraux Intéressant Toutes les Catégories du Personnel du Second Degré,* 1er Fascicule (Paris, 1959), hereafter referred to as *SNES Vade Mécum.* The proposed fusion of 1960 is mentioned in *L'Université Syndicaliste,* 33e année, No. 193 (February 10, 1960), p. 29, hereafter referred to as *U.S.* This publication is the monthly bulletin of the SNES. Consideration of fusion continued in 1961. *Le Monde,* November 1, 1961.

[11] Forty per cent of the pupils already continue their studies beyond that age. Louis Cros, *"L'Explosion" Scolaire.* 2d ed. (Paris: Société d'Editions et de Vente des Publications de l'Education Nationale, 1962), p. 32.

by the Third Republic. It was extended to secondary education in 1933. The FEN has always approved this characteristic of the educational system and has long favored the extension of the compulsory age to eighteen.

In brief, *laïcité* means the neutrality of education with respect to political and religious beliefs. This policy follows naturally from the two doctrines of separation of church and state and compulsory education, since the public schools must be ready to accept children of all faiths and creeds. The defense of *laïcité* claims a major part of the time and resources of the FEN.

It must not be inferred that the role of the state in education is all-inclusive. The state does not have a monopoly of all instruction in France. Laws of 1850, 1875, 1886, and 1919 specifically grant individuals and associations the right to operate schools, while maintaining the right of the state to verify that the instruction given in them is not contrary to the Constitution, the laws, and accepted standards of morality and hygiene. The requirements beyond these are rather limited. For example, the head of a secondary school must have his *baccalauréat* and five years of teaching experience, but no similar qualifications are required of the teachers who work for him (unless the school accepts state financial aid, in which case there is further regulation of teacher qualifications).

The most important organization to take advantage of these laws is the Roman Catholic church. Earlier the principal dispenser of learning, the Church came under the attack of the eighteenth-century *philosophes*. As a result, its role in education expanded and contracted with shifting tides of anticlerical sentiment during the following century. The Law on the Separation of Church and State of 1905, in the eyes of many, definitively settled the boundary lines by treating the Church as a private association. But inadequate financial resources after World War II forced the Church to seek state aid for its schools. The resurgence of this issue renewed the struggle and pitted clerical against *laïque* in the old battle orders. In the front lines of the anticlericals are the members of the FEN—all employees of the public school system. These teachers oppose aid to Catholic schools not only because this diversion of funds means less money for the public schools, but also because it violates their belief in the separation of church and state.

These four characteristics of French education influenced the formation of the teachers' unions in France. Free and compulsory education required a massive teaching force. Liberty of education permitted a private establishment to grow up beside the public system; the teachers' union movement was therefore split, and the FEN came to represent only the public school teachers. *Laïcité*, the doctrine of neutrality which made compulsory education possible, became a cardinal point in their program. Lastly, the centralized organization of French school administration had a direct bearing on the structure of the FEN. The early years of the union movement among teachers showed that local efforts were useless in fighting the Ministry.

UNIONISM'S FIRST FALTERING STEPS

The union movement took root in the fertile soil provided by teacher restlessness and discontent during the "heroic times" of French unionism. While the roles of the primary school teacher as a notable in his community and as a missionary for the Republic were in many ways satisfying, he had numerous causes for complaint, ranging from low salaries to authoritarian administrative structures and practices. Overcentralization put the teacher at the mercy of anonymous government officials; domineering superiors at the school made his daily life miserable. It is not surprising that he demanded a change in his working conditions and the right to take part in decisions affecting his welfare. He therefore joined with his co-workers in a union movement which eventually grew to embrace in a single organization almost all public school teachers.[12]

Condition of the teacher in 1900. In many ways the primary school teacher played an important and rewarding role in French society at the turn of the century. He has been characterized as a "pioneer of the Republic and of Progress at the end of the nineteenth century, man of the Left, defender of *laïcité*, notable in his village."[13]

Recognized in the village because of his education, the local school teacher wielded considerable influence. He not only taught his pupils the rudiments of knowledge necessary for life but counseled them in their career choices, helped them organize their leisure time, and often procured scholarships for them. He fought against alcoholism and promoted hygiene, popularized the latest agricultural methods, and commonly served as the town clerk. He often passed his whole life in devoted service to his village. Usually he was sprung from humble

[12] A summary of this period may be found in Georges Duveau, *Les Instituteurs* ([Paris]: Editions du Seuil [1957]), pp. 140–54.

[13] André Bianconi, "Les Instituteurs," *Revue Française de Science Politique,* Vol. IX (December, 1959), 935. The rest of this description is derived from the same author's article, "Condition de l'Instituteur: Du Maître d'Autrefois à l'Enseignant d'Aujourd'hui," *L'Instituteur,* No. 22 (February, 1960), pp. 5–6.

sources and so possessed the capacity for understanding the people around him. In traditional France the school teacher was a beloved and respected figure.

Seen on a different level, the primary school teacher was much more than just a village notable. He was a missionary and pioneer for the secular Republic. "It was Condorcet who, in his education bill presented to the Legislative Assembly in 1792, was one of the first to use the word *instituteur* [primary school teacher]. But it was the Third Republic which gave the teacher his mission and his condition, which made him the figure we know so well."[14] A celebrated Minister of Education, Jules Ferry, and his fellow exponents of free and compulsory education resolved to end the divisions in the French nation that had come to the surface in the uprising of the Paris Commune. These founders of the Third Republic expected the primary school teachers to implant the republican faith in young hearts and minds, to redress the nation morally after the war of 1870; civic instruction was therefore explicitly included in the program of the primary schools.[15]

The government's attitude toward the school teachers oscillated irregularly. In an earlier epoch the Minister of Education, François Guizot, had furthered public primary education; but he also invited the teachers not to aspire above their "obscure and laborious condition," implying that the government considered the teachers a disturbing force that had to be quieted. In similar fashion the Third Republic, while praising the teachers' civic role, was disturbed by the leftist orientation of many of them. Recruited from the lower strata of society, they tended to be democratic and egalitarian; heirs of the eighteenth-century faith in rationalism, they believed in progress and the ability of man to change the world through science and reason.[16] Unsurprisingly, the government's policy toward the embryonic teachers' unions alternated between approbation and encouragement at one time and suspicion and hostility at another.

It has been observed by Eckstein that government policy is directly related to the scope and intensity of pressure group activity.[17] In this case the policy of free and compulsory education created a large potential interest group in the corps of teachers hired to staff the public schools. Execution of that policy created conditions which led the teachers to organize, despite the vagaries of official attitudes toward teachers' organizations. In addition to the perennial problem of inade-

14 F. Launay, "L'Instituteur," *Avenirs*, p. 62.
15 André Ferré, *L'Instituteur* (Paris: La Table Ronde, 1954), p. 56.
16 *Ibid.*, pp. 31, 70.
17 Eckstein, *Pressure Group Politics*, pp. 26–27.

quate salaries, the teachers' complaints included the tyrannical rule of the school director; arbitrary shifts, promotions, and demotions by the administration; and interference from local politicians.

The school directors exercised over the younger teachers an oppressive tryanny which extended into their private lives. Some directors demanded that the teachers be in their rooms by a certain hour at night, took away their keys, intercepted and sifted their mail, and naturally did not hesitate to judge their political activity "subversive."[18] This authoritarian regime was so oppressive that, according to one union writer, the replacement of school directors with councils of teachers became the "fundamental demand" of the first teachers' unions.[19] In addition, the school teacher had no protection from arbitrary administration. He could be promoted, transferred, or ignored with equal facility. Appointment to an isolated post was a common means of punishment. For example, when a teacher's association (Amicale) voted a motion supporting a teacher who had been brought before the departmental council for political reasons, the president of the association was transferred to a tiny mountain village thirty kilometers from any railroad station. The average teacher was also subject to political pressure. He was appointed by a prefect, a political representative of the central government. The local deputy to Parliament often looked on him as an electoral agent, a notable whose influence could be exploited for political ends. In spite of the resistance of the responsible academy inspectors, "the politicians intervened in favor of such and such a teacher, or to demand the departure of such and such another one who was hostile to them."[20] Such favoritism demoralized the whole service. "All the witnesses agree, both politicians and philosophers who lived through this period and union militants who were caught up in the struggle at its beginnings: nepotism was the first cause, one of the principal causes of unionism among civil servants."[21]

The period of the Amicales. In a sense, the government provided both the motive and the opportunity for teachers' unions. The motive derived from its arbitrary treatment of the teachers; the opportunity arose in the government-created social and political climate of the 1880's which favored the development of associations. The law of

[18] Max Ferré, *Histoire du Mouvement Syndicaliste Révolutionnaire Chez les Instituteurs: Des Origines à 1922.* (Paris: Société Universitaire d'Editions et de Librairie, 1955), pp. 62–63. This thoroughly documented work is a basic source for the early history of the teachers' unions.

[19] *E.P.*, No. 15 (January, 1947), p. 5.

[20] Ferré, *Mouvement Syndicaliste Révolutionnaire*, p. 64.

[21] *Ibid.*, p. 69.

March 21, 1884, granted workers in industry, commerce, and agriculture the right to organize (civil servants were not mentioned). The republican government, dependent on the school teachers for putting into effect its plan for free, compulsory, and secular education, encouraged them to meet together on the local level to discuss common pedagogical problems. In a few years pedagogical circles and normal school alumni groups had been formed. Ideas of union and federation spread.

In 1887 a Syndicat des Instituteurs et Institutrices de France deposited its Constitution with the Prefecture of the Seine in accordance with the law of 1884 and organized a national Congress. This Congress passed a resolution calling for the federation of the various departmental teachers' societies into a Union Nationale des Instituteurs de France. The Minister of Education, remarking that an association with all the characteristics of a union had no meaning for teachers except a seditious meaning, formally condemned every autonomous teachers' association as illegal in a circular of September 20, 1887. With this stroke of the pen he put the union movement among teachers to rest for fifteen years.

In the last years of the nineteenth century, with a change in the political atmosphere marked by the Dreyfus Affair, teachers' organizations sprang up once again. They did not adopt the union name, ideology, or techniques of the union movement, but rather remained pedagogical and mutual aid societies. They called themselves Amicales.[22] After a law of July 1, 1901, had established the right of free association, abolishing the requirement of official approval for any organization having more than twenty members, these Amicales mushroomed. In 1902 a Congress provided the national organization, the Fédération des Amicales, with a permanent apparatus. The highest point in the development of the Amicales was reached at the eminently successful Congress of the Federation in 1903 in Marseilles.

The Amicales differed from unions less in their aims than in their spirit. They were basically professional associations designed to benefit their members through exchange of information, group insurance plans,

---

[22] The story of the Amicales, told by early revolutionary syndicalists who considered them primitive since they lacked class consciousness and revolutionary enthusiasm, can be found in F. Bernard, L. Bouet, M. Dommanget, and G. Serret, *Le Syndicalisme dans l'Enseignement: Histoire de la Fédération de l'Enseignement et du Syndicalisme Universitaire* (Avignon: Edition de "L'Ecole Emancipée," [1924]), Vol. I. Similar mutual aid societies antedated labor unions generally in France and Italy. See Paul Louis, *Histoire du Mouvement Syndical en France 1789–1910*, 2d ed. (Paris: Alcan, 1911), pp. 72–86; and Daniel L. Horowitz, *The Italian Labor Movement* (Cambridge: Harvard University Press, 1963), pp. 12–47.

and joint defense against arbitrary administration. They sought to promote the professional and material interests of their members. Their inspiration was close to the ideals of universal brotherhood and class collaboration which Mazzini had fostered in the Italian mutual aid societies. Unionism of the period, however, was much more radical in spirit; it opposed piecemeal reforms of the existing social and economic structure and wanted to unite all workers, including teachers, in a revolutionary class struggle. It advocated the use of the strike. It condemned the willingness of the Amicales to negotiate, compromise, and collaborate with the administration.[23] Like the dialectical antithesis in a Marxian contradiction, this unionism of a revolutionary syndicalist strain growing within the Amicales constituted a new force that was to supersede them.

Teachers unions to 1919. Shortly after the 1903 Congress of the Fédération des Amicales, numerous new groups were formed under the name of L'Emancipation de l'Instituteur. While not opposed to the Amicales, the Emancipations were closer in spirit to the union movement which they eventually joined. They demanded, for example, a teachers' council to share administration with the school director, the elimination of honorific titles, the banning of directors' secret reports on the teachers, and the exclusion of textbooks which were not inspired by a clearly secular and pacifist educational program.[24] The Emancipations multiplied. Soon, despite the government's ban on civil servants' unions, they began openly to adopt the name of *syndicat* or "union."

In 1905 a number of these Emancipations met in Paris and decided to transform their organization into the Fédération Nationale des Syndicats d'Instituteurs et d'Institutrices Publics de France et des Colonies (FNSI).[25] Indicted for having illegally formed a union among public functionaries, the leaders of the Federation's Paris branch never came to trial. Before they could be tried, the Chamber of Deputies voted their release. The Chamber reiterated, however, that the law of 1884 permitting the organization of unions did not apply to civil servants. Nevertheless, this action did not halt the spread of unionism. In 1906 the Federation called its first Congress, and in 1909 it formally adhered to the nation's largest labor federation, the Confédération Générale du Travail (CGT).

The new unions everywhere taking form did not eliminate the

---

[23] Ferré, *Mouvement Syndicaliste Révolutionnaire,* pp. 28–34.

[24] *Ibid.,* p. 34.

[25] For the report of a participant, see Louis Bouet, *Les Pionniers du Syndicalisme Universitaire* (Bédarrides, Vaucluse: Edition de "L'Ecole Emancipée," n.d.).

Amicales; the national Federation of Amicales lasted until 1919, and many teachers belonged to both organizations. Sometimes union sympathizers merely formed a group within an Amicale; sometimes the Amicales voted to transform themselves into unions. The trend was clear; the unions, led by strong and dynamic personalities on both the national and departmental level, were becoming more numerous and vigorous than the Amicales.

The legal position of the unions remained ambiguous. Persecutions of union leaders continued, particularly under Prime Minister Clemenceau. In 1907 the FNSI sent an open letter to Clemenceau protesting a bill which would end this legal ambiguity by stripping the civil servants' unions of the right to strike and the right to join the Bourses du Travail.[26] This letter, plus the fact that the FNSI also voted the same month to join the CGT, incited the Council of Ministers to undertake action culminating in the dismissal of the president of the FNSI from his teaching position. In 1912, after a misunderstanding which resulted in accusations that the teachers were unpatriotic pacifists, the Minister of Public Instruction ordered the unions dissolved. "These unions are illegal and have only been tolerated pending the vote of a civil servants' *statut*," he wrote.[27] A number of unions were prosecuted, but before the judgments could be executed, Parliament voted an amnesty.

The war years were particularly difficult for the FNSI. Its newspaper, *L'Ecole Emancipée,* was suspended by governmental decree in October, 1914. Many of its most militant members were called to the trenches. Its pacifist reputation won it the suspicion of the public and the close surveillance of the government. As a matter of fact, the pacifist elements remained in the minority until 1916, when they triumphed and called for immediate peace. The national Congress of 1917 was forbidden, but, held clandestinely, it demanded peace based on the right of self-determination and without indemnity, conquest, or annexation. The Congress of 1918 was also forbidden.[28] In the last year of the war, many of the union leaders were either dismissed from

[26] The *Bourses du Travail* were labor exchanges which provided placement services, established funds for unemployed and transient workers, and served as social and cultural centers. Federated in 1892, they came to symbolize working-class unity. Dolléans, *Mouvement Ouvrier,* II, 33–34; and Lorwin, *Labor Movement,* pp. 21–23.

[27] Quoted in Ferré, *Mouvement Syndicaliste Révolutionnaire,* p. 169. A *statut* is a code of government regulations pertaining to the legal rights and duties of a body of government employees.

[28] Finding the entrance of the trade union building blocked by policemen in 1918, the determined delegates adopted the suggestion of a Socialist deputy (and former school teacher) to meet in the Socialists' caucus room of the Chamber of Deputies. Locked out on the following day, they were obliged to conclude their sessions in the Bois de Boulogne, *ibid.,* pp. 182–83.

their teaching posts or sentenced to prison for their pacifist activities. By the end of the war, the Federation was but a shadow of its former self.

Teachers' Unions Between the Wars

The interwar period, which saw the birth of the lineal ancestor of the FEN, the Fédération Générale de l'Enseignement (FGE), was characterized by two developments: the broadening of the union movement to include secondary teachers and professors; and the fusion of two opposing teachers' unions in 1935, uniting adherents of two different ideological tendencies. This period ends with the dissolution of the unions by the Vichy government in 1940.

Growth and rivalry. In August, 1919, the first postwar Congress of the FNSI decided to organize under the new name of the Fédération des Syndicats des Membres de l'Enseignement Laïque de France, des Colonies et des Protectorats (FMEL); it accepted as members of its departmental unions teachers from all branches and levels of education in France.[29] Still affiliated with the CGT, the union now included elementary school teachers, secondary teachers, university professors, student teachers and professors of the normal schools, and teachers in the technical schools. Most of the members of the FMEL, however, continued to be drawn from the ranks of the elementary school teachers.

The interwar period also saw the end of the Amicales and their transformation, after a complex process of maneuvering and bargaining, into the FGE in 1928. Shortly after World War I, the Fédération des Amicales d'Instituteurs became the Syndicat National des Instituteurs (SNI), today the largest FEN member union. Other Amicales of professors, secondary school teachers, etc., also gradually transformed themselves into unions during the same period. Many of these unions wanted to enter the CGT but were prevented from doing so because a general teachers' union, the FMEL, already existed there. Nevertheless, the SNI succeeded in affiliating with the CGT indirectly through the intermediary of a civil servants' union, the Fédération des Syndicats de Fonctionnaires. After the schism of the CGT in 1922 and the departure of the FMEL for the Communist-dominated splinter group, the Confédération Générale du Travail Unitaire (CGTU),[30] and after the

[29] For brief histories of the teachers' unions for the interwar period, see Ferré, *Mouvement Syndicaliste Révolutionnaire*, pp. 219–53; and articles in *E.P.*, No. 1 [1945], p. 2; No. 12 (October, 1946), p. 3; and 6e année, No. 10 (June, 1951), p. 4.

[30] The CGTU was made up of the Communist and revolutionary syndicalist minorities that broke away from the CGT and formed their own labor central in

Fédération des Syndicats de Fonctionnaires had chosen to disassociate itself from all labor centrals, the SNI was able to enter the CGT directly.

Separate unions grouping the members of the various levels and branches of education entered the CGT in 1927 through the intermediary of the Fédération des Syndicats de Fonctionnaires when that organization reentered the CGT. Here they formed a small group known as the Fédération des Membres de l'Enseignement du Deuxième et du Troisième Degré. Under CGT auspices, this group united with the SNI in October, 1928, to form the largest and broadest teachers' union to that date, the FGE. The FGE had 83,000 members; its rival in the CGTU, the FMEL, scarcely exceeded 12,000 members in its best years.

Unification and dissolution. Relations between the moderate FGE and the revolutionary syndicalist Fédération des Membres de l'Enseignement Laïque (FMEL) were poor in the decade before 1935. Even when a conservative government tried to take action against civil service unions, these two teachers' unions were unable to unite against the common foe.[31] Their antagonism stemmed from contrasting inspirations and ideologies. The FGE grew out of the Amicale movement and continued to bear the imprint of its nonrevolutionary origins; the small and militant FMEL was the successor to the revolutionary syndicalist FNSI and kept alive an ideology which condemned collaboration with the administration and the "bourgeoisie." Just as the FGE feared the radicalism of the FMEL, the FMEL abhorred the torpid mass of perfunctory dues-paying members in the FGE.[32]

It was not until after the rightist uprising of February 6, 1934, that these feuding and mutually suspicious teachers' unions were able to reconcile their differences. The rightist demonstrations in Paris encouraged the creation of an anti-Fascist common front. The CGT and CGTU were reunited in September, 1935, and a Popular Front of the

---

1922. This break, reflecting the Moscow-inspired split in the Socialist party which created the French Communist party, stemmed, according to the secessionists, from the failure of the CGT to unleash the general strike and revolution during the war, and the CGT's opposition to the Third International and to the CST (Revolutionary Syndicalist Committees, colonies of militant Communists found in each CGT unit). The revolutionary syndicalists broke away two years later and left the CGTU completely in Communist hands. Dolléans, *Mouvement Ouvrier,* II, 316–51.

[31] Repression on the part of a hostile government was always possible until after World War II. The right to unionize was granted to civil servants by a law of February 16, 1946, although the civil service unions had enjoyed a *de facto* existence for decades. Maurice Duverger (ed.), *Partis Politiques et Classes Sociales en France* ("Association Française de Science Politique: Cahiers de la Fondation Nationale des Sciences Politiques," No. 74; Paris: Colin, 1955), p. 145.

[32] Ferré, *Mouvement Syndicaliste Révolutionnaire,* pp. 224–25.

Communist, Socialist, and Radical Socialist parties was created.[33] The FGE and the FMEL, after lengthy and difficult discussions over structure, joined this stream of anti-Fascist unity by fusing their organizations in December, 1935, to form a new and larger Fédération Générale de l'Enseignement affiliated, as before, with the CGT.

As part of the Vichy regime's National Revolution, the unified FGE was dissolved in August, 1940, and its property confiscated.[34] In a few months its skeletal structure began to take shape underground, in preparation for liberation and the end of the war.

POSTWAR REORGANIZATION

The FGE emerged from the war years with experienced cadres ready to assume the leadership of the organization. The first postwar Congress of 1946 altered the structure and adopted a new constitution. And the withdrawal of the organization from the CGT in 1948 set its political orientation for years to come.

War and reconstruction. As early as August 26, 1940, some members of the Administrative Committee of the CGT met with its secretary general, M. Léon Jouhaux, and decided that the CGT would carry on its activities underground.[35] Several militants of the FGE maintained contacts with each other through the CGT; by February, 1941, the principal teachers' unions were represented on the Administrative Commission of the CGT. Twice an FGE bureau[36] was constituted, and twice it was crushed by the arrest and deportation of some of its members between 1942 and 1944. But by May, 1944, a bureau consisting of the secretary general and five secretaries had been organized. Two members represented the elementary teachers, and one each represented higher education, secondary education, the modern *collèges,* and technical education. After the Liberation a meeting of the FGE provisional Administrative Commission added two more members to the bureau, a treasurer and an assistant treasurer. The bureau thus constituted, aided by several meetings of the Administrative Commission, administered the FGE during the immediate postwar period.[37]

33 Dolléans, *Mouvement Ouvrier,* III, 148–52.

34 The Vichy regime was particularly severe on the school teachers in its analysis of the defeat of 1940. Its principal propaganda themes were that the teachers, and particularly the elementary school teachers, belonged in the great majority to the parties of the Left and the extreme Left which led France to defeat; and that at the root of her troubles was the dechristianization of France for which the public schools were responsible. *E.P.,* No. 1 [1945], p. 9.

35 Dolléans, *Mouvement Ouvrier,* III, 185.

36 The bureau is a small executive committee composed of the secretary general and his assistants. It is responsible to a larger, representative body of union officials, the Administrative Commission.

37 *E.P.,* No. 1 [1945], p. 3.

The bureau of the FGE maintained a high level of activity in these early postwar months. It watched over the interests of its members and brought their claims to the attention of the government in numerous audiences and communications.[38] At the same time, it set about rebuilding the organization.

The Congress of 1946. On July 23–24, 1945, the union leaders convened the FGE National Council, a consultative body made up of members of the Administrative Commission and representatives of the academic regions. Besides considering current questions, this Council appointed a twelve-member Committee on Structure to draw up a new constitution and bylaws before December 1, 1945, in time for discussion and votes at a Congress to be held during the Christmas vacation.

The report of the Committee was published in the December, 1945, issue of *L'Enseignement Public.* It presented the 1928 Constitution of the FGE and the changes it recommended. A preface explained that the Committee favored the development of a unitary organization (instead of a federation of national unions) based on departmental sections grouping teachers of all levels within a given department; however, since loyalties to existing national unions were strong, the Committee settled on a compromise involving the representation of both national unions and departmental sections in a broad federation. Other provisions of the Committee's report dealt with finance, union publications, and membership of the Federation in the CGT.[39]

For a number of reasons, partly because of transportation and communication difficulties in the early postwar period, the Congress had to be postponed until March 4–6, 1946.[40] Few alterations were made in the text proposed by the Committee. One important change which caused considerable discussion was the addition of Article 5bis forbidding a union official from simultaneously holding political office. Deriving from the traditional syndicalist skepticism of political activity, this provision bears witness to a continuing fear of domination by a political party.[41]

In short, the Congress did everything possible to enhance the

[38] A report for the period from January 1 to June 3, 1945, lists thirteen contacts with the Minister of Education or his cabinet, six with the Minister of Finance or his cabinet, four with one of the permanent directors of a department of the Ministry of Education, one with the cabinet of the Minister of Information, and one with the cabinet of General de Gaulle. *Ibid.,* p. 12.

[39] *E.P.,* No. 4 (December, 1945), p. 13.

[40] Minutes of the Administrative Commission of December 1, 1945, in *E.P.,* No. 4 (December, 1945), p. 2.

[41] The constitution (*statuts*) and bylaws (*règlement intérieur*) adopted by the Congress of 1946 may be found in *E.P.,* No. 7 (April, 1946), pp. 15–16.

organization's cohesion. The union's bulletin was to provide a common source of information and inspiration for all members. To reduce the "spirit of category" (the pursuit of the narrow interests of a single branch or level of education), the national unions were to be decreased in number and departmental unions encouraged. The Federation as a whole, not the separate national unions, was to be represented in the newly reorganized civil service union, the Union Générale des Fédérations de Fonctionnaires (UGFF). Finally, the admission of the Federation into the CGT on the same basis as an industrial federation was to broaden this sense of cohesion by identification with members of the working class.[42]

The Congress also changed the name of the organization from the Fédération Générale de l'Enseignement to the Fédération de l'Education Nationale (FEN). The new name reflected a corresponding change in the name of the Ministry of Education. It also evidenced a desire to broaden the union's field of recruitment beyond classroom teachers.[43]

Schism and autonomy. The newly reorganized FEN had barely begun operations when it was faced with schism, a recurrent spectre of the French labor movement. Outwardly unified, with nearly six million members in April, 1946, the CGT was shot through with conflicting currents. Conflicts between revolutionary syndicalists, social reformists, and Communists led to a disintegration of the giant Confederation.[44] In December, 1947, after the CGT had tried to transform a rash of strikes into an insurrectional general strike and had adopted the Stalinist line of opposition to the Marshall Plan, five former CGT secretaries issued an appeal to all CGT dissidents to create a new labor central, the CGT-Force Ouvrière. Many unions and workers responded and joined the CGT-FO, which soon became an important anti-Communist labor federation.[45]

This grave schism, which defined the character of the union move-

[42] The humble social origins, modest salaries, and unremitting toil of the elementary teachers mean that they tend to identify with the working class. The traditional ideology of the union movement reinforces this identification. See pp. 32–37.

[43] *E.P.*, No. 12 (October, 1946), pp. 3–4.

[44] Pierre Monatte described this disintegration as more of a tearing apart (*déchirure*) than a clean break (*cassure nette*). Quoted in Dolléans, *Mouvement Ouvrier*, III, 350.

[45] Soviet policy had smashed the unity of French labor for the third time in twenty-six years, according to a former CGT secretary and a founder of the CGT-FO, M. Albert Bouzanquet. He attributes the schisms of 1921, 1939, and 1947 to Soviet influence. *Combat*, February 10, 1948. Some unions chose autonomy, i.e., they left the CGT but refused to join any other confederation. The Catholic unions, organized as the Confédération Française des Travailleurs Chrétiens (CFTC), were not involved.

ment for the rest of the postwar period, was deplored by the leaders of the FEN. There were advance warnings, however. As early as 1946, the FEN Congress demonstrated the first glimmerings of suspicion when it passed a resolution regretting certain political actions taken by the CGT. The resolution called on the CGT to oppose any attempt to use its organization for partisan purposes and to make certain that its directives came from within. The resolution denounced the CGT's all "too clear tendencies towards bureaucracy and authoritarianism."[46]

After the schism had taken place, the FEN was faced with one of three alternatives: remain a member of the CGT, now clearly under Communist domination; join the new labor central, CGT-FO; or choose autonomy and remain organizationally independent of all labor confederations. It was recognized that each choice involved the risk of producing a schism within the FEN itself. M. Adrien Lavergne, the resolute secretary general of the FEN and a long-time union militant, was faced with a crucial decision.[47] It was clear that the FEN could no longer remain in the Communist-dominated CGT; labor solidarity would have to be temporarily sacrificed. But to join his comrades of long-standing in the CGT-FO would have shattered the FEN, for the Communist teachers and perhaps the revolutionary syndicalists would have broken away. Using the analogy of the school teacher who accepts in his classroom children of all faiths and parties, M. Lavergne reasoned that the ideal of laïcité, that is, political and doctrinal neutrality, could also be applied to a union orientation. With this ideal in mind he made the momentous decision to lead his union into autonomy. Only possible because the Communists were a minority and did not control the leadership organs of the FEN, autonomy meant that the struggles between tendencies in the old CGT would be carried on in an organization uniting all teachers. M. Lavergne's decision, ratified by the discussions and votes which followed, determined the orientation of the FEN for the postwar years.

The decisive votes of Easter, 1948, were preceded by three months of discussion, referenda, and votes in the departmental sections.[48] The

---

[46] E.P., No. 9 (June, 1946), p. 2.

[47] He characterized it as a crise de conscience. Interview, April 25, 1960.

[48] E.P., Nouvelle série, No. 7 (April-May, 1949), p. 15. Proponents of each solution found their forum in the union publications. One of the labor movement's old-timers even took a stand: "Although I am one of those 'pioneers of teachers' unionism' . . . and perhaps one of those who did the most to link the teachers' union movement to that of the working class—and while remaining irreducibly faithful to the ideas of my youth—today I place myself resolutely among the supporters of autonomy for the SNI and the FEN." L'Ecole Libératrice, weekly organ of the Syndicat National des Instituteurs, 15e année, Nouvelle série, No. 17 (February 5, 1948), p. 195, hereafter referred to as E.L.

FEN prepared three questions for a referendum to be held by its member unions:

1. Are you for maintaining your national union's affiliation with the CGT?

2. If the majority votes for withdrawing from the CGT, do you favor affiliation with the CGT-Force Ouvrière?

3. If the majority is against affiliation with either the CGT or the Force Ouvrière, are you for maintaining at any cost the unity of your national union and of the FEN as autonomous organizations, whatever your answer to the preceding questions may be?[49]

The national unions consulted their members and met in congresses to reply formally to the three questions. The most important member union, the SNI, organized a referendum in which almost five out of six respondents answered the third question affirmatively. The SNI then called a special Congress and formally chose complete independence by a vote of 1078 to 253 with 39 abstentions. On the same day, March 23, 1948, two other important national unions also announced their decisions to withdraw from the CGT.[50]

On March 25, 26, and 27, 1948, the FEN met in Congress to vote on the three questions. The results of the votes, mandated by the member national unions, are shown in Table 1. The Congress con-

TABLE 1

FEN VOTES ON AFFILIATION WITH LABOR CONFEDERATIONS, 1948

Question	Yes	No	Abstentions
Affiliation with CGT?	2,089	3,435	76*
Affiliation with CGT-FO?	1,065	4,256	279
Independence?	3,799	1,666	76

* E.P., No. 27 (April, 1948), p. 6.

cluded that it would only accept autonomous unions as members. It also stipulated, in order to minimize the fragmentation of the union movement, that it would accept no factions of unions affiliated with the CGT or the CGT-FO, nor would it allow factions of its member unions to remain outside the FEN; each union would have to be either all in or all out of the FEN.[51] The right of an individual to affiliate with one of the confederations was not denied, however.

[49] E.P., No. 26 (February, 1948), p. 6.

[50] The Syndicat National de l'Enseignement Secondaire (SNES) and the Syndicat National des Collèges Modernes. Combat, March 24, 1948.

[51] Ibid., pp. 1, 6. The SNI had already taken a similar stand: "The Congress . . . declares itself against any fractional organization of one or the other of the centrals

No one knew exactly what would happen when the FEN chose autonomy; disintegration seemed likely to many. One militant condemned the idea of an autonomous FEN. "All interested persons know," he wrote, "that the idea is pure fiction. Autonomy is a position that is untenable for more than several months."[52] On April 29, one month after the vote for autonomy, a questionnaire was sent to all the national unions and departmental sections to determine the impact of the vote on the membership. In November, the FEN Secretary for Structure and Propaganda was able to say:

> More than six months have gone by since the FEN decided to become an autonomous federation. . . . We can affirm that our Federation continues to group the immense majority of French teachers. . . . We can assure you that the FEN now has an autonomous union in every department.[53]

The following year a union official said: "A little over a year ago you would have thought the FEN was done for. . . . We nevertheless were able to keep our membership intact and absolutely independent of everyone."[54]

It is true that the mass of members remained faithful. However, the departure of eight national unions in 1948 depleted the membership rolls considerably. According to the figures furnished by the FEN (but not published at the time), between 1947 and 1948 membership dropped from 187,000 to 148,000, a loss of 39,000 members or about 20 per cent. It was not until 1954, some six years after the decision for autonomy, that the pre-schism membership figures were surpassed.[55]

---

inside the autonomous national union and states that it does not consider itself qualified to authorize or forbid individuals to accept membership cards from a confederation." *E.L.*, 15e année, No. 27 (April 29, 1948), p. 329. The following year referenda were organized by the national member unions to ratify the choice of autonomy. The secretary general of the FEN reported to the Congress of 1949 that these consultations had the following results: the SNI voted approval of the status quo (i.e., affiliation with the autonomous FEN) by 53,788 to 18,641; the SNES also approved by 9139 to 2483 with 1570 abstentions; and the SNET voted the status quo by 2693 to 1347 on a motion to permit the Federation to affiliate freely. *E.P.*, 5e année, No. 1 (September-October, 1949), p. 9.

[52] *E.P.*, No. 25 (January, 1948), p. 9.

[53] *E.P.*, Nouvelle série, No. 2 (November, 1948), p. 3.

[54] *E.P.*, Nouvelle série, No. 7 (April-May, 1949), p. 15.

[55] See Figure 1, Chap. III. After one of the departed unions and five new national unions had added their memberships to the FEN ranks, M. Lavergne, in his report to the 1949 Congress, gave no figures but stated: "Contrary to the predictions of the pessimists, the FEN victoriously weathered the union crisis. . . . The membership figures, which had declined slightly following the departure of several national unions in the course of the year 1948, are already as high as those of 1947." *E.P.*, 5e année, No. 1 (September-October, 1949), p. 3. This statement is in conflict with the figures in the text.

The constitution and bylaws of the FEN changed little after the Congress of 1948 chose autonomy. Despite recurrent demands for working-class unity, the FEN remained autonomous, refusing even to join a labor central made up of autonomous federations.[56] In fact, autonomy became a slogan, watchword, and rallying cry, endowed with an emotional aura and peripheral connotations involving respect for minority rights, opposition to the politicization and disunity of the labor movement, a high evaluation of the free exchange of ideas, and a desire to replace sectarian conflict with human relationships.[57] Autonomy even gave its name to those members of the FEN who supported the break with the CGT and who remain opposed to joining any existing confederations: they are known as the *autonomes*.

However emotionally charged the concept of autonomy may have become, the fact remains that, coldly considered, the choice of autonomy was of decisive importance in the history of the FEN. Autonomy was the only solution which permitted the organization to maintain its unity. Any other alternative would have split the teachers into at least two and perhaps more competing and enfeebled unions. The Federation did not rid itself of conflict by this choice; the legacy of the historic differences between the FNSI and the Amicales and among the revolutionary syndicalists, the Communists, and the reformists was supplemented by a new division rising from the external attraction of a recently created labor confederation, the CGT-FO. But these conflicts remained as more or less permanent internal differences, successfully contained within the organization. Without autonomy, the FEN would be without these factions; but without these factions and their memberships, the FEN would not be the powerful organization that it is today, uniting in its ranks the vast majority of the public school teachers of France.

[56] *E.P.*, 5e année, No. 1 (September-October, 1949), p. 5.
[57] *E.P.*, Nouvelle série, No. 8 (June-July, 1949), p. 7.

Aims

A teachers' union is expected to defend and advance the material interests of its members. As a professional organization it may naturally recommend school reforms and sponsor particular educational policies. But the extension of its activity into the realm of general public policy raises some interesting questions. In the case of the FEN, often these public policy goals are only verbalizations; most in any case are beyond the power of the organization to achieve, and many are even outside the effective range of the teachers' influence. Why then do so many of the positions taken by the FEN go far afield from educational and material matters? Do they represent particular applications of an ideology held by the organization's activists? Or do they perhaps serve other purposes, implicit and unrecognized, such as the reinforcement of group cohesion?

A majority of the official aims listed in the FEN constitution relate to material demands and educational policy. Even those which are inspired by working-class ideology are explicitly related to educational problems.[1] On the other hand, noneducational public policy positions often make up the major share of resolutions passed by the FEN annual Congress. For example, of eleven aims for the year 1953–54 cited in a summary listing, six may be classified as political or ideological, four as educational, and three as material, although one of these refers to the "purchasing power of workers," indicating a scope well beyond the effective bargaining power of the teachers' unions.[2] This

[1] FEN constitution, art. 2.

[2] The aims listed were "the reestablishment of peace in Indochina, normalization of Franco-German relations, condemnation of power politics, simultaneous and controlled disarmament making impossible the hegemony of one nation whatever its economic or military power may be, the participation of the peoples of the French Union in the administration of their own countries, respect for civil and union liberties, maintaining intellectual freedom (*franchises universitaires*), the extension of national education services, the reestablishment of teachers' salary levels, the restoration of order in the civil service, [and] increasing the purchasing power of workers." *E.P.*, 9ᵉ année, No. 8 (August-September, 1954), p. 3.

preponderance of ideological or nonmaterial aims is not unusual among French and other European trade unions.[3]

MATERIAL DEMANDS

Although the FEN leaders may fight for educational reform, intellectual freedom, or peace in Algeria, they can never forget the "bread-and-butter" issues of salaries, hours, pensions, and fringe benefits. Despite an ideology which acclaims the value of fraternal struggle against the bourgeoisie or the state, on the whole people join unions for nonideological, material reasons. If the leaders are to keep their jobs, they must satisfy these demands.

In seeking to satisfy these demands, the FEN has the advantage of a favorable climate of opinion deriving from the social function which teachers perform.[4] The FEN capitalizes on this advantage by promoting the idea of the identification of the welfare of the teachers with the good of the nation. Not unusual are such statements as: "The defense of the legitimate interests of the teaching personnel . . . blends in with that of the whole educational system"; "In adopting this totality of resolutions including the demand that one-sixth of the national budget be assigned to education, the National Council has no other object but the higher interest of the country and the more complete realization of national unity"; and "We must show that our [civil service] reclassification is a way to defend the School and *laïcité*."[5]

As civil servants, teachers are paid by the state according to a salary scale based upon their qualifications, years of service, and responsibili-

[3] "The unions in France are less instruments of collective bargaining than of political action." Lorwin, *Labor Movement,* p. 278. LaPalombara asserts that "European labor was from its inception oriented towards goals transcending the technical, or wages and hours, category." "The Political Role of Organized Labor in Western Europe," *Journal of Politics,* Vol. XVII (February, 1955), p. 80.

[4] A public opinion survey on the status accorded various occupations in France ranked primary school teachers third, on the same level with engineers and scientists but below doctors and movie stars. The report added that professors came immediately after school teachers, probably because they are less well known to the masses of the people. Pierre Marchant, "Les Métiers dont Rêvent les Français," *Réalités,* No. 172 (May, 1960), p. 37. An FEN official noted in 1949 that "we are the most representative organization of the body of teachers; as such we enjoy an incontestable moral credit; this credit rests partly on a traditional prejudice in favor of educated people; it rests, moreover, on our reputation for intellectual disinterest, honesty, and freedom." *E.P.,* Nouvelle série, No. 8 (June-July, 1949), p. 7. A recent UNESCO-assisted publication emphasized the great prestige enjoyed by members of the academic profession in France. Richard H. Shryock (ed.), *The Status of University Teachers* (Ghent: International Association of University Professors and Lecturers, 1961), p. 78.

[5] *E.P.,* No. 9 (June, 1946), p. 1; No. 2 (October, 1945), p. 19; and No. 13 (November, 1946), p. 13.

ties. To the basic salary calculated from this scale are added family and residential allowances paid by the commune if housing is not provided.[6]

The current salary grid, essentially the product of a major overhaul of the salary scheme known as the Reclassification of 1948, is based upon two principles: vertical relations between the several categories of civil servants in the same Ministry, and horizontal relations between the various "pilot" categories of several administrations. That is to say, the raw salary of a certain category of teachers is fixed by multiplying the base salary by a coefficient or index established for that category: for example, if the rank of university professor bears a coefficient of 600, his raw salary will be six times that of a school janitor whose job has a coefficient of 100 (and whose raw salary before supplements and deductions would equal the base salary). According to the principles of the 1948 Reclassification, these salaries should correspond to those paid for similar jobs in other administrations and in private or nationalized industry. The principles of these correlations are often violated, primarily in three ways: salary increases in the nationalized industries and private sector are not reflected in the civil service; employees of other administrations are granted increases or reclassifications which, in effect, declassify the educational employees; and pressures from the numerous lower-level employees for a living wage—which budgetary limitations prevent the government from multiplying for the higher categories—collapse the vertical hierarchy. These departures from the norm regularly move the FEN to demand a restoration of the principles of 1948.[7]

These "bread-and-butter" demands are recurrent. No sooner has the government granted an increase in salaries or an adjustment of the

[6] For a summary of teachers' salaries and conditions of work in France, see UNESCO, International Bureau of Education, *Primary Teachers' Salaries* (Publication No. 147) (Geneva, 1953), pp. 156–63; and *Secondary Teachers' Salaries* (Publication No. 157) (Geneva, 1954), pp. 120–25. The calculations are complex. Teachers have been known to complain that they never know exactly how much they will receive in any one month. In an article entitled "How to Calculate Your Pay," *L'Enseignement Public* listed the elements that go into the computation: annual salary, residence allowance, regressive indemnity, temporary complement of remuneration, hierarchical bonus, special bonus for teachers, Paris transportation allowance, family allowance, and hourly allowances for overtime. Seven pages of charts and instructions follow. *E.P.*, 11e année, No. 3 (December, 1955–January, 1956), p. 7. One excellent detailed analysis of civil service salaries in France is André Tiano, *Les Traitements des Fonctionnaires et Leur Détermination, 1930–1957* (Paris: Génin, 1957).

[7] "Rapport Fédéral aux Membres des Commissions Parlementaires de l'Education Nationale," *E.P.*, 8e année, No. 4 (January, 1953), p. 3; and *E.P.*, 9e année, No. 6 (May, 1954), p. 2. For a fuller explanation of the Reclassification of 1948 and the departures from its principles, see Roger Grégoire, *La Fonction Publique* (Paris: Colin, 1954), pp. 263–82.

classification scheme than the cycle recommences with new demands. For example, in 1957 the FEN noted that an increase promised one year earlier had just been included in members' salaries and said that, in view of the increase in the cost of living and the wage increases in the nationalized sector, it was demanding an immediate increase of at least 10 per cent.[8] The government decisions on salaries two months later were met with "a very deep disappointment" by the civil service unions.[9] On another occasion the FEN accepted a government plan to raise wages as "a first slice of wage increases," as "preparatory measures which have to be inserted in a broad plan of wage increases." Its spokesman concluded: "In other words, the battle for wage increases begins."[10] And so the cycle continues, a perennial series of salary negotiations, punctuated with minimum demands and final offers, frequent strike threats and occasional strikes, and eventually immediate or promised wage-scale adjustments. As a permanent part of the FEN's program, these recurrent struggles fill the pages of the union bulletins and consume a large portion of the time and energy of the union leaders. The demands may be prosaic and repetitious, but they constitute the heart of union activity and require the union to employ its every resource of pressure, influence, and persuasion.

EDUCATIONAL POLICY

A second category of FEN aims relates to the purposes, organization, and functioning of the educational establishment. Representing the teaching profession, the FEN carefully prepares and promotes its own plans for educational reform. Its leaders have served on government study commissions, communicated with members of the appropriate parliamentary committees, discussed education bills in official organs of the administration, and vigorously supported increased school construction and expanded teacher recruitment in planning agencies. It is a constant and diligent advocate of reforms based upon a relatively coherent philosophy.

The underlying impulses which shape the particular pedagogical policies of the FEN may be summarized in the concepts of democratization and modernization. The former attempts to realize the ideals of justice and equality, and the latter seeks to keep pace with the burgeoning needs of a technological society. They are interrelated, of course, as when the development of technical schools not only provides skilled hands for a modern society, but also promotes equality by

[8] *Le Monde,* October 9, 1957.
[9] *Le Monde,* December 12, 1957.
[10] *E.P.,* 6e année, No. 7 (April, 1951), p. 1.

augmenting educational opportunities for all and fosters social justice by developing talents formerly wasted or only partially exploited. From modernization derives the desire to rationalize the educational system: to eliminate its educational dead-ends, to smooth the transition from one level or type of education to another, and to remove its formidable barriers to changes in career choices. Modernization also requires the inclusion of more science and technology in school curricula, the dissemination of new teaching methods and materials, the creation of more technical schools, and the broadening of school services to meet the special needs of an urbanized and industrialized society. From the impulse to democratize stem the aims of establishing counseling systems to assist pupils in choosing careers according to their talents and inclinations unlimited by their parents' income or social class; of expanding educational facilities and the supply of teachers to provide for the increased enrollment that democratization and a higher compulsory-education requirement entail; and, finally, of defending the ideal which favors a school open to children of all races and religions, laïcité.

These goals rise from the conditions of French education and society. Mechanization of agriculture and industry has multiplied the needs for technicians and specialists and made imperative the modernization of traditional school programs which underemphasized scientific training and provided all too few opportunities for mass science education. Teaching methods, traditionally characterized by rote memorization and overly stringent discipline, have only partially yielded to progressive reforms. A jerry-built educational organization which, until the reforms undertaken in the late 1930's, included a primary and secondary education composed of two parallel, closed tracks, each with its own methods, its own teachers, its own spirit, and even its own pupils drawn from separate and isolated social levels, cried out in the postwar years for a continuation of the prewar reforms. The system resulted in a practically irrevocable career choice at the age of eleven.[11] Statistics continue to dramatize the need for democratization. They show that only one-sixth of the students in secondary education are from workers' and peasants' families, although workers and peasants make up more than half of the active population. Forty-five per cent of the university students are children of civil servants and members of the liberal professions, groups that together constitute 8 per cent of the population. Only 3 per cent of the students are offspring of workers,

---

[11] L'Organisation de l'Enseignement en France, pp. 113–14. For an excellent treatment of these problems of educational needs, structures, and methods, see Cros, "L'Explosion" Scolaire.

and only 1 per cent are offspring of farmers.[12] The highest birthrate in Western Europe and the tendency of children to stay in school longer (73 per cent continued their studies beyond the age of fourteen in 1959 compared with 40 per cent in 1945) combined to enlarge the school population from five million in 1948 to over seven million in 1959, necessitating a vast expansion in school facilities.[13] Democratization also means to teachers defense of *laïcité* against the supporters of state aid to Catholic schools who threaten the financial support and religious neutrality of the public schools.

The FEN has made these goals specific in a number of reform projects that were designed to reshape the whole educational system. Teachers' unions before World War II regularly took positions on reforms that were proposed every decade. The predecessor of the FEN, the FGE, sponsored a reform plan of its own as early as 1929.[14] But the FEN participated in the preparation of a comprehensive, long-range plan of reform that, while never actually put into effect, served as an ideal which subsequent, more realistic schemes tried to approximate. This was the plan prepared by the Langevin-Wallon Commission of 1944–47.

The Langevin Commission was constituted by a ministerial decree of November 8, 1944, and directed to study the complete reorganization of education in the broadest and deepest manner. The FEN reacted immediately by appointing its own pedagogical committee to debate the questions under consideration by the Langevin Commission in order to establish an FEN position harmonizing the views of the member unions. At the same time the FEN contacted the Minister of Education and used its influence to have four of the members of its pedagogical committee appointed to the Commission and four others made members of the specialized subcommittees. As finally constituted, the Commission had twenty-five members named by the Minister: the four directors of primary, secondary, technical, and higher education in the Ministry, representatives of teachers' unions, and educational experts. The Commission drew inspiration from the 1937 reform plan of the then Minister of Education Jean Zay and guidance from the

[12] Christiane Peyre, "L'Origine Sociale des Elèves de l'Enseignement Secondaire en France," *Ecole et Société*, ed. Pierre Naville (Paris: Rivière, 1959), p. 17; "France at School—II," *Economist*, January 9, 1960, p. 116; and *Le Monde*, October 15, 1960.

[13] Minister of Education André Boulloche in *Avenirs*, p. 9. Eleven million pupils and students are predicted for 1970. Cros, "*L'Explosion" Scolaire*, p. 5.

[14] I. L. Kandel, *The Reform of Secondary Education in France* (New York: Teachers College, Columbia University, 1924), pp. 5–6; and *E.P.*, No. 1 [1945], p. 2.

basic principles of educational reform laid down by the provisional French government's Algiers Commission of March-September, 1944. After the death of the Commission's first president, Paul Langevin, the Commission was headed by Professor Henri Wallon. The Commission's report to the Minister of Education was published as a brochure in September, 1947.[15]

The principles of the Langevin Commission project were approved by the FEN at its first National Council in July, 1945. Among them were the principles of justice in the school, education for work and for life, delayed and flexible differentiation into specialties, and the extension of compulsory education. Justice in the school meant that every child was to be provided the opportunity of developing his aptitudes and enriching his life to the limit of his talents and efforts. For this the school was to be open to all, regardless of creed, wealth, or social class. Furthermore, the school was to have the task of preparing the child for an occupation without sacrificing general culture. The artificial barriers isolating the branches of education were to be toppled so as to allow changes from one program to another. Differentiation into these various orders of education was to be delayed as long as possible to provide for a maximum of common culture and to allow time for the talents and interests of pupils to develop before career choices were made. The compulsory school age was to be extended to eighteen years in order to raise the national educational level as much as possible.[16]

The specific plan for implementing these principles, briefly described, involved nursery schools for children between the ages of three and seven; a four-year primary school; a four-year cycle of orientation; a secondary cycle for children between the ages of fifteen and eighteen; and two years of pre-university training followed by two years in the university for the *licence*. The cycle of orientation was potentially the most significant and consequently the most controversial part of the reform. This four-year period, also known as the "common trunk" because all children would pass through it before branching out into their respective specialties, was to be divided into two equal parts: two years of observation during which pupils' talents and capacities would be evaluated, as general instruction and some optional courses continued; and then two years of determination during which pupils

15 *E.P.*, No. 1 [1945], pp. 2, 6; No. 7 (April, 1946), p. 11; No. 20 (June 10, 1947), p. 5; 5e année, No. 5 (January, 1950), p. 11; and Donald W. Miles, *Recent Reforms in French Secondary Education* (New York: Teachers College, Columbia University, 1953), pp. 36–55.

16 *E.P.*, No. 1 [1945], p. 6; No. 2 (October, 1945), p. 20; and No. 20 (June 10, 1947), p. 5.

would be guided into practical and vocational courses or into theoretical courses by means of counseling and meetings with parents. Supporters maintained that the whole reform would benefit both national productivity and national unity. In the words of a member of the Commission: "By grouping on the same benches children of the same age, whatever may be the fortune of their families, [the plan] will equalize the chances of all for learning and make possible greater national cohesion."[17]

Since the plan called for massive investments and expenditures for education, it was never wholly put into effect. Some of its recommendations, however, appeared in later reform proposals. Ministers of Education Yvon Delbos in 1949, Jean Berthoin in 1955, and René Billères in 1956 each prepared reform plans which tempered the earlier ideals with realistic consideration of financial limitations. But no general reform was put into effect until the de Gaulle transitional government issued on January 6, 1959, two decrees and an ordinance instituting certain moderate reforms.[18] For example, where the Langevin-Wallon Commission recommended a four-year cycle of orientation and the Billères plan cut it to two, the de Gaulle reform reduced it to three months. One FEN leader labeled the 1959 reform "segregative" and "profoundly reactionary."[19] It did, indeed, constitute a retreat from the union ideals embodied in the Langevin-Wallon report as regularly revived and modernized by the Pedagogical Committee of the FEN. While cooperating with the government to put the 1959 reform into effect, the FEN at its 1961 Congress continued to call for "a real democratization of education."[20]

Support for expansion of the nation's educational facilities is an important part of the FEN's pedagogical policies. Leaders of the organization often cite the recommendations of the Le Gorgeu Commission in this respect. Formally known as the Commission de l'Equipement Scolaire, Universitaire et Sportif, a section of the General Planning Commission, this Commission was assigned the tasks of forecasting the future numbers of students and needed teachers, of determining how many new schools and additions to old ones would be necessary, and of estimating how much all this would cost. Originally established in 1951, the Commission was reconstituted in 1956 and

17 E.P., No. 1 [1945], p. 6; and No. 20 (June 10, 1947), p. 5.
18 Ordonnance No. 59–45, Decret No. 59–57, and Decret No. 59–58. J.O., Lois et Decrets, January 7, 1959, pp. 376, 422–30.
19 E.L., 26e année, No. 16 (January 16, 1959), p. 510; and E.P., 14e année, No. 4 (February-March, 1959), p. 15.
20 E.P., 17e année, No. 2 (November, 1961), p. 16.

1960 to make recommendations for the Third and Fourth National Economic Plans. The FEN maintains a representative on the Commission.[21] Expansion, however, failed to keep up with need. For example, in forty-nine "deficient" departments in the North and East of France persons lacking the necessary credentials were provisionally appointed elementary school teachers pending the completion of their professional preparation through correspondence courses and special monthly meetings.[22] Of the 28,200 positions in secondary education, 10 per cent were filled with persons lacking regular qualifications in 1959.[23] The shortage of qualified teachers will continue until about 1968, when the increase in the school population is expected to slacken.[24] Meanwhile, the teachers' unions regularly demand more attractive salaries and the creation of new teacher training institutes to help alleviate the shortage.[25] The major motion on educational policy of the 1959 FEN Congress emphasized "the very grave situation created by difficulties of recruiting teachers on all levels of public education" and proposed reforms in selection, training, certification, and assignment.[26]

IDEOLOGICAL AND PUBLIC POLICY POSITIONS

The third and final category of FEN aims extends far beyond the purview of special teacher competence. It includes positions taken on public issues as broad as disarmament and as specific as the Rosenberg case. It takes in aims which are parts of larger ideologies such as syndicalism and *laïcité*. This last category of ideological and public policy positions illustrates a common tendency among many groups organized for the promotion of the relatively narrow interests of members to take positions on broad questions of national policy. The FEN shares this practice with French trade unions generally.[27]

Laïcité. Although at first view the doctrine of *laïcité* has its prime application in the question of government aid to religious schools, its ramifications extend so much beyond that single question that it cannot

[21] E.P., 14e année, No. 1 (October, 1958), p. 4. A description of the Commission and summary of its findings may be found in Documentation No. 32 of the French Cultural Services, French Embassy, New York, N.Y.

[22] Le Monde, May 29, 1959.

[23] J.O., Documents de l'Assemblée Nationale, No. 328–29 (1960), p. 660.

[24] R. Naudin et al., "Les Besoins en Maîtres de l'Enseignement dans la Métropole," Avenirs, p. 34.

[25] Le Populaire de Paris, March 29, 1956.

[26] E.P., 15e année, No. 2 (November, 1959), p. 13.

[27] Meynaud argues that these positions logically flow from the basic goals of the organization. For example, an increase in teachers' salaries is easier to obtain if military expenses caused by the Algerian war are reduced. In addition, many leaders view their unions as communities of citizens as well as of workers. Nouvelles Etudes, pp. 118–22.

be considered just a part of the FEN's educational policy; it must be viewed as an ideology underlying a multitude of its policy decisions. *Laïcité* has been translated as "secularism" and *laïque* as "lay," but the French words have a broader and, in certain circles, a more emotional connotation than their English translations. *Laïcité* implies not only anticlericalism,[28] but also rationalism, humanism, and tolerance. Perhaps the most sweeping definition was put into words in 1956 by M. Adrien Lavergne, then secretary general of the FEN:

> What is *laïcité?* The culmination of the evolution of French thought marked by the Reformation, Humanism, the practice of tolerance, the philosophical development of the Eighteenth Century, the practice of fraternity, the revolutionary social movements of the Nineteenth Century, [and] the necessary humanist resistance to the dizzying developments of new techniques capable of suffocating the human personality, if unionism doesn't take care.[29]

This definition, which makes of *laïcité* the distilled essence of the historical currents that produced the modern world, is enthusiastically shared by many other union educators. Some explain *laïcité* in even more expansively abstract language. For example, one writer claims that the essential element of *laïcité* is a kind of dialectical rationalism.

> It is identified with human reason moving towards the future, a future that we build each day, without being able to foresee surely what it will be in twenty, thirty, or fifty years. It has taken in the course of the ages diverse names, including that of humanism four hundred years ago. But the name that could have been given it permanently is that of an historic law of the evolution of free human thought. Thus *laïcité* appears not as a fixed concept, but as the very movement of critical thought, capable itself of destroying its own errors, indeed, open to all currents, but capable of sorting them to choose those which are motors of progress and to reject without brutality those which are retrograde. Its essence is discovery, constant adaptation, and that is what makes it superior to metaphysics or religions whose tactics alone evolve.[30]

In the terms of these authors *laïcité* is the modern spirit of rationalism, opposed to superstition and ignorance, impatient of restraints

---

[28] FEN Secretary General Georges Lauré emphasized that the clericals are not to be confused with the Catholics who as believers in a faith claim no special privileges for their religion. Interview, May 11, 1960.

[29] *E.P.*, 12e année, No. 2 (November-December, 1956), p. 1.

[30] *E.L.*, 26e année, No. 22 (February 27, 1959), p. 849.

on thought and communication, dedicated to seeking and disseminating the truth wherever it may be found. It admits the free competition of ideas—intellectual pluralism—but vigorously rejects institutional pluralism, as exemplified by the existence of the Catholic school system alongside the public schools, on the grounds that the Church not only constitutes a state within a state, but that it also maintains exclusive control of a part of the population by not allowing a free flow of ideas among them.[31] The logical conclusion derived from this line of reasoning is not simply the mild expedient of opposing state aid to Catholic schools; it is nationalization of all private educational establishments, a measure discussed by the primary school teachers' union, the SNI, as early as its 1927 Congress, and now a recurrent feature of its program.[32]

In addition to the question of the schools, the doctrine of laïcité is applied to other public matters with such vehemence that its supporters have been accused of narrow sectarianism and exaggerated anticlericalism. Laïcité, as conceived by its adherents, demands absolute separation of church and state. One MRP member of the National Assembly was severely criticized for invoking the aid of God after his election as president of that body.[33] The 1959 Congress of the FEN passed a motion which "denounced the abandonment of the principle of the laïcité of the state in very numerous cases, and particularly: obligatory masses for certain young soldiers, the visit of the President of the Republic to the Vatican, and the place occupied by religious ceremonies in the newspapers, radio, and television."[34] Articles in the union press, especially that of the SNI, regularly attack clericalism, the "clericalism of the twentieth century, clericalism of all time, symbolically represented by two swords, one belonging to Peter and one at his orders."[35] The titles of these articles reveal their orientation. For example, two are "The Incurable Diseases of the Church" and "The So-Called Social Doctrine of the Church." Secularization of the schools and the state is justified, not as an attempt to de-Christianize, but as "a reaction against the totalitarian pretensions of Roman clericalism."[36]

The peculiarly virulent brand of anticlericalism that passes for

31 Cf. Robert Escarpit in Le Monde, August 24, 1959.

32 E.P., Nos. 17–18 (1947), p. 5.

33 The MRP (Mouvement Républicain Populaire) is a progressive Catholic party. E.P., 10e année, No. 5 (February, 1955), p. 1. His words were "with your permission, and as for me personally, I invoke the aid of God." J.O., Assemblée Nationale, January 13, 1955, p. 59.

34 E.P., 15e année, No. 2 (November, 1959), pp. 11–12.

35 E.L., 26e année, No. 21 (February 20, 1959), p. 840.

36 Minutes of the 1957 Congress, in E.P., 13e année, No. 3 (January, 1958), p. 16.

laïcité among the primary school teachers has been the subject of repeated controversy. One incident which began with a verbal engagement in the National Assembly between an MRP deputy, M. Charles Viatte, and an outspoken Socialist, M. Maurice Deixonne, demonstrated that many who consider themselves *laïque* are repelled by the narrow and sectarian *laïcité* of the SNI. In the course of a debate on school reform in 1957, M. Deixonne said he wanted an explicit statement in the law requiring that the public schools be *laïque*. M. Viatte supplied a clause that would apply his conception of *laïcité* by permitting religious instruction in the public schools by outside teachers. Aroused by interruptions, M. Viatte launched into an attack on the *laïcité* of the SNI:

> I question very plainly the false conception of *laïcité* of the National Teachers Union [SNI] and its directors, a conception which seems to me to have slipped progressively from the conception of Jules Ferry, who wanted the souls of the children of every faith and of every tendency to be respected, to a certain conception of anticlericalism. . . . They have come to confuse *laïcité* and irreligion.

M. Viatte protested the systematic campaign of opposition to religion that goes on, not just in the SNI, but in the organizations of parents and supporters of the public schools linked to it. He labeled M. Clément Durand of the SNI and the FEN a doctrinaire supporter of *laïcité*.[37] In commenting upon this exchange, Secretary General Denis Forestier of the SNI stated that his organization intended to remain *laïque* within the framework of the following definition: "*Laïcité* is neither a dogma nor a religious persuasion. Its purpose is to free from religions and dogmas all the common institutions and services of the nation and of the state."[38] M. Viatte answered in the press with an even stronger attack on the SNI. He concluded: "Very few know that the sectarian intransigence of M. Forestier and his friends has . . . prevented all conversation between Frenchmen seeking the good of France."[39]

These examples show the spirit that pervades the teachers' affirmations of *laïcité*. Rationally expressed, *laïcité* is the complete separation of church and state; emotionally considered, it is a secular faith whose devotees can be as sectarian as the adherents of any religion.[40] As a

---

37 *J.O., Assemblée Nationale,* July 27, 1957, pp. 4024–25.
38 *Combat,* August 2, 1957.
39 *Ibid.,* August 17–18, 1957.
40 In the strong words of a Catholic writer, *laïcité* is "anticlerical, anticatholic, antiecclesiastical, and antireligious, in order to become in its turn by an immanent

basic ideological orientation of FEN leaders, it has influenced their decisions from opposition to Catholic youth hostels to the choice of union autonomy.

Syndicalism. A second ideological complex underlying a number of FEN aims is that of syndicalism.[41] More accurately it should be called reformist syndicalism to differentiate it from its more aggressive ancestor, revolutionary syndicalism. Reformist syndicalism is the product of a union history rich in combat and comradeship. Although still given to the language of economic warfare and class struggle, as its weakness for extravagant verbal irrelevancies attests, syndicalism today can be described in terms of its two essential elements: independence of government, parties, and sects; and solidarity with the working class in its struggle for emancipation. The choice of autonomy in 1948 may be regarded as the result of a conflict between these two principles in which the second was temporarily sacrificed to preserve the first. Nevertheless, both elements continue to mold the public behavior of the FEN. As Eckstein has observed, attitudes affect the choice of the channels and targets of pressure group action and influence the scope and intensity of group activity.[42]

Still cited frequently by FEN leaders as a guide for union activities, the Charter of Amiens, drafted and passed by the 1906 Congress of the CGT, summarized the position of the revolutionary syndicalists. It declared in part:

> This declaration is a recognition of the class struggle which opposes, on the economic level, the workers revolting against all forms of material and moral exploitation and oppression undertaken by the capitalist class against the working class. . . .
>
> Syndicalism prepares the total emancipation [of the working class] which can only be realized by expropriation of the capitalists; it recommends the general strike as a means of action. . . .
>
> The Congress affirms complete liberty for the union member

necessity all that it condemns, a sort of clergy, church, and religion but in caricature only, that is, a sect that is usurping, violent, monopolistic, and despotic." Sister M. Justine Redmond, *Laicism in the Schools of France* (Washington: Catholic University of America, 1932), p. 1. In my conversations with both union leaders and union critics in France, the element of strong feeling on the question of *laïcité* could not be overlooked. One union militant urged that my report on their mission be written with heart and feeling, as a crusade would be treated. One critic whose application to teach had reportedly been turned down at the behest of the union representative on the grounds that she had been educated in the Catholic schools considered the SNI to be narrowly sectarian.

41 For a discussion of the impact of syndicalism on the French labor movement, see Lorwin, *Labor Movement,* pp. 29–46.

42 Eckstein, *Pressure Group Politics,* pp. 16–31.

to participate, outside of the corporate group, in such forms of struggle as correspond to his political or philosophical conceptions, confining itself to ask him in return not to introduce into the union the opinions that he professes outside. . . .

The Congress decides that . . . economic action must be taken directly against the employers since the confederated organizations, as syndical groupings, do not have the right to preoccupy themselves with parties and sects.[43]

Often references are also made to the preamble of the CGT constitution of 1936, sometimes called the Charter of Toulouse, which listed the principles by which the reunified Confederation was to function. It reasserted the independence of the union movement.

The union movement, in all its echelons, administers itself and determines its action in absolute independence of employers, governments, political parties, philosophical sects, or other outside groups.[44]

Although a small number of revolutionary syndicalists continue their activity within the FEN, the majority group is explicitly reformist.[45] The vocabulary of struggle and the myth of the general strike persist, but the leaders of the majority place their faith in gradual ameliorations won through all the techniques available to a union within a democratic system. Only political independence and a sense of solidarity with the working class in its struggle for democratic and human rights remain of the syndicalist ideology among the FEN operative ideals.

The FEN constitution embodies these two principles. It suspends members of the Federation's executive committee from their positions for the duration of any electoral campaign they may undertake and requires them to resign if they are elected.[46] It also requires the FEN leaders to work for the unity of the working class:

Convinced that the defense of the educational system and its personnel is inseparable from the general action of the working class, the Federation works for the reunification of the union movement in a democratically organized confederation indepen-

[43] Jean Maitron, *Le Syndicalisme Révolutionnaire: Paul Delesalle* (Paris: Editions Ouvrières, 1952), pp. 31–32.
[44] Jean Montreuil, *Histoire du Mouvement Ouvrier en France: Des Origines à Nos Jours* (Paris: Montaigne, 1946), p. 465. Both Charters were reprinted in *E.P.*, 17e année, No. 1 (October, 1961), p. 30.
[45] In the words of M. Denis Forestier of the SNI, "We are not revolutionaries; we are convinced reformists." *Le Monde*, July 20, 1956.
[46] Constitution, art. 9.

dent of all governments and of all political, philosophical, or religious organizations.[47]

Public communications have reiterated the official FEN position. Before the schism of the CGT, the FEN National Council of June 23, 1946, affirmed "the entire solidarity of the members of education with the whole of the working class in its struggle for the maintenance and improvement of the living conditions of all workers."[48] In 1949, M. Henri Aigueperse, the first postwar secretary general of the SNI, deplored the CGT schism, but set as the essential condition for a return to unity the absolute independence of the unions with respect to sects, parties, governments, and blocs of states.[49] M. Lavergne of the FEN said that his organization would endlessly affirm that "the reconstitution of syndical unity is only possible within a confederation respectful of union democracy and independent of political parties, religions, and philosophies."[50] M. Lavergne's successor, M. Georges Lauré, considered it incontestable that the division of the working world had made the "progressive disaggregation" of the Fourth Republic possible.[51]

These quotations make clear that the autonomy chosen by the FEN was an unpleasant expedient made necessary by the subjection of the CGT to the Communist party. The teachers' unions did not want to splinter the union movement, but the threat of political domination in violation of the traditional syndicalist faith in apolitical unionism obliged them to break with the CGT. However, the syndicalist faith was by no means dead. While clinging to autonomy as the best safeguard against colonization by and subjection to outside political forces, and ignoring leftist criticism that "autonomy has brought nothing to the teachers,"[52] the FEN continued to make repeated appeals for "the reconstitution of a solid and durable union unity."[53]

In 1957 certain union leaders moved to translate this sentiment from the realm of slogans and manifestoes to that of action. M. Forestier of

[47] Ibid., art. 2.
[48] E.P., No. 10 (July, 1946), p. 3.
[49] Le Monde, July 24–25, 1949.
[50] E.P., [10e année], No. 9 (August-September, 1955), p. 3.
[51] E.P., 14e année, No. 7 (August-September, 1959), p. 13.
[52] Roger Hagnauer, "Dans l'Enseignement: Bilan de Six Années d'Autonomie," Revue Prolétarienne (December, 1953), p. 338.
[53] Le Populaire de Paris, July 22, 1957. It has been remarked that as the only major union which succeeded in maintaining its unity, the FEN feels it has the particular destiny of reuniting the working class. Contrary to most unions which are interested almost exclusively in material demands, unless they have been subjected to Communist political control, the FEN has intellectualized a complete proletarian ideology with which it would like to lead the working class. François Goguel, interview, May 20, 1960.

the SNI, joined by the leaders of two other rather small unions, founded a movement aimed at the reunification of labor in a democratic organization, the Mouvement Syndical Uni et Démocratique.[54] Apparently inspired by the experience of the SNI and the FEN, the new organization was to be based on the frank recognition of differing ideological tendencies and acceptance of majority rule.[55] The founders felt that with such a realistic and democratic organization working-class unity could be restored. Supported fully by the SNI and FEN congresses (but opposed by the CGT), by 1958 the movement claimed a membership of nineteen national organizations having a total membership of 400,000.[56] Although it was originally conceived as a loosely organized "movement," in late 1958 it was transformed into an association regulated by the law of 1901. This change permitted it to have a responsible treasurer and an official accounting.[57] On December 12, 1959, the association held its first General Assembly.[58] In 1960 union leaders expressed confidence in the future growth of the movement; by early 1961 reported membership exceeded 500,000.[59]

Two other intellectual currents in addition to laïcité and syndicalism have played a significant role in the union movement among teachers. Both pacifism and internationalism characterized the inter-war years, particularly among the elementary school teachers.[60] The Vichy regime indicted the teachers' unions for their alleged anti-patriotism which had purportedly weakened France, but the heroic participation of numerous teachers in the Resistance wiped out these charges. However, strains of both ideologies persist in modified form. This is apparent from some of the particular policy positions taken by the FEN.

Policy positions. The general ideological attitudes of laïcité and reformist syndicalism explain many of the policy positions of the FEN, but there are others which stem from a cluster of principles which are somewhat difficult to summarize except in very broad terms. These principles are essentially those of liberalism; they include: defense of the Republic, defense of civil liberties and human rights, and defense

---

[54] *Le Monde,* July 4, 1959.

[55] *E.P.*, 13e année, No. 1 (October, 1957), p. 8.

[56] *Combat,* July 6, 1959; and *E.P.*, 14e année, No. 1 (October, 1958), p. 3.

[57] It also helped to refute charges that it was financed by the Freemasons. Minutes of the SNI National Council of Christmas, 1958, in *E.L.*, 26e année, No. 17 (January 23, 1959), p. 575; and Minutes of the Administrative Commission of January 15, 1959, in *É.P.*, 14e année, No. 4 (February-March, 1959), p. 14.

[58] *E.L.*, 27e année, No. 15 (December 18, 1959), p. 789.

[59] Pierre Dhombres, secretary general of the SNES, interview, April 25, 1960; and *Le Monde,* March 2, 1961.

[60] Ferré, *Mouvement Syndicaliste Revolutionnaire,* pp. 280–86.

of the right of peoples to self-determination and self-government. They are also the principles of socialism. In the words of M. Forestier, "We believe in a constructive socialism, in a directed economy. We are against all discrimination and for emancipation of the School by the working class with whom we share solidarity."[61] These principles, applied with a ready impartiality which is the pride of the FEN leadership,[62] are revealed in the public stands taken by the FEN on both international and domestic issues.

In the arena of international politics, the FEN supported the strikers in the Berlin riots of June, 1953; consistently opposed atomic bomb tests, even for France; favored a reduction in the length of military service; opposed German rearmament; favored the admission of Red China to the United Nations as early as 1950; and opposed the execution of Julius and Ethel Rosenberg, Americans convicted of espionage for the Soviet Union. In the latter case, a strongly worded resolution of the FEN Administrative Commission expressed regret over "the refusal of a stay of execution or a pardon which would have permitted the non-application of a verdict judged extraordinarily severe by world opinion, when the very guilt of the accused seemed far from being proved and when they proclaimed their innocence to the end." The FEN wanted "to bear witness to the protest of French teachers against a measure which marks the contempt into which individual liberties fall when Reason of State is imposed on peoples."[63] In December, 1955, the FEN made an appeal for general disarmament and sent copies to the chiefs of government and foreign ministers of France, the United Kingdom, the United States, and the U.S.S.R., as well as to the United Nations. This action won the FEN an invitation to a Soviet-sponsored meeting on partial disarmament; the FEN, however, refused to attend on the grounds that the other organizations invited to attend were political. That fall the FEN secretary general reported to his Congress that replies had been received from all except the United States.[64] The FEN also took a stand on the war in Indochina. From its 1953 Congress to the Geneva Accords of 1954, the FEN demanded a cease-fire as a preliminary condition for establishing peace. On April 29, 1954, it sent telegrams to the heads of

[61] *Le Monde,* July 20, 1956.

[62] *E.P.,* 9e année, No. 1 (September-October, 1953), p. 9.

[63] *E.P.,* 6e année, No. 3 (December, 1950), p. 9; 9e année, No. 1 (September-October, 1953), pp. 9, 40; 15e année, No. 2 (November, 1959), pp. 6–7; and 17e année, No. 2 (November, 1961), p. 11.

[64] *E.P.,* 11e année, No. 5 (March, 1956), p. 4; Minutes of the Administrative Commission of March 15, 1956, in *E.P.,* 11e année, No. 6 (April-May, 1956), p. 13; and No. 8 (August-September, 1956), p. 6.

government or delegations meeting in Geneva to inform them of the
FEN position. On July 16 a telegram to Premier Mendès-France
declared that the teachers would be profoundly satisfied if a cease-fire
should be obtained by July 20.[65] The FEN also resigned from the
French National Commission of UNESCO in 1952 as a protest over
the admission of Spain to the United Nations. After a stormy session,
the FEN Congress of 1956 condemned both the Franco-British inter-
vention in Egypt and the Soviet repression of the Hungarian Revolution.[66] In 1959 the Congress passed a motion on "peace" which approved the international relaxation of tension, expressed hostility to
power politics, advocated controlled general disarmament, approved
the development of atomic energy for peaceful purposes, and called
for ending nuclear tests.[67]

In the area of domestic politics, the FEN has vigorously defended
individual liberties. In particular, it has spoken out for intellectual
freedom in an atmosphere of war and domestic unrest which threatened it. It has expressed little sympathy for capitalism and none for
colonialism. It took a relatively moderate stand on Algeria, rejecting
both independence and integration, but was adamant in its opposition
to the Fifth Republic.

The FEN has never hesitated to take a position in support of human
rights and civil liberties whenever they are threatened. As the pro-
longed Algerian conflict grew in bitterness and in the gravity of its
threats to civil liberties, the FEN spoke out against the confiscation
of newspapers, the use of torture, and arbitrary arrests and confine-
ment. The FEN protested the suppression of M. Henri Alleg's *La
Question,* a book which exposed the use of torture in Algeria.[68] But
loyal to its role as the spokesman of the teaching intellectuals of
France, the FEN was particularly sensitive to attacks on intellectual
freedom. The 1950 Congress passed a resolution condemning the dismissal of eight teachers in New York City and requested the school
board to reinstate them.[69] The FEN condemned the dismissal of the
Communist scientist, M. Frédéric Joliet-Curie, from his position in
atomic research the same year. In 1953 the Congress of the SNES and
M. Lavergne of the FEN protested the treatment accorded certain
civil servants because of their political views. M. Lavergne wrote:
" 'McCarthyism,' which is neither French nor proletarian, is practiced

---

[65] *E.P.,* 9ᵉ année, No. 8 (August-September, 1954), p. 3.

[66] *E.P.,* 12ᵉ année, No. 2 (November-December, 1956), pp. 3, 5.

[67] *E.P.,* 15ᵉ année, No. 2 (November, 1959), pp. 6–7.

[68] Minutes of the Administrative Commission of April 24, 1958, in *E.P.,* 13ᵉ
année, No. 7 (June-July, 1958), p. 21.

[69] *E.P.,* 6ᵉ année, No. 3 (December, 1950), p. 9.

in the civil service. Under the pretext of political ideology, candidates for certain public jobs are rejected or researchers whose professional activity has nothing to do with the security of the state are discharged."[70]

A motion passed by the first postwar FEN Congress demonstrates the socialist economic orientation of the organization. This motion called on the CGT to institute a workers' plan of reconstruction, "not for the trusts and the shareholders, but for the interests of the working world alone." This plan was to entail the expropriation of key industries, the control of production by workers' representatives in Plant Committees, a national plan, and the establishment of cooperatives, especially in agriculture.[71] Except for the role of the CGT, the orientation has not basically changed since. M. Lavergne in 1956 favored a fiscal reform that would provoke a leveling of the inequalities between standards of living.[72] M. Forestier, in the following quotation, reveals the basic hostility to capitalism that pervades most FEN pronouncements on economic life:

> That there was anarchy in the expansion, resulting in disequilibrium in the economy, is a fact which would demand a rather austere directed economy and not the competitive economic liberalism that people extoll; that there were abusive profits accompanied by the investment of French capital abroad is a fact; that there was a kind of "socialization of losses" resulting in state subsidies to weak sectors is a fact; that tax frauds, the huge frauds known and never reduced, reach the level of a trillion francs is a fact. These are facts inherent in every capitalist society.[73]

It is not surprising that the FEN took a moderate stand on the Algerian conflict. Belief in the assimilating power of French culture is probably stronger among teachers than any other occupational group. There is no apparent difference between the doctrine of assimilation and the slogan of "integration" espoused by the French settlers of Algeria. Most FEN teachers in Algeria became supporters of integration. Even venerable President Albert Bayet of the Ligue de l'Enseignement, an educational organization closely associated with the teachers, was a leading member with M. Jacques Soustelle of the Union pour le Salut et le Renouveau de l'Algérie Française, an organization sup-

[70] *Combat*, April 1, 1953; and *E.P.*, 9e année, No. 1 (September-October, 1953), p. 1.

[71] *E.P.*, No. 7 (April, 1946), p. 14.

[72] *E.P.*, 12e année, No. 3 (January, 1957), p. 11.

[73] *E.L.*, 26e année, No. 15 (January 9, 1959), p. 454.

porting integration. M. Bayet believed that France had the duty of continuing her civilizing mission in Algeria. But the policy of integration conflicted with another principle, that of self-determination. One of the most vociferous minorities in the FEN carried this principle to its logical end by favoring independence for Algeria, but the majority would not go so far. The compromise resulting from these conflicting views was the FEN demand, as early as 1955, for a cease-fire followed by peaceful negotiation at a round table of the participants in order to agree on a system of specially tailored institutions. The 1959 FEN Congress approved of de Gaulle's declaration of September 16 offering self-determination to the Algerian people. It requested that the negotiations for a cease-fire and the conditions of the referendum be undertaken immediately. The FEN insisted that guarantees for the European minority were necessary, largely reflecting the influence of the union's members in Algeria.[74] A motion calling for the resumption of negotiations between the French government and the provisional government of the Algerian Republic received the nearly unanimous approval of the 1961 FEN Congress.[75] After the negotiations at Evian had ended the war, the FEN called for the "loyal and effective application" of the agreements.[76]

The FEN reacted vigorously to developments in the course of the war. When a number of French intellectual and artistic leaders signed a "Manifesto of the 121" condemning the war and advocating insubordination in Algeria, the FEN published in October, 1960, an "Appeal to Opinion for a Negotiated Peace in Algeria." The FEN opposed the solution recommended by the Manifesto and sought to strike at the heart of the problem—the war itself. It rallied other organizations behind the appeal, and together they organized on October 27, 1960, a demonstration for a negotiated peace which drew over ten thousand participants and ended with five hundred arrests and one hundred injured persons, including thirty-eight policemen.[77] Work stoppages were organized in cooperation with the national labor confederations on April 24, 1961, to mark the teachers' support for the Republic when threatened by a revolt of four generals in Algeria, and on December 19, 1961, to demonstrate against the terrorist Secret

[74] *Combat,* July 18, 1956; *Le Monde,* July 22, 1958 and June 15, 1960; *Tribune du Peuple,* August 26, 1958; *E.L.,* 27e année, No. 10 (November 13, 1959), p. 517; and *E.P.,* 15e année, No. 2 (November, 1959), p. 7; and 17e année, No. 3 (November, 1961), p. 28.

[75] *Le Monde,* November 5–6, 1961.

[76] *E.P.,* 17e année, No. 6 (March-April, 1962), p. 2.

[77] *Le Monde,* October 6, 19, 27–31, November 2, 1960.

Army Organization (OAS) and for a negotiated peace in Algeria.[78] In the spring of 1961, when negotiations between the French government and the Algerian nationalists were about to be resumed, the FEN engaged in direct discussions with representatives of the General Union of Algerian Workers (UGTA), as did the major labor and student organizations, over the conditions of self-determination and guarantees for the European minority.[79]

Probably the most controversial political policy position of the FEN was its decision actively to oppose the granting of special powers to General Charles de Gaulle in May, 1958, and to condemn the Constitution of the Fifth Republic the following September. This action won the FEN both warm support and deep hostility. The Federation's leaders were supported by the highest favorable vote at the annual Congress since 1946, but they were also soundly attacked in the press for their alleged partisan and short-sighted action.

From May 13, when the insurgents sacked the government offices in Algiers, to the end of the month, the FEN sent out ten circulars to keep its member unions and local leaders informed of developments and alerted for possible action. They announced the position of the union in a large number of communiqués and press conferences. They maintained contact with other unions and federations, including all three labor confederations. On May 15, two days after the demonstrations in Algiers, they sent this telegram to the President of the Republic and to the Premier:

> The FEN and the SNI are anxious to make clear to you their unfailing attachment to republican institutions and the constitutional regime.
>
> In the grave hours which the country faces there is no solution outside of republican legality and the legitimate government.
>
> The regime of personal power is contrary to that legality.
>
> The granting of the powers of the Republic to one man, however great his past, would be incompatible with our institutions and would even more atrociously tear the country apart.[80]

M. Forestier pointed out that it would be easy to call a general strike in the case of a coup d'état, but that a union response to a revolution

---

[78] In September, 1961, the OAS bombed the offices of the FEN and the SNI in Algiers in reaction to the unions' liberal policy. *E.P.*, 16e année, No. 7 (May-June, 1961), p. 15; 17e année, No. 1 (October, 1961), p. 2; No. 3 (December, 1961), p. 1; and *Le Monde*, December 12, 17–18, 20, 1961.

[79] *E.P.*, 16e année, No. 5 (March, 1961), pp. 7–8; and No. 6 (April, 1961), pp. 13–14.

[80] *E.P.*, 13e année, No. 7 (June-July, 1958), p. 14.

which respected the legal forms would be much more difficult.[81] On May 28, the FEN announced that it was calling a strike for May 30 "to protest with force against the injuries inflicted on the republican regime and the free functioning of its institutions." The CFTC teachers' union, the Syndicat Général de l'Education Nationale (SGEN), joined in this political strike, relatively rare among teachers. The FEN maintained that through all of this action it had "succeeded incontestably in influencing the course of events,"[82] although the impartial observer would be hard put to demonstrate how.

One month later the FEN issued an appeal to the non-Communist left to end "the divisions of the left which have been a source of weakness and inefficacy in the past" and to join together in an appropriate organization. Political groups, members of Parliament, and other non-Communist opponents of the investiture of General de Gaulle formed the Union des Forces Démocratiques (UFD) with which the FEN maintained constant liaison throughout the summer. M. Lauré assured the Congress in November that he was resolved to continue to encourage such friendly relations among these groups.[83]

At the July Congress of the SNI, political questions overshadowed economic and pedagogical problems. Almost all of the speakers proclaimed their hostility to a government "brought to power by sedition." Some of the spokesmen of minority opinion wanted the Congress to condemn the referendum on the new Constitution without further ado, but the majority felt that it was impossible to make a decision before publication of the text. In the end, the SNI declared that it had "the right and duty as a union organization to pass judgment on the constitutional texts" and listed the principles on which this decision would be based. These included *laïcité* of the state and schools, freedom of information, independence of the judiciary, individual and union liberties, and popular sovereignty. It rejected in advance "any caricature of a parliamentary regime actually alienating the rights of national representation and establishing a regime of personal power in any form whatsoever."[84]

After the publication of the text of the new Constitution, a special FEN National Council was called to consider the union's position. Many speakers felt that the FEN should limit itself merely to providing full information; others believed that the FEN should follow the

[81] Minutes of the Administrative Commission of May 22, 1958, in *E.P.*, 13e année, No. 7 (June-July, 1958), p. 23.

[82] *E.P.*, 13e année, No. 7 (June-July, 1958), pp. 14–15.

[83] *E.P.*, 14e année, No. 1 (October, 1958), p. 3.

[84] *Le Monde*, July 18, 20, 1958; and *France-Observateur*, July 31, 1958.

example of the SNI and take a definite stand. M. Forestier said to the Council: "To take a stand on the constitutional problem is not a matter of politics, but of simple civic responsibility. In this respect educators have the duty of formulating an opinion." The Council examined the text and had it published in the FEN bulletin accompanied by a critical analysis.[85]

All this markedly political activity was not without its repercussions on the teaching profession. Many teachers supported de Gaulle and his Constitution for various reasons or felt that the union was overstepping its rightful sphere of activity. M. Jacques Narbonne of the National Center of Scientific Research wrote in the press: "It is beyond doubt that certain teachers' unions were among . . . the strongest opponents of the investiture of General de Gaulle." He said that the action of these unions ranged the educators "among the most irreducible adversaries of a republican renewal and practically among the defenders of an order responsible for the decline of France." M. Narbonne joined with others to form a group opposing the politicization of the teachers' unions.[86]

In his report to the 1958 Congress, M. Lauré said that the criticism of the union's political activities would have led one to expect an exodus of members to nonpolitical groups. On the contrary, he said, the increase in membership of all the member unions was greater than the increase in the number of employees of the Ministry of Education. He also asserted that the congresses of the member unions had approved their leaders' actions by unprecedented majorities.[87] The Congress of the FEN followed suit with an enthusiastically overwhelming approval. In his report M. Lauré defended the position of the FEN leaders and summarized his conception of the role of unions in politics:

> Faithful to its principles, the FEN deemed it its duty to examine the constitutional text. Then adversaries from outside, and sometimes union members, accused us of meddling in a purely political problem. According to our adversaries, unionism must be apolitical.
>
> What does that mean? If it is exact to say that certain problems depend on parties alone . . . , unionism cannot limit its objectives

---

[85] E.P., 13e année, No. 8 (August-September, 1958), pp. 4–6.

[86] Combat, July 10, 1958; and Le Monde, December 25, 1958. The creation of a Syndicat Indépendant de l'Enseignement Public claiming to be apolitical was reported in 1960, but apparently it has not generated much interest. Le Monde, December 9, 1960.

[87] E.P., 14e année, No. 7 (August-September, 1959), p. 3.

to purely professional and material problems, it cannot be assimilated to a "pressure group" in the service of solely material interests such as that of the beet-growers. . . .

The most bread-and-butter minded [*corporatistes*] cannot be indifferent to the opportunities that the regime provides for the workers. That is so true that not only all union organizations but also the "pressure groups" were interested in the question of the referendum.

Unionism, which has the task of hastening the emancipation of the workers, seeks to promote a social democracy which can only be born of political democracy. That is why it could not be indifferent to everything which threatens that democracy.[88]

At the beginning of this chapter, it was noted that the operative goals of the FEN fall into three general categories: material interests, pedagogical questions, and public policy. While the first two are important, constituting as they do the initial reasons for creating the teachers' unions, the third category comprises the policy positions that have not only absorbed much of the time and energy of union leaders but have also brought the unions into public controversy. This chapter has made clear that these policy positions are applications of the principles of *laïcité*, reformist syndicalism, socialism, and liberalism. But the third question posed at the beginning of this chapter, whether pronouncements on public issues serve an organizational function beyond their avowed purpose of fulfilling the organization's civic responsibilities, cannot be answered without first understanding the strains and stresses running through the structure of the FEN.

[88] *E.P.*, 14e année, No. 3 (January, 1959), p. 10.

Units of Organization

The internal organization of a group seeking to influence governmental decisions has important implications for the nature and potential efficacy of its efforts. An organization with homogeneous membership and a tightly knit, coherent structure ordinarily lacks the force of numbers. A loosely structured organization may have the advantage of numbers and yet find itself debilitated by internal stresses and strains rising from the heterogeneity of its membership. The FEN is a federation, composed of units of disparate size and occasionally conflicting interests. Its major organizational problem has been to accommodate the SNI, the Federation's largest and richest member union, without permitting it to dominate. Organizational problems also rise from the diversity of the Federation's members, for they are as different in professional status as they are in ideological orientation. The FEN includes teachers from all levels, and its political coloring covers the whole left half of the political spectrum from revolutionary syndicalists to moderate reformists. The success of the FEN in maintaining unity amid the scattered debris of shattered union organizations, despite its diversity of membership and its potential for conflict, is in large measure attributable to organizational ingenuity. And unity is one of the organizational attributes, along with size and resources, correctly stressed by Eckstein to help explain the political effectiveness of pressure groups.[1]

MEMBERSHIP

While a sound case could be made for the importance of the teachers' Federation based upon its role as the spokesman for the educators of youth and the leaders of opinion, it must be recognized that the FEN wears a mantle of significance merited by sheer bulk alone. In November, 1961, it had 281,000 members, and its growth curve was upward. In 1951 the maximum possible membership figure was estimated to be 200,000; in 1959 the SNI alone reported that many mem-

[1] Eckstein, *Pressure Group Politics*, p. 33.

bers.[2] Inspection of Figure 1 shows this over-all increase in membership. It also shows how severely the Federation was shaken by the schism of 1948.

FIGURE 1
GROWTH IN FEN MEMBERSHIP*

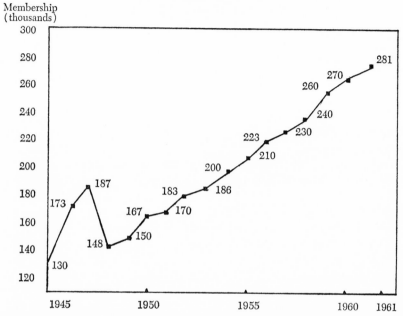

* Based on reports published in *E.P.* and figures furnished by the FEN for 1948, 1950, 1952, and 1953.

[2] Statistics from *E.P.*, 7ᵉ année, No. 1 (October, 1951), p. 9; *E.L.*, 26ᵉ année, No. 30 (May 8, 1959), p. 1294; and the table below. The reported statistics of FEN membership are reasonably accurate, although less so for the immediate postwar years, according to an employee of the Paris office. A case in point: in the morning of July 23, 1945, the FEN secretary general reported a membership of 130,000; in the afternoon of the same day another spokesman claimed 150,000 members. *E.P.*, No. 2 (October, 1945), pp. 11–12. Since membership figures are not always reliable, and since some of the smaller member unions do not always publish them, the following figures are the results of calculations based on the number of votes allotted each national union represented at the 1961 Congress. Since the number of votes depends on the number of paid-up members according to a regressive scale, these figures may be considered accurate to with ten members for the smallest union and two hundred members for the largest. Cf. *E.P.*, November, 1961, p. 12; and FEN bylaws, art. 11.

Ministry of Education

1.	Personnel Administratif de l'Administration Académique	1,700
2.	Enseignement Supérieur	1,460
3.	Personnel Technique de l'Enseignement Supérieur	860
4.	Personnel Contractuel de l'Education Nationale	200

The FEN includes most of the public school teachers in France. The unorganized potential is not large,[3] and the competing teachers' unions

5.	Censeurs	460
6.	Enseignement Secondaire (SNES)	30,000
7.	Principaux et Administrateurs de Collèges	520
8.	Proviseurs et Directrices de Lycées	340
9.	Enseignement Technique (SNET)	12,120
10.	Centres d'Apprentissage (SNET-AA)	5,120
11.	Ecoles Normales (Directeurs)	200
12.	Ecoles Normales (Professeurs)	1,140
13.	Inspecteurs Primaires	800
14.	Institutrices et Instituteurs (SNI)	203,000
15.	Chercheurs Scientifiques	1,060
16.	Enseignement d'Education Physique et Sportive (maîtres)	1,680
17.	Education Physique de l'Enseignement Public (professeurs)	2,330
18.	Inspecteurs Principaux de la Jeunesse et des Sports	30
19.	Inspecteurs de la Jeunesse et des Sports	200
20.	Techniciens du Service de l'Equipement Sportif	20
21.	Personnel des Bibliothèques	280
22.	Assistantes et Adjointes du Service de Santé Scolaire et Universitaire	1,560
23.	Médecins Départementaux	60
24.	Médecins de Secteur du Service de Santé Scolaire et Universitaire	280
25.	Agents de l'Education Nationale	9,680
26.	Intendance et Economat	1,220

Ministry of Culture

27.	Enseignement Artistique	1,240
28.	Enseignement Supérieur des Beaux-Arts	180
29.	Personnel des Manufactures Nationales d'Art	120
30.	Personnel des Archives de France	140
31.	Personnel Ouvrier et de Surveillance des Services Extérieurs	330

Ministry of Agriculture

32.	Personnel Enseignant des Ecoles d'Agriculture et Ecoles Assimilées	130
33.	Personnel Enseignant des Ecoles Ménagères Agricoles	460
34.	Personnel Administratif des Etablissements d'Enseignement Agricole	30

Ministry of Justice

35.	Personnel de l'Education Surveillée	740
36.	Personnel Educateur des Services Pénitentiaires	50

Ministry of Public Health

37.	Union des Personnels Enseignants des Instituts Nationaux des Sourd-Muets et Aveugles	150

Other

38.	Professeurs Spéciaux de la Ville de Paris et du Département de la Seine	1,200
	Total	281,090

[3] The total number of teachers employed in higher education and primary, secondary, and technical schools, exclusive of physical education teachers, was 292,800 in 1960. See Commissariat Général du Plan d'Equipement et de la Productivité, *IVe Plan de Développement Economique et Social 1962–1965, Rap-*

are either small in size or shadow organizations existing mostly on paper. The only competing teachers' federation of any importance is the Syndicat Général de l'Education Nationale (SGEN) affiliated with the CFTC. In 1960 the SGEN, made up of Catholic public school teachers, had a membership of 20,000 to 25,000.[4] After the labor schism of 1947, an FEN-CGT and an FEN-FO were created by their respective labor confederations to compete with the independent FEN. Neither of the two new groups was very successful in recruiting members, and at one time it was reported that the leaders of the Communist party had decided to lay the FEN-CGT to rest, preferring that its militants work among the mass membership of the FEN rather than exhaust their energies in a tiny organization already under their control.[5] The FEN-FO and the FEN-CGT still exist, however, the former insignificant in membership, and the latter reduced to skeletal form and actually only a façade for its two lively member unions, the Syndicat National des Agents des Etablissements de l'Education Nationale and the Centres d'Apprentissage, FEN-CGT.[6] There are no other general teachers' federations, but only limited organizations recruiting members from particular categories of teachers, such as the Société des Agrégés or the Fédération des Syndicats Autonomes de l'Enseignement Supérieur.

It has been officially recognized that the FEN represents the bulk of the teaching profession. The Ministry of Education conducts elections in which teachers select their representatives to Education Councils which are consulted by the administration on professional and pedagogical questions. In the 1954 elections to these Councils the FEN took ninety-two out of ninety-eight seats. Five of the six remaining seats went to the FEN-CGT affiliate which organizes teachers in the Apprenticeship Centers. The sixth went to the SGEN of the Catholic labor confederation.[7] The government has also recognized the FEN as a union representing an important bloc of civil servants. On July 2, 1954, the Council of State declared that the FEN, by virtue of its

port Général de la Commission de l'Equipement Scolaire, Universitaire et Sportif (Paris, 1961), p. 253. This document is hereafter referred to as Rapport Général. Physical education teachers numbered about 7,100 in 1960–61. French Cultural Services, Documentation No. 32 (New York: French Embassy, n.d.), p. 15. The FEN includes several nonteaching categories of educational workers.

[4] Dhombres, interview, April 25, 1960.

[5] Lauré, interview, May 11, 1960.

[6] These two unions linked their recruitment efforts in 1960. See the common supplement to Le Travailleur de l'Enseignement Technique, No. 158 (February, 1960); and to L'Agent des Lycées et des Etablissements de l'Education Nationale, No. 72 (January, 1960).

[7] E.P., 10e année, No. 3 (December, 1954), p. 32.

membership and activity, was legally regarded to be among the most representative of the civil servants' unions and denied the claim of the Fédération Générale des Syndicats Chrétiens de Fonctionnaires that a decree attributing two seats to the FEN on the Higher Council of the Civil Service was illegal.[8]

NATIONAL UNIONS

The member unions which make up the Federation are so different in size and in the composition of their membership that at first it seems impossible to find a common element permitting the unions logically to be grouped together. All union members must be employees of the state,[9] but not necessarily of the Ministry of Education. They are not all teachers, although by far the greatest proportion of them are. In terms of skills and titles, members range from university professors to cooks and gardeners, from master craftsmen at the National Factory of Sèvres to researchers in agronomy. In his first activity report to a national Congress after he became secretary general of the FEN, M. Georges Lauré noted this diversity of membership and stated that the common unifying element of FEN members is that all are engaged in the public service of education. He did not deny that the member unions are conscious of their importance and jealous of their independence, but he claimed that these attitudes contribute to the originality of the organization and are "at the same time its strength and its weakness."[10]

The FEN is composed of thirty-eight member unions known as "national unions." The largest and most important national union, one which prides itself on a long, independent history and which enjoys a virtual monopoly of representation of primary school teachers is the Syndicat National des Instituteurs (SNI).[11] The other important national unions of classroom teachers are the Syndicat National de l'Enseignement Secondaire (SNES) for secondary teachers; the Syndicat National de l'Enseignement Technique (SNET) for teachers in technical schools; and lastly, the Syndicat National de l'Enseignement Supérieur for teachers in higher education. Other national unions represent teachers from specialized fields or schools, such as professors of physical education or persons teaching in penitentiaries. Personnel working in school administration are organized in separate national

8 *E.P.*, 9e année, No. 8 (August-September, 1954), p. 2.
9 *E.P.*, 12e année, No. 4 (February-March, 1957), p. 16.
10 *E.P.*, 12e année, No. 8 (August-September, 1957), p. 2.
11 The Le Gorgeu Commission reported 234,000 primary school teachers for 1961. *Rapport Général*, p. 253. The membership of the SNI was 203,000 in 1961. See footnote 2 above.

unions: the school bursars are grouped in a national union that is distinct from the union of principals of *collèges* which, in turn, is distinct from the union of *lycée* headmasters. Occasionally persons working in the same discipline are found in different unions because of differences in rank. For example, the union of professors of physical education does not admit instructors (*maîtres*) of physical education. The latter are therefore obliged to organize and maintain their own national union.[12]

The Syndicat National des Instituteurs is the backbone of the FEN. The organization of the SNI is relatively simple; its basic unit is the section in each department (*département*). Members join the section located in their department and participate in local activities as well as in the election of delegates to the annual Congress. The annual Congress receives the reports of the secretary general and decides upon a motion of orientation to guide the leadership for the following year. Current policy is in the hands of the SNI's executive committee known as the bureau. Its twenty members are elected every two years by the secretaries of the departmental sections gathered together in a National Council. This election is organized so as to insure proportional representation of ideological currents. The secretary general is the head of the bureau and the union's chief executive officer.[13]

The SNI provides the FEN with three-fourths of its membership and furnishes it with a good proportion of its dynamic and outspoken leaders. It also transmits to the FEN the dues which it collects on behalf of the Federation. These dues from the SNI constitute about two-thirds of the FEN's total annual revenue. In 1957–58 the annual budget of the SNI was more than nine times as large as that of the FEN; the SNI spent thirty-eight times as much money on the defense of *laïcité* as the FEN did.[14] Like the state of Prussia in the German Empire, the SNI is rich and powerful enough to dominate;

[12] A similar desire to safeguard the status and privileges of a more highly trained group separated grades of archivists at one time. On March 20, 1957, the FEN Administrative Commission admitted the Archivists Union although the FEN already included a union of sub-archivists (*sous-archivistes*). It was reported by the FEN Committee on Structure that a single union representing all archivists was impossible because of the "hostility of the two categories. The sub-archivists demand mainly the right to attain . . . the rank of archivist. The archivists, all graduates of the School of Charts, refuse." *E.P.*, 12e année, No. 5 (April, 1957), p. 15.

[13] For the SNI constitution see *E.L.*, 27e année, No. 5 (October 9, 1959), p. 236. Also see *E.L.*, 26e année, No. 20 (February 13, 1959), p. 746; and *E.L.*, 27e année, No. 16 (January 2, 1960), p. 863.

[14] Figures derived from a comparison of financial reports published in *E.P.*, 14e année, No. 1 (October, 1958), p. 12; and *E.L.*, 26e année, No. 30 (May 8, 1959), p. 1334.

indeed, it has been called a steam roller and accused of imperialism by critics fearing its overbearing weight.[15] M. Georges Lauré admitted to the 1952 Congress the existence of a certain malaise resulting from the domination by the FEN's "most powerful union."[16]

This malaise, this quiet fear of domination by the largest union, has existed in the FEN since its earliest moments. The 1946 Congress was the scene of a debate which articulated the reservations of the smaller unions about having the SNI in their midst and which resulted in a lasting, if uneasy, accommodation. In the discussion of the committee report on structure, M. Aigueperse of the SNI refused to accept that his union be given only ten seats out of twenty-five on the governing body of the FEN, the Administrative Commission; he demanded that his primary school teachers be granted half of all the seats reserved for the national unions. The spokesman for the committee on structure explained that the total number of seats had been increased from twenty to twenty-five to give the primary school teachers and the secondary school teachers equal representation. The remaining five seats were reserved for higher education and non-teachers. Another speaker urged the primary teachers not to take advantage of their mass and force, and to let the other categories live within the organization. Another wanted the primary teachers to withdraw their demand for fear that the FEN would appear to be but a reflection of the SNI. M. Lavergne of the FEN warned that the primary teachers ought not give the impression that they are always and everywhere trying to impose their point of view; this would imperil the very existence of the Federation. The discussion ended with a vote which overruled objections of M. Aigueperse and accepted the committee report by a large majority.[17] A step had been taken towards the accommodation of "Prussia."

From time to time the SNI finds itself in disagreement with the second largest member union, the Syndicat National de l'Enseignement Secondaire. The SNES represents some 30,000 of the approximately 37,600 teachers in nontechnical secondary schools.[18] Its basic units are more than 1000 locals (*sections d'établissement*) which in-

[15] E.P., 9e année, No. 3 (December, 1953), p. 30; and 15e année, No. 3 (December, 1959), p. 23.
[16] Minutes of the 1952 FEN Congress, in E.P., 8e année, No. 3 (December, 1952), p. 25.
[17] E.P., No. 9 (June, 1946), p. 2.
[18] The SNES figure is for 1961. See footnote 2 above. The number of secondary teachers is for 1961 and was extrapolated from data in *Rapport Général*, p. 253. The same report predicted 41,700 secondary teachers for 1962; the SNES was reported to have 38,000 members at that time. *Ibid.;* and E.P., 17e année, No. 7 (May, 1962), p. 13.

clude teachers at a single institution. The locals are organized into departmental sections. The organizational pyramid continues with units on the Academy and national levels. At the top is the secretary general and his bureau of twenty-six members, charged with current policy-making and execution. The bureau is elected from and by an Administrative Commission of fifty-eight members which is chosen by the whole membership in such a way as to insure representation of all significant categories of teachers and ideological tendencies.[19]

The structure of the other national unions is similar to these two. Even most of the small ones have an elected Administrative Commission, bureau, and usually an annual Congress. For example, the 1,000-member Syndicat National des Chercheurs Scientifiques has an Administrative Commission of twenty members and a small bureau but no permanent staff or headquarters.[20] The Syndicat National de l'Enseignement Supérieur has an Administrative Commission which brings together its fifteen Parisian and fifteen provincial members quarterly, but it suffers from lack of followers.[21] Regional organizations are emphasized in the 10,000-member Agents' Union.[22]

The number of member unions increased from thirty in 1945 to

[19] *SNES Vade Mécum.* The 1960 Congress appointed a committee to study proposals for reforming the organization's structure in order to "reinforce the cohesion and efficacy of SNES." Criticism had fallen heavily upon the mode of electing the Administrative Commission; it was held that the current method increased the distance between the union member and his elected representative and practically freed the latter from the control of the former. Two proposals aimed at stimulating the Academy unions by making their secretaries automatically members of the Administrative Commission or by having a majority of the Administrative Commission elected by the Academy unions. Secretary General Dhombres opposed both plans and, supported by his Administrative Commission, proposed the appointment of a study committee to consider reform proposals. *U.S.,* 33e année, No. 193 (February 10, 1960), pp. 26–29; and No. 197 (May 15, 1960), p. 6.

[20] This union includes about one-third of the personnel of the National Center of Scientific Research. *La Vie de la Recherche Scientifique,* No. 28 (*sic:* should be No. 23) (January, 1960), folder insert, p. 1; No. 25 (April, 1960), p. 1. Also see footnote 2 above.

[21] In 1961 the Ministry of Education employed about 11,000 teachers in higher education. *Rapport Général,* p. 253. The Syndicat National de l'Enseignement Supérieur had a membership of 860 the same year. See footnote 2 above. The union's own publication reported that in the course of an audience the Minister of Education questioned the delegates about the representativeness of their union; and that at the FEN Congress of 1959 the union abstained from voting on certain ideological questions because of the small number of its members. *Bulletin du Syndicat National de l'Enseignement Supérieur,* No. 39–40 (March-April, 1959), p. 3.

[22] *La Tribune des Agents de l'Education Nationale,* 12e année, No. 15 (June-July, 1959), p. 6; and *E.P.,* 17e année, No. 3 (December, 1961), p. 21. This union represents school janitors, cooks, concierges, and other service personnel.

thirty-eight in 1961.[23] One cannot conclude from this that expansion has taken the form of the simple addition of eight national unions, for schisms and fusions as well as withdrawals marked this period of the union's history. In the year following the vote for withdrawal from the CGT in 1948, for example, eight unions left the FEN, one of these rejoined, and five new ones entered.[24] The SNES itself was the result of a fusion, and the Syndicat National de l'Enseignement Supérieur et de la Recherche Scientifique split into two national unions in 1956.[25]

DEPARTMENTAL SECTIONS

The national unions constitute one type of organizational unit of the FEN; the departmental sections are a second type. An FEN departmental section is made up of all members of FEN national unions who reside in the same department. The section, therefore, is a very heterogeneous grouping.[26]

The early postwar leaders strongly favored the development of the departmental sections. They recognized the difficulty of combining educational workers of all types in a single organization and hoped to reduce tension between professional categories by utilizing geographic units as elements of organization. It was hoped that frequent contact with other educators in the same area would encourage members to think of themselves first as teachers and secondly as elementary teachers or physical education teachers. The syndicalists saw the departmental sections as vehicles for enhancing the unity and mutual sympathy of all members of the working class. The mood of the time was clearly "hostile to the narrow spirit of category."[27]

In accordance with this thinking, the Congress of 1946 expressed its desire "to reduce as much as possible the number of national unions" and "to create everywhere departmental unions gathering together in a spirit of fraternal collaboration every category of teaching personnel."[28] The intention was ultimately to create single unions of all educators in a department; the Federation then was to be formed from these departmental unions, while the national unions were to be transformed into technical sections on the national level. It was in order to emphasize the departmental sections that ten of the thirty

23 *E.P.*, No. 1 [1945], p. 3; and 17e année, No. 2 (November, 1961), p. 12.
24 *E.P.*, 5e année, No. 1 (September-October, 1949), p. 3.
25 *E.P.*, 12e année, No. 3 (January, 1957), p. 17.
26 Organization along vertical and horizontal lines is typical of French trade unions. Lorwin, *Labor Movement*, pp. 145–56. In Italy for a number of reasons the horizontal "chambers of labor" dominate the vertical category unions in their area. LaPalombara, *The Italian Labor Movement*, pp. 37–41.
27 *E.P.*, No. 1 [1945], p. 2.
28 *E.P.*, No. 12 (October, 1946), p. 4.

members of the Administrative Commission were to be nominated by the departmental sections; that the departmental sections, not the academic regions as formerly, were to be represented in the National Councils; and that the departmental sections were to be allotted more votes at the annual Congress than before the war.[29]

But even at the beginning the skeptics of this plan to promote the departmental sections were numerous. A delegate to the first postwar National Council asserted that during thirty years as a union militant he had never seen a single really active departmental union in the FGE.[30] M. Lavergne believed that the national unions would naturally be powerful since most important questions are decided on the national level. He insisted that he did not oppose the departmental unions; but the facts did not justify the forecasts of certain militants. "You don't build an imposing edifice on uncertain foundations," he concluded.[31]

Experience has substantiated the reservations of M. Lavergne. The national unions have grown in number and power, while the departmental sections have diminished in importance. It is true that some of the ninety-four departmental sections are active. Some are tightly organized unions which discuss common problems and split into "technical sections" to study problems of particular educational levels.[32] Some prepare resolutions for FEN Congresses, send reports for publication in *L'Enseignement Public* under the rubric "Our Departmental Sections in Action," and work with other departmental union and *laïque* organizations; some even print local membership bulletins. On the other hand, indications of the weakness of departmental sections appear regularly. Sections fail to answer questionnaires and have to be prodded from the center. They complain that they have nothing to do, since it is difficult to interest members in questions already studied by the national unions.[33] When a delegate to the FEN Congress of 1959 condemned factional struggles between ideological tendencies, another replied that in his department there were "no struggles between tendencies, only an absolute emptiness. The departmental assembly preparing for the Congress gathered together only 28 out of 2,700 union members."[34]

29 *E.P.*, No. 4 (December, 1945), p. 13.
30 Minutes of the National Council of July 23, 1945, in *E.P.*, No. 2 (October, 1945), p. 12.
31 *E.P.*, No. 1 [1945], p. 3.
32 *Supplément à l'Enseignement Public* [No. 16 (1947)], p. 8.
33 *E.P.*, 6e année, No. 2 (November, 1950), p. 24.
34 Minutes of the 1959 Congress, in *E.P.*, 15e année, No. 3 (December, 1959), p. 21. In 1961 Lauré stated that meetings of the departmental section of Bouches-du-Rhône attracted only 400 out of 6,000 members. *E.P.*, 17e année, No. 3 (December, 1961), p. 21.

In short, it can be said that, despite the confidence which the post-war fathers of the FEN placed in the departmental sections as means of enhancing unity, of reducing the "spirit of category," their unimportance relative to the power and prestige of the national unions means that they cannot be regarded as highly significant organizational techniques for accommodating the SNI and other unions of teachers with dissimilar interests. They exist and some are very active, but a good number are dormant. In any case, power is focused in Paris. Most of the FEN leaders are simultaneously officials in the top levels of the national unions. The power and importance of the national unions viewed against the weakness of the departmental sections, which were supposed to foster working-class unity and oppose the "narrow spirit of category," suggest that the syndicalist ideal is not much more than a myth which gives way before the imperatives of interest.[35]

CENTRAL ORGANS

The representative and administrative organs of the FEN consist of three major units on the national level: the annual Congress, the Administrative Commission, and the executive committee or bureau.

The Congress brings the rank-and-file militants face to face with the union leaders once a year. It obliges the leaders to defend their actions. It provides the arena where partisans of different ideological currents may clash. It permits the ventilation of irritations arising from frictions between different categories. By its motions it takes stands on current public issues. And by its votes it orients the activities of the leadership for the following year.

The schemes for representation and voting at the Congress are clearly designed to prevent domination by the SNI. Individual mem-

[35] One interesting FEN unit which is treated as a departmental section despite its differences is the active Foreign Section. The Foreign Section includes those teachers on detached service to the Ministry of Foreign Affairs who are working in French institutions abroad, in joint Franco-foreign schools, or in purely foreign universities. Its three-member bureau, elected by a General Assembly, promotes the interests of the more than 1,000 members scattered in forty-nine foreign countries by representing them on the Interministerial Comittee on French Education Abroad, by keeping them informed of governmental regulations, vacancies, union activities at home and abroad, and by defending before critical budgetary authorities and before public opinion the mission of France to spread its language and culture throughout the world. Emile Hombourger, secretary general of the Foreign Section, interview, February 7, 1960; his article "La Section Etranger de la Fédération de l'Education Nationale" in France, Ministère de l'Education Nationale, de la Jeunesse et des Sports, Institut Pédagogique National, L'Enseignement Français à l'Etranger ("Mémoires et Documents Scolaires," No. 11 [January, 1959]; Paris: Société des Editions et de Vente des Publications de l'Education Nationale, 1959), pp. 244–47; and E.P., 16e année, No. 8 (August-September, 1961), p. 24.

bers of the FEN have double representation at the Congress: they are represented first by a number of delegates allotted to their national union, and second, by delegates from their departmental section. The allotment of delegates for both is determined by regressive scales. As a result the SNI with 72 per cent of the Federation's members has only 22 per cent of the total number of delegates representing national unions, while the SNET with 4 per cent of the members has 8 per cent.[36] Moreover, each delegate does not have one vote. National unions and departmental sections are awarded a number of votes or "mandates" according to the number of FEN dues-stamps purchased. The total number of mandates is about equally divided between national unions and departmental sections. Mandates allotted to the national unions are distributed according to a regressive scale which favors the small unions. The Syndicat National de l'Enseignement Supérieur, for example, has only 0.5 per cent of the FEN's members but 2 per cent of the national union mandates at the Congress.[37]

The Congress normally meets for three days in November. Since the SNES and the SNET normally hold their conventions during the spring vacation in April and the SNI meets in July, the FEN Congress comes after its constituent unions have met.[38] Also, as Secretary General Lavergne pointed out in 1950, a fall meeting coincides with the beginning of the school year and the opening of Parliament "when it is important to give precise mandates to the Administrative Commission and its bureau."[39] The proceedings adhere to a pattern: fraternal greetings from foreign teachers' unions; an activity report given by the secretary general and approved by the delegates; the discussion and

[36] Departmental sections of less than 6,000 members are permitted one delegate for each 1,000 members or fraction thereof; for those with more than 6,000 the proportion is reduced to one delegate for each 2,000 members after 6,000. For the national unions, the allotment is made as follows: 100 or less—one delegate; 101 to 500—two delegates; 501 to 1,000—three delegates; 1,001 to 15,000—three plus one for each 1,000 beyond the first thousand; 15,000 to 50,000—seventeen plus one for each 5,000 over 15,000; over 50,000—twenty-four plus one for each 10,000 over 50,000. Constitution, art. 12. See note 2 above for membership figures.

[37] A departmental section is awarded one mandate for each fifty members or fraction thereof. Article 11 of the FEN bylaws gives the following scale for allotting mandates to the national unions:

7– 400 paid-up members: one mandate for each	10	members
401– 2,000 paid-up members: one mandate for each	20	members
2,001– 5,000 paid-up members: one mandate for each	30	members
5,001–15,000 paid-up members: one mandate for each	40	members
15,001–25,000 paid-up members: one mandate for each	50	members
25,001–50,000 paid-up members: one mandate for each	100	members
over 50,000 paid-up members: one mandate for each	200	members

[38] E.P., 5e année, No. 1 (September-October, 1949), p. 3.
[39] E.P., 6e année, No. 1 (October, 1950), p. 1.

vote of committee reports and resolutions; and elections of officers. The sessions are far from somnolent, however. Criticism from the floor is perceptive and barbed, and the secretary general is always called upon to defend his activity report. Such criticism often leads to action. For example, delegates to the 1954 Congress complained that they had not been informed of the matters to be taken up by the Congress early enough so that member units could discuss the questions and instruct their delegates on how to vote. In October, 1955, FEN officials published a table of the votes to be taken at the Congress in November.[40] The bitterest criticism, and usually the most ineffective, is inspired by the several ideological currents that strive for dominance. The discussion of the "motions of orientation" presented by each current evokes an especially sharp debate, for the motion approved by the majority is expected to guide the union officials for the following year. Usually, however, the end of the Congress brings a closing of ranks and a revival of solidarity marked by the delegates singing the "Internationale" together.[41]

The Administrative Commission represents the membership between Congresses and by its decisions guides the union's executive officers. It is designed to permit the representation of both national unions and departmental sections as well as to give a sounding board to minorities within the organization. Its discussions bring to the surface the underlying tensions of category and ideology.

Two-thirds of the body of fifty-one members represent the national unions. Each union has the right to a certain number of these national union seats as indicated in the bylaws; the annual Congress merely ratifies the lists of candidates presented by each national union. Alternates are chosen at the same time and in the same way. It is instructive to note once again the underrepresentation of the SNI. Of the thirty-four seats reserved for the national unions, the SNI has only thirteen or slightly more than one-third.[42]

---

[40] E.P., 11e année, No. 1 (October, 1955), p. 2.

[41] An incident marred this concluding harmony in the SNI Congress of 1950. According to a newspaper report, the pro-Communist delegates walked out of a session of the Congress. "The majority of the Congress, which was not otherwise troubled by the ridiculous exit of the CGT-supporters, gave an ovation to the national secretary and, standing, sang the 'Internationale' while the Communists sang their own 'Internationale' in the wings." Le Populaire de Paris, July 22, 1950.

[42] The SNES has five seats; SNET, three; the Agents, two; and the following have one seat each: Higher Education; Scientific Research; Principals and Assistants; Apprenticeship Centers; Normal School Professors; Normal School Directors and Primary Inspectors; Physical Education Professors; Physical Education Instructors; Managers and Bursars; Outer Administrative Services; and the School and University Health Service. Bylaws, art. 6.

The other seventeen members of the Administrative Commission are supposed to represent the departmental sections; the mode of their election insures the representation of minority currents as well. After the split with the CGT, the 1949 Congress decided to elect the representatives of the departmental sections proportionally from lists in order to insure minority representation.[43] Each ideological current which presents a motion of orientation to the Congress also proposes a list of candidates and alternates for these seventeen seats. The seats are then distributed in proportion to the vote received by each motion of orientation. For example, at the 1959 Congress the majority tendency, the *autonome*, was awarded twelve seats; the supporters of union with the CGT received four seats; and the revolutionary syndicalists were allotted one seat.[44] The strength of minorities on the Administrative Commission is augmented by the practice of some national unions, notably the SNI, of selecting their representatives for the Commission in proportion to the strength of the various minority tendencies within them.

It is clear that of the two kinds of members on the Administrative Commission, those emanating from the national unions and those from the departmental sections, the former are the more significant. They are usually powerful figures in their own right, since they are normally the officers of the national unions. When changes are made in the size of the Commission (usually increases representing concessions to vociferous unions and to tactics of recruitment), the decision is made first on the number to represent the national unions; practice then requires that the departmental sections get half as many.[45] Almost all the members of the Federation's executive committee, or bureau, are drawn from their ranks: between 1946 and 1961 five members of the

[43] *E.P.*, 5e année, No. 1 (September-October, 1949), pp. 17–19; and No. 4 (December, 1949), p. 15.

[44] The Congress also agreed that the FEN representative on the Economic Council should be permitted to sit in on meetings of the Administrative Commission. Constitution, art. 5; and *E.P.*, 15e année, No. 3 (December, 1959), p. 27.

[45] The provisional Administrative Commission of 1945–46 had twenty-seven members. The 1946 Congress instituted the system of two kinds of representation, allotting twenty-five seats to the national unions and twelve to the departmental sections. In 1948 the numbers were changed to thirty and fifteen, giving new representation to the Agents, to the Principals and Assistants, and to employees of the newly established School Health Service; the SNET and the SNI each received one additional seat. In 1958 membership was increased by four. The Agents received another seat, the Managers and Bursars who had formerly shared a seat with the Normal School Professors got a seat of their own, and one additional seat each went to the SNET and to the SNI. *Supplément à l'Enseignement Public* [No. 16 (1947)], p. 10; *E.P.*, 5e année, No. 4 (December, 1949), p. 10; and 14e année, No. 1 (October, 1958), p. 31.

bureau were representatives of the departmental sections while twenty-seven were from the national unions. Even more striking is the comparison of the aggregate number of years of service on the bureau for the same period. The total for the national union representatives is 152 years; the corresponding figure for the departmental section representatives is thirteen years, a ratio six times as great as one would expect from the observation that the former are twice as numerous as the latter.[46] The predominance of the national unions is not surprising when it is remembered that the departmental sections are more or less artificial creations, fathered by syndicalist ideology and its ideal of working-class unity and born of the sentiments for solidarity that characterized the Liberation.

The Administrative Commission meets monthly and extraordinarily when convoked by the bureau or ten members. Its usual business consists of hearing and discussing reports from the bureau and from the study committees. These committees, varying in number from time to time, are appointed by the Administrative Commission. Decisions on study committee reports are made by the Commission as a whole. In short, the Administrative Commission guides and controls the bureau, admits new member unions, and generally determines union policy between Congresses.[47]

Another body which sometimes meets on the national level is the National Council. The Council is composed of the members of the Administrative Commission together with one delegate from each national union and one from each departmental section. While rather important in the immediate postwar years, the National Council met less frequently thereafter. Its decreased importance was officially recognized by the Congress of 1949 which changed the FEN constitution in order to restrict the National Council to consultative and informative functions only.[48] The decline of the National Council is probably due to its large size, which makes it unwieldy for studying complex problems; and to its apparent superfluity, since the departmental sections are regularly represented in the Administrative Commission. It appears to be better suited for organizing campaigns and arousing enthusiasm than for discussing issues and making policy.

[46] Figures calculated from reports on elections of officials published in *E.P.*

[47] Constitution, arts. 7, 8. On November 26, 1959, the Administrative Commission chose members for the following ten commitees: Corporative (for matters pertaining to salaries, conditions of work, etc.), Pedagogical, *Laïque* Action, Personnel Working Abroad, Social Works, Pensioners, Structure, Overseas, Social Education, and Culture and Youth. *E.P.*, 15ᵉ année, No. 3 (December, 1959), p. 31.

[48] *E.P.*, 5ᵉ année, No. 1 (September-October, 1949), pp. 17–19.

The bureau is the action nucleus of the organization. It is a twelve-member executive committee, chosen by and from the members of the Administrative Commission. It includes the union's top, full-time executive officer, the secretary general, who, with the treasurer, is elected by and from the Administrative Commission. It meets often, usually every week, and conducts union affairs on a regular basis. Its members negotiate with the government, hold seats in the consultative councils of the Ministry of Education, maintain liaison with other civil service unions and labor confederations, serve on study committees, and usually play an active role in their respective national unions.

Members of the bureau include the most important figures in the Federation. M. Adrien Lavergne, pioneer militant and devoted laïque, filled the post of secretary general until his retirement was announced in December, 1956. He was replaced by M. Georges Lauré, former secretary general of the SNET and a member of the FEN bureau since 1949. The bureau elected on November 23, 1961, also included the leaders of the largest member unions: Secretaries General Dhombres of the SNES, Astre of the SNET, and Forestier of the SNI.[49] Certain specialists with rich experience in union activities were also elected to the bureau. These included: M. Clément Durand, an expert on laïcité; Mlle. Jeanne Borgey, a member of the bureau for the preceding eight years and the editor of the SNES bulletin; and M. Emile Hombourger, a member of the bureau for a dozen years, a regular union representative to international teachers' organizations, and the head of the Foreign Section. The only representative of the departmental sections was M. Georges Aulong, elected secretary-treasurer of the FEN.[50]

The size of the bureau was increased twice after 1946. These changes were supposed to make the body more representative, but at the same time tactical ends were not ignored. In 1948, following the schism, membership was increased from eight to ten. These seats were filled with members of the SNI and the SNES, and one of the two seats formerly occupied by the SNET was given to a representative of a departmental section.[51] The SNET had apparently suffered a considerable loss of membership because of the union schism. The bureau was

[49] M. Forestier had been a member of the FEN bureau since 1949 and head of the SNI since 1953. At the time of the postwar reorganization, the Administrative Commission considered barring the secretaries of the big unions from membership on the bureau on the grounds that they would not have enough time to be active in both; it concluded, however, that the authority of the secretaries before both "the comrades of the base" and the government could only strengthen the FEN bureau. Minutes of the Administrative Commission of March 21, 1946, in E.P., No. 7 (April, 1946), p. 4.

[50] E.P., 17e année, No. 4 (January, 1962), p. 15.

[51] E.P., No. 20 (June 10, 1947), p. 3; and No. 27 (April, 1948), p. 2.

again increased by two at the 1958 Congress in order, according to the minutes of the Congress, to "permit the association of a greater number of categories in union work."[52] More specifically, the leaders desired to strengthen the competitive position of the FEN in relation to the CGT. These two additional seats were destined for the Agents' Union and the Apprenticeship Centers Union. Both unions suffer from the keen competition of strong CGT unions active among these same lower-level civil servants. It was felt that these two seats increased the prestige of the FEN unions and gave them an additional selling point in their competition with the CGT unions. Furthermore, representatives of these employees sitting in the highest union organ could better convey the plight of the lowest ranks to the bargaining agents of the Ministry of Finance as well as obtain for their members a better understanding of the limitations of the bargaining process.[53] At a meeting of the Agents' Executive Committee on December 21, 1958, it was proudly noted that "for the first time in the union's annals, a seat on the bureau of the Federation is occupied by our secretary general."[54] It should be noted that the SNI is underrepresented on the bureau as it is on all other FEN organs. Only three representatives of the SNI sit on the twelve-member board, compared with the same number for the much smaller SNES and two for the SNET.

Unlike the Congress and the Administrative Commission where the several ideological currents are represented, the bureau adheres to a policy of "homogeneity": only members of the majority ideological current may be elected to the bureau. The adoption of this policy was surrounded with no little controversy in the early postwar councils of the union. The supporters of the Communist-led CGT, a minority group in the union, demanded representation on the bureau so vigorously that it required votes at two successive Congresses to get the policy of homogeneity put into effect.[55] M. Lavergne, after one year's experience with homogeneity, concluded that he preferred a bureau made up of members of the majority tendency alone.[56]

While not integrally part of the FEN's basic structure, three other organizations are related to it by virtue of overlapping membership and interlocking directorships. The Mutuelle Générale de l'Education

[52] Minutes of the 1958 FEN Congress in *E.P.*, 14e année, No. 3 (January, 1959), p. 31.

[53] Dhombres, interview, April 25, 1960.

[54] *La Tribune des Agents de l'Education Nationale*, 12e année, No. 13 (February, 1959), p. 13.

[55] Minutes of the 1949 Congress, in *E.P.*, 5e année, No. 4 (December, 1949), p. 15.

[56] *E.P.*, 6e année, No. 1 (October, 1950), p. 10.

Nationale is a highly successful mutual welfare society composed of about 560,000 members recruited from among the employees of the Ministry of Education, retired employees, and their families. It provides insurance against a variety of risks, maintains rest homes and sanatoriums, and administers the Social Security program for its members. Its long-time president, M. Marcel Rivière, was concurrently a member of either the FEN bureau or Administrative Commission from 1946 to 1956.[57] The Société Universitaire d'Editions et de Librairie was founded before World War II by the SNI in order to provide textbooks considered desirable by the teachers. It is now controlled by the SNI, the SNES, and the SNET.[58] The Union Sportive de la Fédération de l'Education Nationale organizes sporting events and promotes athletic activities among members.[59]

A union with as many varied interests as the FEN is bound to experience conflicts over policy. The structure of the FEN is designed to attenuate conflicts, particularly those stemming from the position of the giant SNI in the Federation; but structure alone cannot solve the problem. Reconciliation of interests is a function of both high political skill and external necessity.

[57] Lauré, interview, May 11, 1960; and *E.P.*, 7e année, No. 1 (October, 1951), p. 7.

[58] *E.P.*, 12e année, No. 7 (June-July, 1957), p. 14.

[59] *E.P.* [10e année], No. 9 (August-September, 1955), p. 10.

Conflict and Cohesion

Organizational ingenuity provided the basis for accommodating the giant SNI in a Federation made up of smaller unions. But the SNI with its impressive numbers and relatively well-stocked treasury is not the only source of friction in the organization. Other member unions have their own particular interests which the organization is expected to promote. Occasionally these interests, both material and moral, are in conflict, and the FEN must work out an acceptable compromise or risk defections. And, as if this task of deftly balancing the particularistic goals of the member unions with the general goals of the total membership were not enough, the Federation is also obliged to contend with the stresses and strains introduced by conflicting ideological crosscurrents and their organized factions which reflect France's fragmented political culture and which cut across the boundaries between national unions. Furthermore, parallel and related organizations, some having identical bases of recruitment, some made up of general categories of civil servants, and some predominantly ideological in nature, exert a magnetic attraction on disgruntled or disoriented segments of the Federation to threaten its unity.

Ingenuity in structural arrangements alone obviously fails to explain the enduring unity of the FEN. Important as they are, schemes of regressive representation and a decentralized federal structure could not in themselves nullify the centrifugal tendencies of internal conflict. Continued organizational cohesion demands further explanation. Counterforces rising from the recognized need for unity, from the successful compromising of demands, from leadership concessions to minority opinions, and from broad agreement on certain ideological views, help check the disintegrative tendencies and create an organizational equilibrium of lasting although varying stability. These positive forces for cohesion, supplementing structural arrangements, are additional and necessary explanatory factors.

64

CONFLICT

The intramural conflicts of the FEN are no secret. They are manifest for all to see at sessions of committees, Congresses, and departmental sections; both the press and the union leaders are fully aware of them. During his long tenure as secretary general, M. Lavergne often spoke of the FEN as "imperiled by the collisions of its national unions"; his successor, M. Lauré, was no less concerned about "these quarrels whose sharpness could have sterilized all FEN action."[1] Journalists have occasionally written about the "centrifugal tendencies" of the FEN; one blamed them on the multiplicity of kinds of educational workers represented by the organization.[2] These conflicts between categories justifiably claim first importance. However, conflicts also rise from differences between ideological factions and from controversial positions taken by the union leaders on particular public issues.

Conflict between categories. Disagreements having their source in the diversity of educational employees organized in the FEN recurrently plague the union leadership. Since practically every category of educational employees has its own national union, the conflicts between categories take the form of disputes between national unions. The most serious differences of view arise between the two largest unions, the SNI and the SNES, over matters of salary and educational policy.

The disagreements over salary are sharp and recurrent. The essential disagreement is this: the SNI, like most unions of relatively low-level civil servants, tends to favor across-the-board increases which raise the salary of every category a fixed amount, while the SNES, like most unions of higher-level civil servants, favors "hierarchized" salary increases. When a salary increase is "hierarchized," the higher-level categories get a larger raise than the lower ones do because the former have higher coefficients.[3] Since the same sum promised by the Ministry of Finance can be distributed either way, the choice is one that may be made by internal compromise between the member unions.[4] Sometimes external compromise with the other civil servants' unions is also necessary. Examples of these differing points of view are not difficult to find. The press reported in 1950 that a special FEN committee was appointed to reconcile, on the one hand, the demand that salaries be based on the minimum living income and "hierarchized" and, on the other, that 4,000 francs be paid monthly to the least favored categories,

[1] *E.P.* [10e année], No. 9(August-September, 1955), p. 3; and 12e année, No. 2 (November-December, 1956), p. 2.
[2] *Combat,* November 2, 1954.
[3] Cf. Chap. II, p. 24.
[4] Dhombres, interview, April 25, 1960.

thereby collapsing the salary scale established by the Reclassification of 1948.[5] In 1956 internal compromise succeeded, but apparently external compromise failed. The CGT and CFTC civil servants' unions (composed mostly of lower-echelon employees) demanded an immediate bonus of 4,000 francs a month for the least favored categories, while the FO and the FEN wanted a base salary of 200,000 francs that would be "hierarchized."[6] In 1951 the differing viewpoints of the SNI and the SNES posed a grave threat to FEN unity. Having lost confidence in FEN support and hoping to protect the gradations of the salary scale which favored them, the leaders of the SNES joined other secondary teachers, not members of the FEN, to form a delegation which appeared before representatives of the Ministry of Education. They did not inform the FEN of their action. In a subsequent stormy session of the FEN Administrative Commission, M. Aigueperse of the SNI declared that "it is inadmissible for comrades to undertake moves outside of the FEN. The SNI has never made a separate move; the SNES must adopt the same attitude as long as the action for salary increases lasts."[7] The independent action on the part of the SNES leaders, for which they were roundly chastized, was rightly seen as a threat to organizational unity. However, the SNES continued "to protest against the slight case that the FEN makes of the SNES demands as opposed to the support that the FEN constantly and unreservedly gives to every demand, even the most debatable, which comes from a certain direction (never ours)." M. Lavergne in reply called for mutual comprehension and added that "there is not an important claim of the SNES which the FEN has not supported."[8]

The SNES has sometimes received the support of other national unions in its skirmishes with the SNI. For example, in the 1954 Congress the SNET joined the SNES in support of a motion on material questions opposed by a contrary motion of the SNI. M. Lavergne was obliged to assume the role of mediator and present a compromise text acceptable to both sides which then dropped their respective propositions.[9]

Differences over educational policy divide national unions, particularly the SNI and the SNES, almost as sharply as salary disputes. The summer vacation dates, the nature of the proposed cycle of

[5] *Le Populaire de Paris*, November 13, 1950. This disagreement was also cited by Lavergne in *E.P.*, 6e année, No. 4 (January, 1951), p. 3.

[6] *Le Monde*, November 4–5, 1956.

[7] Minutes of the Administrative Commission of April 11, 1951, in *E.P.*, 6e année, No. 8 (May, 1951), p. 23.

[8] *E.P.*, 8e année, No. 2 (November, 1952), pp. 1–2.

[9] *E.P.*, 10e année, No. 3 (December, 1954), pp. 3–4.

orientation, and the disposition of the Complementary Courses have provided the main topics of controversy.

Teachers' representatives are normally consulted each year by the Minister of Education before he announces the dates for the beginning of the long summer vacation and the reopening of school in the fall. At first view a simple matter, the question is complicated by the fact that secondary teachers are normally expected to administer and grade examinations for the *baccalauréat* during a two-week period in July and a second, "make-up" period in September. If these periods are added to the normal school year, the secondary teachers are deprived of two weeks of vacation (not a full month since a teacher usually works during either the summer or the fall examination session but not both).

In 1959 the primary and secondary teachers were unable to agree on vacation dates when the Administration consulted their representatives. Therefore, when the Minister announced his acceptance of the dates proposed by the primary school teachers (July 1–September 15), the members of the SNES were highly indignant. The SNES Congress voted to organize a national day of protest with a one-hour strike, meetings, contacts with parents, and similar public demonstrations of their discontent.[10] The threat of a strike at examination time was successful in obtaining action. The Minister issued an amendment to his decree postponing the reopening of senior classes until September 21, while retaining the September 15 date originally decreed for all other classes. The second session of the *baccalauréat* examinations was scheduled for September 7–20.[11] Nevertheless, M. Dhombres of the SNES maintained that the secondary teachers had been divested of two weeks of vacation and concluded, "We shall not accept, we will never accept this new amputation of our vacation; we will struggle as long as necessary until the secondary teachers' summer vacation has again found its traditional dimensions."[12]

At the subsequent 1959 Congress the FEN leaders were criticized for their handling of the vacation problem. A half-dozen orators cited it to explain the votes of their unions against the FEN leadership. One delegate regretted that the bureau had not tried to harmonize the demands of the various unions prior to consultation with the Administration. Another orator accused the SNI of "hiding behind" a motion of its Congress without regard to the harm done to the SNES. M. Dhombres declared that the whole problem of the distribution of holidays

[10] *Le Monde*, March 27, 1959.
[11] *E.P.*, 14e année, No. 6 (May-June, 1959), p. 4.
[12] *U.S.*, 33e année, No. 193 (February 10, 1960), p. 7.

throughout the school year needed review. M. Lauré's reply was essentially a confession that compromise had failed. He said:

> We must stop accusing the SNI of imperialism. Indeed, the interests of the national unions are sometimes contradictory. In this case the FEN tries to arrive at a synthesis. If it proves to be impossible, the FEN has nevertheless not become bankrupt.
>
> The vacation example is quite poorly chosen. The attitude of the FEN in this matter is not a carbon-copy of that of the SNI. . . . Those who dare to affirm that efforts at conciliation were not undertaken prior to [consultation with the Administration] are indeed poorly informed.[13]

While the perennial vacation controversy generates internal friction, it is not a crucial matter. Much more important to France and to the teachers is the question of educational reform. This question transforms the fraternal ties between the SNI and the SNES into bitter antagonisms. The FEN leaders regularly and courageously seek a compromise plan which will satisfy them both, but their efforts are rarely successful.[14]

The points of conflict between the SNI and the SNES rise essentially from their differing conceptions of education which, in turn, are related to their occupational roles. Sketched in broad strokes, the SNI ideal is an educational system which democratically educates a maximum number of students, differentiated at the latest possible moment in accordance with their talents and educated to the extent of their capacities, especially in those disciplines crucial to modern civilization. The SNES is more conservatively oriented. It refuses to risk the debasement of standards by broadening an elite education which has traditionally sought to turn out a relatively small number of highly cultured ladies and gentlemen rather than a popularly educated mass. It opposes raising the age at which students begin secondary studies because there is already too little time for serious subjects. Its subject-matter approach is traditional and emphasizes such studies as Latin and literature. The SNET is usually on the side of the SNI.

These opposing viewpoints clashed most obviously on two issues involved in educational reform plans: the cycle of orientation or "common trunk" and the Complementary Courses. The SNI was a

---

13 Minutes of the FEN Congress, November 3–5, 1959, in *E.P.*, 15e année, No. 3 (December, 1959), pp. 12ff.

14 In 1953 the FEN made a typical effort when it intervened to seek a common accord among the interested national unions on a reform project. This attempt at synthesis ended in failure. *E.P.*, 9e année, No. 1 (September-October, 1953), p. 8.

vigorous supporter of a long cycle of orientation designed to guide
pupils into the proper career channels for which their capacities best
suited them. The SNES just as vigorously opposed such an innovation
because it would delay the commencement of Latin and other secondary studies. It also maintained that mixing manually and theoretically
inclined students for the duration of the cycle would lower standards.[15]
The disagreement over the Complementary Courses was generated by
a mixture of ideal and material motives. Originating in the upward
extension of the elementary school parallel to the already existing
secondary schools, these secondary courses were taught by primary
school teachers. The SNI was naturally interested in maintaining and
improving them, and in coordinating them with the rest of the educational system so they would no longer be educational dead ends.[16]
The SNES looks on them with distaste, claiming that their course
offerings are too limited in scope and that they are taught by persons
without secondary qualifications. Indeed, primary school teachers are
sometimes found teaching the same courses as secondary teachers, in
the same building, and yet they lack the professional titles demanded
of secondary teachers. It is not difficult to comprehend the unsympathetic attitude of the SNES towards these courses.[17]

Stemming from both intellectual convictions and occupational situations, these differences on educational reform are not easily com-
promised. Sometimes a resolution dealing with these matters is made
vague enough to receive general approval at a Congress. For example,
in 1955 M. Dhombres of the SNES, after obtaining the consent of the
SNI and the SNET, proposed that the Congress change the wording
of the motion on reform so that the orientation period would be
described not as "also common," but as "progressively differentiated."[18]
This phraseology kept the way open for the introduction of secondary
studies into the cycle of orientation. The following year the Congress
similarly voted a motion which was "so balanced that it lost all

[15] *E.P.*, 10ᵉ année, No. 8 (June, 1955), pp. 3, 23.

[16] To the SNI these courses bear witness to the missionary zeal of the primary
school teachers for spreading popular education. They were "BORN OF THE
DEVOTION OF THE SCHOOLMASTERS OF FORMER TIMES WHO BE-
NEVOLENTLY PUT THEIR TIME AND KNOWLEDGE AT THE SERVICE
OF POOR CHILDREN WHOSE APTITUDES THEY HAD NOTICED." (Caps
in original.) *E.L.*, 26ᵉ année, No. 23 (March 6, 1959), p. 911.

[17] Dhombres, interview, February 6, 1960.

[18] M. Lavergne noted his satisfaction with this tenuous compromise: "Isn't it
comforting to note that after the collisions without amenities which succeeded each
other for more than a year . . . the delegates were able to vote almost unanimously
for an FEN motion on educational reform?" *E.P.*, 11ᵉ année, No. 2 (November,
1955), pp. 1, 11.

meaning." These equivocal verbal compromises were necessary; a clear motion only publicized internal divisions. For example, in 1957 the Congress adopted a clear and precise text. The SNES considered it unacceptable and voted against it, objecting particularly to the definition of the "common trunk," its excessive duration, and the institution of special middle-level schools for it.[19] In 1960 the FEN Congress was faced with two resolutions prepared by its Pedagogical Commission which had been unable to reconcile the conflicting positions on the "common trunk." The SNI plan received 5,025 votes and the SNES plan received 1,703 votes; there were 2,712 abstentions, mostly supporters of an SNET plan which was not put to a vote.[20]

As the second largest union in the Federation, the SNES is the member union which is most often moved to express its frustration. In the course of one debate an SNES spokesman complained that his union always seemed to be opposed by the whole FEN Administrative Commission. Another questioned whether it was right for a majority in the Federation to overrule the congress of a national union. M. Lavergne replied that union democracy is nothing but the rule of the majority,[21] but this answer could hardly satisfy the SNES. The spokesmen of the SNES were articulating tensions inherent in the nature of the organization. Their complaints raise the analytic question of why they remain in the Federation. But before considering this question, a second major source of disunity must be noted.

Conflicts between tendencies. Cutting across the divisions between national unions and constituting the second major source of centrifugal tension in the FEN are the ideological currents or "tendencies," as they are known in French. Rooted in the history of French unionism and officially recognized by the FEN constitution, four currents have vied for dominance: the supporters of independence for the FEN, known as the majority tendency or the *autonomes*; the supporters of con-

---

[19] *Le Monde*, November 13, 1957.

[20] *Le Monde*, November 5, 1960; and *E.P.*, 15ᵉ année, No. 10 (August-September, 1960), p. 31; 16ᵉ année, No. 1 (October, 1960), p. 16; No. 2 (November, 1960), p. 24; and No. 3 (December, 1960), pp. 12, 26–27. The failure of the cycle of observation to reorient students from one type of secondary education to another led the FEN Congress of 1962 to advocate comprehensive middle-level schools for all students, a solution that was gaining widespread acceptance among parents and even members of the SNES. Cf. the excellent articles on the consequences of the 1959 reform by Bertrand Girod de l'Ain in *Le Monde, Sélection Hebdomadaire*, 16ᵉ année, No. 744 (January 17–23, 1963), pp. 1, 8; and No. 745 (January 24–30, 1963), p. 8. A ministerial decree requiring such schools had been partially rescinded because of the opposition of the SNES, the Society of *Agrégés*, and parents' organizations as recently as 1961. *Le Monde*, December 5, 13, 1961.

[21] *E.P.*, 9ᵉ année, No. 3 (December, 1953), pp. 29, 35.

federation with the CGT, known as the *cégétistes*; the supporters of affiliation with the CGT-Force Ouvrière, called members of the FO tendency; and the revolutionary syndicalists who identify themselves by the title of their bulletin, the *Ecole Emancipée*. The FO tendency was disbanded in 1954, but the other three tendencies continue to compete for membership support.

The recognition of ideological tendencies is not new in French organizational life; both parties and unions have known organized factions.[22] This feature of organizational life in France is well known in the literature on political culture.[23] But in the FEN their nature and their organization owe much to the circumstances of the schism of 1948. In order to preserve the unity of the FEN and to avoid the disintegration of the national unions themselves, it was necessary to give all significant tendencies their proper place. The 1948 Congress therefore provided for the representation of minority currents. While the bureau is restricted to members of the majority tendency, representatives of the departmental sections on the Administrative Commission are nominated by the tendencies and seats are distributed to each tendency in proportion to the votes received by its motion of orientation.[24] As a result, each important ideological current has a voice in the union's councils. There is no doubt that the presentation of conflicting motions and the discussions between tendencies are healthy for the preservation of the union. Repression of these differences would only lead to sudden explosions; open debate which recognizes the points of disagreement increases organizational self-confidence.[25]

The largest or majority current is the *autonome* tendency, so named because it opposes affiliation with any of the labor confederations. Despite a general belief in the desirability of labor unity, it was this

[22] Minority factions have been represented in organs of the Socialist party (SFIO); even the Force Ouvrière had been a minority faction within the CGT before the schism of 1947. Cf. Williams, *Politics in Post-War France*, pp. 65–66; and Georges Lefranc, *Le Syndicalisme en France* ("Que Sais-je?" No. 585; Paris: Presses Universitaires de France, 1959), pp. 111–13.

[23] Cf. Gabriel A. Almond, "Comparative Political Systems," *Journal of Politics*, Vol. XVIII (August, 1956), 405–407; Gabriel A. Almond and James S. Coleman (eds.), *The Politics of the Developing Areas* (Princeton: Princeton University Press, 1960), pp. 20–25; and Gabriel A. Almond and Sidney Verba (eds.), *Political Culture and Political Development* (Princeton: Princeton University Press, 1965).

[24] Constitution, art. 5. On one occasion the *Ecole Emancipée* tendency sought to force the resignation of one of its representatives from the SNI bureau, but the bureau refused to permit it. *E.L.*, 24e année, No. 39 (September 20, 1957), p. 1001. Apparently representatives of tendencies on the FEN Administrative Commission are likewise not subject to recall.

[25] *E.P.*, 8e année, No. 2 (November, 1952), p. 6.

tendency which engineered the departure of the FEN from the Communist-dominated CGT. Since this critical decision, the FEN has
jealously guarded its independence of party, government, and the great
labor confederations; it has repeatedly insisted that it takes orders
from no one except its members.[26] The social policy of the *autonome*
tendency is reformist rather than revolutionary. Reform, its supporters
claim, must come through the efforts of the working class, democratically organized into unions which remain independent of parties and
the state. *Laïcité* and human rights must be defended whenever and
wherever they are threatened. The very system of representation of
ideological currents and of their honest confrontation within union
councils is a tenet of *autonome* belief.[27] The *autonome* tendency is
supported by about 70 per cent of the membership according to votes
on the motions of orientation.[28]

The second largest tendency is composed of the *cégétistes*, those
who opposed leaving the CGT in 1948 and who repeatedly urge re-
affiliation with that organization to reestablish working-class unity.
While it is impossible to determine what percentage of this tendency's
supporters are Communist party members or sympathizers, the high
degree of conformity of its political policies with the current Communist party line, even when the latter is highly unpopular, strongly
suggests that at least its leaders are active party members. For example, amid outraged exclamations of obvious scorn and indignation,
the *cégétiste* spokesmen attempted to defend the 1956 Soviet interven-
tion in Hungary. The Congress soundly rejected their defense, 6,089 to
653 votes and 1,284 abstentions.[29] The militant doctrine of this tendency is distinctly revolutionary. It favors direct action by the working
class itself through the CGT rather than "collaboration" with the
existing institutions of the state and the employer class. It opposes

26 Cf. Lavergne in *E.P.*, Nouvelle série, No. 6 (March, 1949), p. 1; and
Forestier in *Le Monde*, July 18, 1953.
27 *E.P.*, 14e année, No. 7 (August-September, 1959), p. 15.
28 Cf. Fig. 2, Chap. IV.
29 *Combat*, November 21, 1956; and *E.P.*, 12e année, No. 3 (January, 1957),
p. 18. Similarly, a *cégétiste* spokesman attempted to stall FEN support of the
1953 workers' uprising in East Berlin. He maintained that the FEN should be
prudent and gather exact information about the uprising before taking a position.
Another FEN member replied that numerous motions of solidarity on other issues
had been passed without waiting for the least information. *E.P.*, 9e année, No. 1
(September-October, 1953), p. 38. On another occasion, a *cégétiste* representative
condemned members from Algeria who refused to take a stand on the rebellion
there on the grounds that the total situation was not known. He was condemning
a tactic that had been used by his own group. Minutes of the Administrative
Commission of March 15, 1956, in *E.P.*, 11e année, No. 6 (April-May, 1956),
p. 13.

"futile" ideological discussions within the FEN, and would prefer to see the divergent tendencies submerged in common action; it particularly objects to the homogeneity of the bureau as that practice has eliminated its devoted militants from the councils of union leadership.[30] It preaches hostility to clericalism, capitalism, colonialism, militarism, and imperialism. In fact, it is clearly anti-American and pro-Soviet. This excerpt from the report of a speech at the 1949 FEN Congress gives the tone of the attitude of this tendency:

> War is the weapon of capitalism and not of revolution, and it is unworthy to put on the same level fascism and the Soviet Union, that is, racism and the construction of socialism. . . .
> The only imperialism is American imperialism, which does not hide its will for war, even preventive war. [One cannot] give a single proof of the will for war of the USSR.[31]

The cégétiste tendency has been in the minority and excluded from the bureau for more than a decade. At no time did its support rise above one-fourth of the FEN membership or drop below 15 per cent, according to votes at the Congresses. Frustrated by its exclusion from the power center and restless because of a sense of isolation, this tendency attempted a number of maneuvers. Underlying them all was the desire to dispense with the organized tendencies or at least to blur the dividing lines between them so as to permit loyal militants to infiltrate and capture positions of influence. It was reported that in 1952 M. Benoît Frachon of the CGT called upon the cégétistes "to renounce the sterile game of confrontation of tendencies which are only the scarcely veiled expression of different political currents of the French left."[32] Beginning in 1952, the cégétiste tendency no longer presented its motion of orientation under its own name at the FEN Congress. That year the motion was simply entitled: "Contributions to the Preparation of the Congress." For elections to councils which represent teachers in the Ministry of Education an alphabetical list of names labeled "Independent" appeared in opposition to the lists presented by the autonome and Ecole Emancipée tendencies; almost all on the list were either members of the Communist party or of the rival CGT teachers' union, the FEN-CGT.[33] At the 1953 FEN Congress the cégétistes abstained from voting on the motions of orientation,

---

[30] E.L., 27e année, No. 10 (November 13, 1959), pp. 511–17.
[31] Minutes of the 1949 Congress, in E.P., 5e année, No. 4 (December, 1949), p. 13.
[32] L'Observateur d'Aujourd'hui, November 19, 1953.
[33] Le Populaire de Paris, December 4, 1953.

calling the debate over orientation superficial and useless. In subsequent years the *cégétiste* motion of orientation was presented under the name of one of the departmental sections, usually that of Bouches-du-Rhône. This maneuver apparently fooled no one.[34] It is clear that by this policy of confusion and concealment the Communists and their sympathizers were attempting to gain entry to the positions of authority in the union. It was even reported that the directors of the Communist party in 1953 gave precise directives to supporters among the primary school teachers.[35] According to M. Forestier of the SNI the *cégétistes* attempted to create confusion "by the application of a tactical action determined by the . . . Communist primary teachers and the Political Bureau of their party."[36]

In 1961 the leaders of the FEN became increasingly impatient with the *cégétiste* tactics of confusion and concealment, particularly when the Communist party and the CGT began to attack the FEN position on the war in Algeria. The union leaders let it be known that the *cégétiste* minority was an instrument of Communist policy. M. Forestier reported that in the SNI the very faction which advocated the abolition of tendencies never voted with the majority but always with one tendency, the *cégétiste*. M. Lauré remarked to the 1961 FEN Congress that the Syndicat National de l'Enseignement Supérieur claims to be "without tendencies" but always adopts as a bloc the positions of the CGT. M. Lauré added that the CGT

is not independent. [*sic*] and all the positions of the CGT reappear systematically in a tendency of the FEN which nevertheless denies being "*cégétiste*."

The independence of the union movement from political parties and the state must be manifested in daily action. . . . We defy anyone to accuse the FEN of collusion with one or the other. As much cannot be said of our *cégétiste* comrades who have never distinguished themselves from the CGT. . . . We are waiting until the CGT does not adhere systematically to the positions of the C[ommunist] p[arty] and until the latter puts an end to that

[34] The editors of the FEN bulletin least of all. In reporting the names of members elected to the Administrative Commission, they referred to the "*cégétiste* list." The following month they printed a correction which changed the name of that list to "a list presented by a group of departmental sections, under the title of the general motion of Bouches-du-Rhône." *E.P.*, 10ᵉ année, No. 4 (January, 1955), p. 2. A delegate to the Congress stated baldly, "The names at the head of the list 'Motion of Bouches-du-Rhône' are militants of the Communist party." Minutes of the 1954 Congress, *ibid.*, p. 21.
[35] *L'Observateur d'Aujourd'hui*, November 19, 1953.
[36] *France-Observateur*, July 22, 1954.

unconditional fidelity [to Moscow] which characterizes it in all circumstances.[37]

The third tendency, supported by 5 per cent to 9 per cent of the membership, is composed of the "heirs of the pioneers" of unionism among teachers, the spiritual descendants of the founders of the FNSI and the FMEL. Members of this tendency call themselves "Friends of L'Ecole Emancipée," after the bulletin of their faction. They cling to the ideology of revolutionary syndicalism. They believe in the class struggle, in revolution, and in proletarian internationalism. They claim an attitude of defiance against the state which employs them. In the words of a representative of this tendency on the National Bureau of the SNI, "the reformist seeks amelioration of the regime through endless reforms; the revolutionary syndicalist conceives of all action in terms of the destruction of the regime."[38] They oppose militarism, colonialism, imperialism, and clericalism, and reject reform of the capitalist system as ineffective. In all this they resemble the cégétistes. But they differ sharply from them in that they vigorously support genuine internal democracy for the FEN: respect of the rights of tendencies, particularly their freedom of expression; proportional representation of tendencies on union councils; publicity of votes, objective reporting, and space for minority tendency views (tribune libre) in union publications; and the regular reporting of representatives to their constituents. They favor working-class unity but not at the expense of domination by political parties.[39] They pursue an aggressive anti-Communist policy. Articles in L'Ecole Emancipée score the hesitation of the Communist party to support Algerian independence and their readiness to compromise with the regime.[40] In fact, their dislike for the Communist party is part of a broader distrust of all political parties; they even accused the leaders of the SNI of politicizing the union by refraining from making demands while a Socialist government was in office.[41]

[37] E.P., 17e année, No. 3 (December, 1961), p. 21. For the position of the Syndicat National de l'Enseignement Supérieur, cf. E.P., 15e année, No. 9 (June-July, 1960), p. 7.

[38] Minutes of the 1956 SNI Congress, in E.L., 23e année, No. 39 (September 21, 1956), p. 961.

[39] E.L., 27e année, No. 10 (November 13, 1959), pp. 511–17; and E.P., 15e année, No. 10 (August-September, 1960), p. 23. Members of this tendency are sometimes called Trotskyites to describe their simultaneous devotion to the revolutionary class struggle and espousal of internal union democracy.

[40] Cited as evidence of compromise was the fact that party leaders had gone to a reception given by the President of the National Assembly in January, 1959. L'Ecole Emancipée, 44e année, No. 11 (January 23, 1960), pp. 96–99.

[41] Combat, July 19, 1957.

This tendency has a particular penchant for strong language. An excerpt from the *Ecole Emancipée* motion of orientation of 1959 illustrates some of the stock phrases of this group.

> In conclusion, THE CONGRESS finds it more than ever indispensable to reaffirm the value of the CLASS STRUGGLE and to proclaim its faith in the REVOLUTIONARY SENSE OF UNIONISM whose profound mission remains to develop and coordinate the secular struggle of the workers for the disappearance of the EXPLOITATION OF MAN BY MAN and to recall that only the union of the workers of all countries will be able to assure world peace.[42]

The language of its virulent anticlericalism is sometimes abusive. In special numbers of *L'Ecole Emancipée* devoted to topics such as "The Church Clericalism," there appear sentences such as: "The *blousons noir* ["black jackets" or juvenile delinquents] wear cassocks and their rosaries are worse than bicycle chains."[43]

The fourth, smallest, and now defunct tendency, Force Ouvrière, supported affiliation with the CGT-FO. At the time of the schism of the CGT in 1947, the members of this tendency opposed autonomy for the FEN, feeling that it should add its forces to the anti-Communist labor confederation. This tendency's motion of orientation received 6 per cent of the votes at the 1949 Congress but only 3 per cent in 1950. For the next four years the FO tendency joined with the *autonomes* to present a common motion of orientation. The tendency disappeared completely when, in 1954, the Executive Committee of the CGT-FO forbade double affiliation for its member teachers.[44]

The relative strength of these tendencies has varied little since 1948. Figure 2, based on the votes on the motions of orientation published yearly in the FEN bulletin, shows this continuity. A similar chart for the SNI would show that the *cégétiste* minority is somewhat stronger in the SNI than in the FEN while the *Ecole Emancipée* supporters are almost twice as numerous. The *cégétiste* minority is very strong in the SNET where it includes about 40 per cent of the members.[45]

These tendencies, then, and the varying interests of the national unions are responsible for most of the important internal tensions. Naturally, there are other sources of dissidence. Occasionally, depart-

[42] (Caps boldface in original.) *E.P.*, 14e année, No. 7 (August-September, 1959), p. 19.
[43] *L'Ecole Emancipée*, 44e année, No. 11 (January 23, 1960), p. 101.
[44] Minutes of the 1954 Congress, in *E.P.*, 10e année, No. 4 (January, 1955), p. 9.
[45] *Le Monde*, March 26–27, 1961.

FIGURE 2
STRENGTH OF IDEOLOGICAL TENDENCIES IN THE FEN*

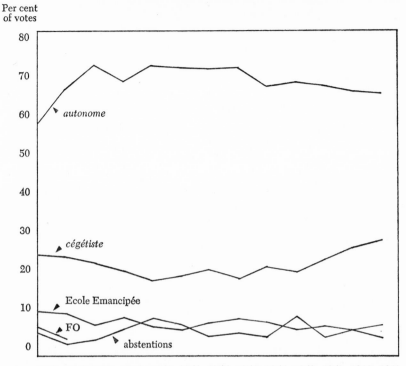

Per cent
of votes

1949 1950 1951 1952 1953 1954 1955 1956 1957 1958 1959 1960 1961

* Based on votes on motions of orientation at FEN Congresses as reported in *L'Enseignement Public.*

mental sections demonstrate too much independence. One section in 1960 admitted members of the rival FEN-CGT to membership until the FEN leaders ordered their exclusion. Some departmental sections announced their stands on the referendum of January 8, 1961, on Algerian self-determination before the national organization had taken a position; FEN leaders learned of these actions in the press. Secretary General Lauré reminded the delegates to the 1961 FEN Congress that "the sections are not unions. Committed by the decisions taken on the Federation's national level, they may not publicly go against a position taken by the FEN. . . ."[46]

[46] Minutes of the Administrative Commission of February 25, 1960, in *E.P.*, 15e année, No. 6 (March, 1960), p. 24; of January 19, 1961, in *E.P.*, 16e année, No. 5 (March, 1961), p. 21; and Minutes of the 1961 FEN Congress, in *E.P.*, 17e année, No. 3 (December, 1961), p. 11.

Some teachers would like to see the FEN refrain from all political activity, particularly the taking of stands on questions of public policy. The Federation's attitude towards General de Gaulle and the Fifth Republic aroused some criticism among members. Speakers at the FEN Congress questioned the political strike of May, 1958, and expressed concern about political positions taken by the Federation's officers.[47] One group of critics, without suggesting withdrawal from the FEN, whose effectiveness in furthering occupational and professional demands they did not dispute, invited all educators to unite in a Mouvement National Universitaire d'Action Civique "to struggle against deviations of union activity" and to come to "the defense of the seriously threatened political neutrality of education."[48] While this group never became a serious threat to the FEN's unity, it illustrates both the internal tensions of the organization and its possibilities for spinning off dissident groups into the eagerly waiting arms of competing unions and groups. These quiescent counter-organizations (such as the FEN-CGT) would be delighted by such contributions to their strength. Why more dissident groups do not "spin off" remains to be explained.

COHESION

As potent as these centrifugal tendencies are, the FEN remains the only mass organization of French teachers. The explanation for this seeming paradox lies in the existence of compensating forces which nullify the inner disintegrative impulsions and the outward-pulling attractions to hold unions and tendencies together.

Certainly one of the most important of these forces is widespread recognition that the Federation's considerable influence is dependent on its continued unity;[49] all groups of teachers would lose effectiveness if they were to dissipate their efforts in uncoordinated, isolated action. The small unions which constitute the vast majority of FEN member organizations particularly appreciate the active support given them by FEN leaders.[50] Common action, however, requires some sacrifice on

[47] Minutes of the 1958 Congress, in E.P., 14e année, No. 3 (January, 1959), p. 22.

[48] Le Monde, December 25, 1958; L'Express, December 18, 1958; and Combat, November 26, 1958.

[49] E.P., 9e année, No. 1 (September-October, 1953), p. 11.

[50] FEN leaders support the demands of each national union in contacts with the "very diverse ministries" which employ union members. E.P., 5e année, No. 1 (September-October, 1949), pp. 3–4; and 12e année, No. 8 (August-September, 1957), p. 2. The rather small National Union of Scientific Researchers declared: "Our membership in the FEN . . . opens certain doors which would be closed to us if we were alone." From a recruitment folder inserted in La Vie de la Recherche Scientifique, No. 28 [23] (January, 1960), p. 2.

the part of individual unions. It is therefore necessary for the union leaders to draw upon their ample store of political and diplomatic skills to harmonize these demands. It is a point of pride with FEN leaders that they are normally successful in reconciling conflicting union positions;[51] it is also a point of great concern, for they realize that the penalty for failure is disintegration and disunity.

But the logical need for unity is not by itself a sufficient explanation for the lasting cohesion of a Federation beset with strong internal conflicts. Besides the structural devices, such as underrepresentation of the SNI, already considered in chapter III, two major countervailing forces help preserve the unity of the organization: a common ideology of *laïcité* and syndicalism, and agreement on "great issues" such as peace, disarmament, and colonialism; and opportunities for criticism of the leaders and consultation of the members which promote mutual understanding and provide safety valves for releasing tensions.

Ideology and the great issues. The question has already been raised[52] whether some of the aims of the organization, particularly those exceeding its capacities for realization, might not serve organizational ends. It seems clear that certain broad and ill-defined ideological attitudes operate as unifying factors, providing slogans and symbols that all members can support without compromising their conflicting material and pedagogical claims. Paradoxically, ideology is both a unifying influence and a divisive one, since the tendencies already described are expressions of differing ideologies. But the ideologies of *laïcité* and syndicalism have been so generalized, so emotionalized and "sloganized," that they are able to bring all tendencies together under their broad umbrella. In addition, certain great issues such as the defense of peace and the protection of human liberties have sufficiently general support so that union positions on them may rally members of all categories and tendencies.

A very revealing article by M. Lavergne in the FEN bulletin dramatically illustrated the role of the ideologies of *laïcité* and unionism in enhancing organizational cohesion. It also took note of divisive ideologies.

> And if the rupture of the unity of the Federation of National Education should pave the way for a retreat of *laïcité*, what teacher would not then regret having failed to forget . . . his

[51] *E.P.*, 5e année, No. 1 (September-October, 1949), pp. 3–4; and 12e année, No. 8 (August-September, 1957), p. 2.
[52] See Chap. II, p. 22.

ideology, his philosophy, or his convictions in order to cement the agreement of all members?

Indeed, the unity of all teachers is impossible. The unity we are seeking is that of the *laïcs*, that of the true unionists, whose affiliation with a labor confederation translates their resolution to defend *laïcité*.[53]

One critic concluded similarly that every time the SNI encountered a thorny problem, it retreated into *laïcité*, "the only theme capable of forging a semblance of unanimity."[54] Syndicalism is perhaps a less effective cohesive force than *laïcité* because there are many interpretations of how best to "emancipate" the working class. But its phrases perform symbolic functions and serve as rallying points. M. Lauré employed characteristic language when he said in 1958 that the national unions "have the duty of hastening the emancipation of the workers and their preparation for the role which will be theirs in a more just society."[55]

The great issues also provide opportunities for bridging internal conflicts. Questions of international politics and human rights may be passionately discussed and firm positions adopted while underlying and divisive union questions are glossed over. Indeed, representatives of the SNES have complained that "taking positions on the grand problems, often exceeding the grasp of the teachers' unions, hides the difficulties resulting from conflicts between large national unions on pedagogical and corporative questions."[56] This process of diverting attention to the great issues submerges real differences within the FEN and fosters the image of unity. For example, M. Lauré reported in 1958 that FEN cohesion was "exemplary" on the problems of educational reform, the defense of *laïcité*, and the defense of peace and liberty. All but one of these problems were of the ideological, "great-issue" type.[57] The "majority without precedent" that supported the FEN leadership in its opposition to the Fifth Republic is another case in point.[58]

Criticism and consultation. Fortunately, opportunities for criticism of the leadership and consultation of the membership exist in the FEN and permit the release of tensions without damage to organizational unity. Dissidents who might otherwise organize counter-groups instead

[53] *E.P.*, No. 25 (January, 1948), p. 1.
[54] Roger Chabaut, "Situation du Syndicalisme Enseignant," *Esprit* (January, 1952), p. 143.
[55] *E.P.*, 14e année, No. 1 (October, 1958), p. 1.
[56] *E.P.*, 9e année, No. 1 (September-October, 1953), p. 14.
[57] *E.P.*, 14e année, No. 1 (October, 1958), p. 1.
[58] *E.P.*, 14e année, No. 2 (November-December, 1958), p. 1.

take advantage of these opportunities to air their grievances against the leaders. Consultation not only reinforces members' identification with the organization but also helps to avoid communication gaps between the leaders and followers which, if sufficiently aggravated, could jeopardize unity.

Ideally, as in the eyes of one union writer, the leaders simply carry out the orders or "mandates" of the union members.[59] If this were true, there would be no possibility of tension between the mass base and the leadership structure. But critics have claimed that the relationship between base and superstructure is much different, for the leaders often act without consulting the base. On the question of the Fifth Republic, for example, one journalist wrote:

> Dizzied by the numerical importance of the organization . . . and mentally clouded by the grandeur of the role that they attribute to teachers' unions, these leaders come to make categorical political choices at the summit. In the name of a scarcely consulted organization, they have condemned the Atlantic Pact, condemned the EDC, condemned Suez, [and] brought a "solution" to the Algerian problem. . . .
> The teachers were not consulted by their leaders.[60]

Neither the union writer nor the newspaper critic gives a fair picture, for the truth lies somewhere between the two. The leaders do not act only in accordance with strict "mandates" from the base; sharp criticism leveled at them from the base for their actions demonstrates that they do not always do what the members have instructed them to do. Nor do they act independently of members' wishes; they utilize consultative techniques to keep themselves informed of the feelings of the rank-and-file.

The major opportunity for criticism of the leadership by the militants occurs at the annual Congress. In August or September the FEN bureau approves and publishes an activity report. At the November Congress the secretary general supplements this report with an up-to-date oral summary. Discussion follows. Delegates announce their complaints and satisfactions and explain why the unions or sections they represent have decided to vote for or against the activity report. Discussions on the motions of orientation proposed by the tendencies and on other motions of guidance or complaint also provide occasions for criticism.[61]

[59] E.P., Nouvelle série, No. 3 (December, 1948), p. 15.
[60] Combat, September 24, 1958.
[61] For example, three motions presented in 1956 observed that the union press was too sad, that the motions presented to the Congress were too long and heavy,

Figure 3 shows that while the Congress has always approved the activity report, the degree of approval has varied from year to year.

FIGURE 3
VOTES ON FEN ACTIVITY REPORTS, 1946–59*

Per cent of
favorable
vote

* Source: *L'Enseignement Public*, issues reporting on annual Congresses.

An analysis of the discussion of one or two years shows the type of criticisms made. The precipitous drop in support of the leadership in 1948 is due to the decision to leave the CGT and requires no special explanation. In 1957 the percentage of votes favoring the report also dropped noticeably. Speakers criticized the leadership for failing to harmonize the demands of the national unions with each other and with the other civil servants' unions in order to face the government with a united front; for being too reluctant to call a strike when there was no government in May and June; for refusing to support the strikes of the SNES and the SNET with an FEN work-stoppage; for failing to take a more positive stand for Algerian independence; for the paucity of material concessions wrung from the government; and for letting the bill for educational reform die a parliamentary death through post-ponement.[62]

In 1958 the reverse process occurred. In that year the majority favoring the activity report was the largest since 1946, some twenty percentage points higher than the average for the previous ten years.

and that the activity report ought to be shorter and more to the point. *E.P.*, 12e année, No. 3 (January, 1957), p. 22.

[62] *E.P.*, 13e année, No. 3 (January, 1958), pp. 18–22.

As one union official was quick to point out, the determining factor in this favorable vote had been the FEN's opposition to the Constitution of the Fifth Republic.[63] M. Lauré explained the vote as a shift of *cégétiste* strength from opposition to support of the *autonome* majority in its stand against the Fifth Republic; he added that they returned to their more traditional stance of opposition the following year.[64]

In 1961 the precipitous drop in favorable votes was traceable to several causes. Most important, however, was the failure of the FEN to win for many of its non-teaching categories the same benefits which its measures against the government in the spring had obtained for the teachers. The *cégétistes* claimed the FEN had given in too soon.[65]

Consultation in the FEN takes several forms: it may consist of a referendum in which all members are expected to participate; questionnaires may be sent to the national unions and departmental sections for discussion and report; a National Council may be called to get a broad representation of militant opinion; or leaders of accessible units may be informally sounded out.

A common criticism leveled at the leadership in its 1958 Congress, coming from both within and without the union, was that the membership had been insufficiently consulted on the decision to oppose the Fifth Republic. One member complained: "The mass of the union members were not consulted; the activity report has not been submitted to the individual vote of every member; the FEN remains too much an association of union notables." In reply Secretary General Dhombres of the SNES used strong language: "To claim that the FEN did not consult the base is a lie. Rarely has an organization composed of so many unions proceeded as democratically (consultation of the SNI Congress, of all the regular organs of the other unions) and, as far as the SNES is concerned, a precise mandate was given by the National Council."[66]

It is noteworthy that Secretary General Dhombres did not dispute the contention that not every individual member had voted on the matter. A referendum involving the vote of every member is not a commonly used device in the FEN. It was used for the critical decision on disaffiliation from the CGT in 1948; but even then it had to be confirmed in a mandated vote at the Congress.[67] The usual method of consultation is to circulate a questionnaire to the national unions and

[63] *E.P.*, 14e année, No. 3 (January, 1959), p. 23.
[64] Interview, May 11, 1960.
[65] *Le Monde*, November 1, 1961; and *E.P.*, 17e année, No. 3 (December, 1961), pp. 13–14, 19–21.
[66] *E.P.*, 14e année, No. 3 (January, 1959), pp. 22, 24.
[67] *E.P.*, No. 27 (April, 1948), p. 6.

departmental sections. These units discuss the questions and send in reports which are collated and printed in the union bulletin or presented orally to the Administrative Commission. Sometimes a National Council is called to discuss and summarize the results and to draw up a formulation of union policy.

Examples are numerous. In December, 1951, a decree to alter the vacation dates was proposed to teachers' councils in the Ministry of Education. The union representatives on the councils requested time to consult the union members. Fifty departmental sections answered the questionnaire which they circulated; the replies were discussed by the FEN's Pedagogical Committee. The FEN Administrative Commission then decided to have the union representatives on the councils prepare a unanimous position for presentation to the government.[68] A similar procedure was proposed in 1954 to prepare a union project for educational reform. The Administrative Commission was to prepare the FEN position from the reports of the national unions and departmental sections.[69] Sometimes very broad questions are treated in this way, such as "the responsibilities of the school and university facing the problems imposed on them by the development of youth" or "the reorganization of the school year in terms of the possibilities, the health of the child, and the conditions of present-day social life."[70]

Although channels of consultation exist, they are not always utilized. Only thirty-one departmental sections replied to the 1954 questionnaire on reform.[71] The response to a questionnaire on the proposed pupil orientation period was so meager (the principal national unions answered, but only six of the departmental sections did) that the Pedagogical Committee of the Congress declared that these several responses did not constitute a sufficient base for determining the Federation's position.[72] In 1959 it was decided to replace the questionnaire on educational reform with a "very general canvass" of unions and sections.[73]

The National Council is also a means of consultation since its composition includes the numerous departmental secretaries who occupy positions at the base. A meeting of the National Council often caps the process of general consultation of militants described above. For example, a National Council met on September 9, 1958, to consider the de Gaulle Constitution. Preparations for this meeting took place in the

[68] *E.P.*, 8e année, No. 1 (October, 1952), p. 6.
[69] *E.P.*, 9e année, No. 8 (August-September, 1954), p. 7.
[70] *Le Monde*, July 22, 1958.
[71] *E.P.*, 9e année, No. 4 (March-April, 1954), p. 7.
[72] *E.P.*, 8e année, No. 3 (December, 1952), p. 30.
[73] *E.P.*, 12e année, No. 4 (February-March, 1957), p. 10.

unions and sections. The SNES held a National Council of its own to assess opinion. The results of these discussions were pooled at the meeting of September 9. No vote was taken, but one man, appointed to draw the conclusions of the debate, declared that "the A[dministrative] C[ommission] now knows the sense of the position prevailing in the N[ational] C[ouncil]." On the following day, the Administrative Commission met to declare formally the hostility of the FEN to the Constitution.[74]

The confluent forces of a recognized need for unity, structural devices, agreement on the great issues, and safety valves of criticism and consultation help compensate for the strong centrifugal tendencies of the organization. They help answer the fundamental and difficult question of why a large and significant union such as the SNES should remain in the FEN when it finds itself so often opposed by the other unions. They also help explain why the SNI accepts underrepresentation and makes concessions to the other unions when it has the mass and power to go its own independent way.[75] No single force but a combination of them all is necessary to explain the obvious sacrifices that these two unions make in order to maintain the unity of the FEN.

But one may speculate that an equally important explanation for the continuing unity of the organization lies in the possibility that the ideological tendencies are not weaknesses at all but elements of strength. In an organization that reproduces in microcosm the cleavages of France's fragmented political culture, or at least those on the left, organized factions operate as political parties in a small-scale political system with spokesmen, programs, candidates, and elections. These factions legitimize and channel dissent which might otherwise jeopardize unity. They make it possible for teachers of different ideological persuasions to coexist in a single organization that thereby becomes at least a potential force to be reckoned with on the political scene.[76]

[74] *E.P.*, 13e année, No. 8 (August-September, 1958), pp. 1, 6; and 14e année, No. 1 (October, 1958), p. 31.

[75] Forestier stated in 1960: "We must be careful of the tactics used: defense by category or within the framework of the FEN. In the first case it would be easy for the primary teachers to prove that they are the most disadvantaged [*déclassés*], but that could only be done to the detriment of the Federation's cohesion. Therefore we must all face the problem together." Minutes of the Administrative Commission of February 25, 1960, in *E.P.*, 15e année, No. 6 (March, 1960), p. 24.

[76] A two-party system in trade union government is analyzed in the classic work by Seymour E. Lipset, Martin A. Trow, and James S. Coleman, *Union Democracy: The Internal Politics of the International Typographical Union* (Glencoe: Free Press, 1956).

Methods of Action

One spokesman of an FEN member union has described the methods of action employed by the Federation as the "traditional means of unionism." He listed them as petitions, appeals to members of Parliament, audiences with ministers, contacts with officials in the Ministry of Education, communiqués, press conferences, and strikes.[1] With the exception of strikes, these action techniques are more commonly associated with pressure groups than with unions. They are typical of those described not only in the literature on American pressure groups but also in the increasing number of books and monographs on foreign pressure groups. Inspection of the patterns of FEN activity gives additional support to some of the hypotheses about them developed by Eckstein, Ehrmann, LaPalombara, and others and raises some questions as well.[2]

Most of the methods utilized by the FEN can be discussed in terms of the target of their action: the government and administration, the Parliament and parties, and public opinion. While directed against the government, the strike must be considered separately because of its broad impact on all the target areas.

GOVERNMENT AND ADMINISTRATION

The most important and the most frequent contacts take place between the teachers and their employer, between the FEN on the one hand and the government and administration on the other. Contacts with the administration are institutionalized, multi-purposed, and normally prosaic. Contacts with the government are irregular, pointed, and often climactic. In both cases the FEN seeks the support of its natural allies where appropriate.

[1] From a recruitment folder in *La Vie de la Recherche Scientifique*, No. 28 [23] (January, 1960), p. 2.
[2] See Chap. VIII for a brief survey of recent developments in group theory and a summary of the findings of this study in relation to them.

Contacts with the government. Interviews and communications with members of the government, particularly with the Minister of Education, are frequent. In 1946 M. Lavergne, after a meeting of the FEN bureau with the Minister of Education and the director of his cabinet, requested regular exchanges of views every fortnight.[3] While this request was not formally granted, contacts with the Minister and his cabinet take place from time to time. A newly invested Prime Minister ordinarily calls in the FEN leaders in order to establish good relations.[4] When he or one of his ministers decides to consult union leaders during the course of his administration, the FEN is normally included. In 1956, for example, Prime Minister Guy Mollet received the representatives of the CGT, CGT-FO, and CFTC labor confederations, spokesmen of the civil service unions, and a delegation from the FEN; he assured the delegation that the FEN would be invited to future meetings between the government and the labor confederations. M. Lavergne considered this equality with the labor confederations to be a clear FEN success.[5] These contacts deal most often with economic demands; sometimes they are taken up directly with the Minister of Finance.[6] Negotiations for wage increases in 1961, carried on under the pressure of FEN strikes and strike threats, involved several ministers and eventually the Prime Minister and President de Gaulle themselves.[7]

Occasionally the contacts are of a more general nature. In September, 1958, Prime Minister de Gaulle took the initiative in arranging an interview with the secretaries general of the FEN, the SNI, the SNES, the SNET, and the Syndicat National de l'Enseignement Supérieur. In this meeting the Prime Minister asked the delegates to summarize the essential problems currently facing education and its personnel.[8] The FEN does not hesitate to initiate contacts. In 1954, for example, it sent telegrams to Prime Minister Mendès-France to inform him of the FEN position on the war in Indochina.[9] Its contacts with the Minister of Education in 1944 were successful as it obtained the appointment of four of its members to the Langevin Commission.[10] One of the more important successes of the FEN resulted from an

[3] *E.P.*, No. 7 (April, 1946), p. 2.
[4] Lauré, interview, May 11, 1960.
[5] *Le Populaire de Paris*, October 9, 1956; *E.P.*, 12ᵉ année, No. 1 (October, 1956), p. 7; and No. 2 (November-December, 1956), p. 23.
[6] *Combat*, January 8, 1958.
[7] *Le Monde*, March 31, 1961.
[8] *Le Monde*, September 11, 1958.
[9] *E.P.*, 9ᵉ année, No. 8 (August-September, 1954), p. 3.
[10] *E.P.*, No. 1 [1945], p. 6.

audience with Prime Minister Guy Mollet. On May 13, 1957, the Prime Minister promised to make passage of a particular educational reform bill a question of confidence. It was, however, a short-lived triumph, for the Mollet government resigned one week later.[11] In short, the FEN is able to reach the top levels of government; the efficacy of its contacts depends upon the issues, the political situation, and also personalities.[12]

Contacts with the administration. However important audiences granted by the members of the government are for matters of top-level policy, the frequency and regularity of contacts between the FEN and the administration suggest that it is on this level that the most significant exchanges occur. FEN leaders have occasional meetings with directors and bureau chiefs in the Ministry of Education. But more important than these typical pressure group contacts are the permanent beachheads that have been won in the administration; unions have achieved "penetration into the administrative machinery," in the words of M. Lavergne.[13] Union leaders are elected by the employees of the Ministry of Education to advisory councils in the administration. They have direct, institutionalized access to the decision makers in education. In this way, the downward flow of hierarchical commands is attenuated by the organizationally articulated upward flow of teachers' objections and suggestions.

The organization of these consultative councils is somewhat complex because of the overlapping jurisdictions of the prewar councils and those established by the General Civil Service *Statut* of October 19, 1946. The prewar representative organs were basically of two types: first, the Education Councils (*Conseils d'Enseignement*), charged with advising the Minister on pedagogical and other questions of a general nature, and including the High Council of Public Instruction (*Conseil Supérieur de l'Instruction Publique*); and second, the Consultative Committees (*Comités Consultatifs*) in the various branches and levels, created to consider personnel nominations, transfers, and promotions. The 1946 law affected both types; their reorganization is not yet complete.[14]

---

11 *E.P.*, 12ᵉ année, No. 6 (May, 1957), p. 6.

12 A former Minister of Education, Senator Jean Berthoin, emphasized that the Minister of Education is normally a *laïque* sympathetic to teachers' demands. Interview, June 1, 1960. A high-level civil servant cited personality factors, noting that the then Minister of Education, M. Louis Joxe, a former ambassador and diplomat, seemed to be enjoying smoother relations than his predecessor, M. André Boulloche, who, as a graduate of Ecole Polytechnique, tended to have a less flexible, technical approach to problems. Interview, May 20, 1960.

13 *E.P.*, No. 2 (October, 1945), p. 13.

14 *L'Organisation de l'Enseignement en France*, p. 9.

The 1946 legislation created five Education Councils (first degree, second degree, technical education, higher education, and adult education and sports) and one High Council of National Education (*Conseil Supérieur de l'Education Nationale*), the latter to replace the prewar High Council of Public Instruction. Each council is composed of ex officio members, members named by decree, and members and alternates elected by the personnel. Since the unions present lists of candidates for these elections, these members are usually union leaders, but *de jure* they are only representatives of the personnel.[15]

The High Council of National Education is the highest consultative body of the Ministry of Education. It must be consulted on bills and decrees which affect several levels of education, on questions raised by the Minister or sent it by an Education Council, and on all questions concerning private education. The High Council of National Education also serves as a court of final appeals for disciplinary cases such as the decision of a lower body to bar a teacher from further employment in the public schools. The High Council is made up of seventy-nine members. Fourteen are officials who sit ex officio; ten are appointed by decree and include largely rectors and inspectors general; and five are selected to represent private education. Fifty members, a majority of the Council, are chosen by the five Education Councils.[16] Each Education Council elects ten of its elected members to serve on the High Council. It is in these elections that the teachers' unions play a dominant role. For example, the Primary Education Council (*Conseil d'Enseignement du Premier Degré*) elected on November 17, 1958, met on February 4, 1959, to elect its ten representatives to the High Council of National Education. The SNI reported to its members:

> On the proposal of our comrade Mounolou (Normal School Professor), the Council first decided to renew the distribution adopted in 1946 of these ten members, namely: seven primary school teachers, one Primary Inspector, one Normal School Director, and one Normal School Professor.

[15] This difference is a nuance insisted upon by certain members of the administration in conversations with the author. It may be evidence of the administration's traditional lack of amity for the civil service unions or simply a reminder that elected members are not always FEN officials.

[16] The Secondary Education Council (Conseil de l'Enseignement du Second Degré), composed of fifty-nine members, is one of the five Education Councils and fairly typical of them all. The three ex officio members are: the Director of Secondary Education (who also serves as president of the Council), the Director of Technical Education, and the head of the Pedagogical Research and Studies Service. The fourteen members named by decree include five Academy rectors, six inspectors general, one functionary from the central administration, and two representatives of parents' associations. The forty-two other members are elected

Then, by secret and unanimous ballot, it elected the candidates presented by the Primary Inspectors Union, the Normal School Directors and Professors Union, and the National Teachers Union [SNI].[17]

All were FEN unions. It is therefore not surprising that the voice of the High Council often seems to be the echo of the FEN.

Union militants regard the creation of the consultative councils as one of their proudest accomplishments. Suggesting the syndicalist ideal of workers' councils, these organs allow direct and regular communication between the unions and the administration. The unions protest vigorously when they believe the government is slighting or ignoring the decisions of the councils. On October 27, 1950, the High Council of National Education recalled that "it is regularly competent to give its opinion on all questions concerning education. Consequently, the High Council declares that respect for legality requires that every proposal or recommendation concerning education be submitted to the High Council of National Education before being decided by the government or presented to Parliament."[18] In 1951 the FEN protested that the High Council had not been properly consulted on a government bill to grant scholarships to private school students; it had the Council approve a resolution condemning such scholarships. When the administrative regulations governing the distribution of the scholarships were published, the Council realized its advice had not been strictly followed and registered a sharp complaint.[19] Slightly more than a year later an unpopular summer vacation scheme proposed by the government furnished the occasion for the elected members to resign in face of "the scorn that the government had not ceased to show . . . for the highest instance of the educational establishment." L'Enseignement Public printed an explanation:

Our colleagues wanted to protest . . . against the attitude of the Minister towards the High Council of National Education. They

---

by members of specified categories. They include one director of a girls' lycée elected by the directors of girls' lycées; five professors teaching in boys' lycées, and elected by the professors of philosophy, history, geography, literature, grammar, and modern languages in such schools; and other similarly chosen representatives of educational employees. France, Ministère de l'Education Nationale, de la Jeunesse et des Sports, Bulletin Officiel, Institut Pédagogique National, Fascicules de Documentation Administrative, Brochure No. 97 (Paris: Imprimerie nationale, 1959), par. 2/A, pp. 1–4, 7–9. This series is hereafter cited as Documentation Administrative. A recent structural change in the High Council has been reported in Education in France, No. 26 (December, 1964), pp. 16–17.

17 E.L., 26e année, No. 21 (February 20, 1959), p. 791.

18 E.P., 6e année, No. 2 (November, 1950), p. 6.

19 E.P., 7e année, No. 1 (October, 1951), p. 6; and No. 3 (December, 1951), p. 3.

do not indeed forget that that organ is only consultative, but they feel that there is no reason for consulting it if, in all important circumstances, the recommendations it formulates are ignored; and they consider it useless to give their opinion on a question if, even before asking for it, the Minister has made his decision.[20]

Under the Fifth Republic complaints that the government has failed to consult the Education Councils have increased. They were not consulted on the reorganization of the Ministry of Education in 1961.[21] The High Council was not consulted on the 1959 bill to aid private schools; all the elected members resigned in protest on December 21, 1959.[22] The High Council was not consulted on the scheme for classifying private school teachers for pay purposes under the new law.[23] It was not consulted on a plan to create separate institutions for the cycle of orientation period. M. Lauré declared: "We are astonished that texts which absolutely overturn [educational] structures could be published without the least consultation. This deeply shocking procedure implies either distrust or scorn of us."[24]

Besides these Education Councils, a system of committees was developed to further the principle of employee consultation. The committees created in accordance with the General Civil Service *Statut* of October 19, 1946, are of two types: the Joint Technical Committees (*Comités Techniques Paritaires*) and the Joint Administrative Committees (*Commissions Administratives Paritaires*).[25] The latter propose appointments, transfers, and promotions of personnel and suggest sanctions when necessary; they have largely replaced the prewar Consultative Committees. The former are supposed to submit advisory opinions on new civil service regulations and particularly on personnel regulations for the different categories.[26] The unions proudly claim credit for their creation.[27]

A Joint Technical Committee was established on each level and in each branch of the Ministry of Education. The highest one, appointed to work with the Minister of Education and known as the Ministerial Joint Technical Committee (*Comité Technique Paritaire Ministériel*) is

[20] *E.P.*, 8e année, No. 5 (February-March, 1953), p. 5.

[21] *Le Monde*, November 2, 1961.

[22] *E.L.*, 27e année, No. 15bis (December 26, 1959), p. 844. See Chaps. VI and VII for a full discussion of the 1951 and 1959 controversies.

[23] *E.P.*, 16e année, No. 3 (December, 1960), p. 6.

[24] *Le Monde*, December 5, 6, 1961. Partially as a result of union protests, a later decree narrowed significantly the application of the texts. *Le Monde*, December 13, 1961.

[25] These committees are provisional, pending the creation of a special *statut* for the personnel of the Ministry of Education.

[26] *L'Organisation de l'Enseignement en France*, p. 9.

[27] *E.P.*, No. 25 (January, 1948), p. 1.

composed of fifteen members named by the Minister to represent the administration, and an equal number of members (hence the name *paritaire*) designated by the unions "regarded as the most representative of the personnel at the moment the appointments are made." A decree of February 25, 1948, awarded fourteen seats to the FEN and one to the Syndicat Général de l'Education Nationale (CFTC).[28] The union representatives are chosen from among the members of the Administrative Commission of the FEN and appointed with the agreement of the national unions.[29] Other Joint Technical Committees, usually composed of ten representatives of the administration and ten members selected by the unions, function in the various Directions of the central administration and on the Academy and departmental levels.

Joint Administrative Committees were created for each body and level of civil servants with the same rule of equality between representatives of the administration and of the personnel. For example, a decree of February 11, 1957, created such committees for laboratory assistants and service personnel (concierges, office boys, watchmen, etc.) in a number of higher educational establishments. Two members were to represent the administration and two the personnel.[30] FEN members tend to dominate these councils as well. For example, in 1960 the secretary general of the SNET announced that at the last council elections his union won forty-nine of the fifty seats.[31]

The FEN is represented in another consultative body, the High Council of the Civil Service (*Conseil Supérieur de la Fonction Publique*). Although the FEN is only a minority member, this important council represents the whole body of civil servants. It speaks for them on such matters as reclassification, defense of their legal rights, and interpretation of the General Civil Service *Statut* of 1946.[32] Originally, the FEN was represented on the High Council of the Civil Service by Secretary General Lavergne; M. Aigueperse of the SNI served as alternate. In 1949 the FEN bureau declared that, since the Federation represented about a third of all civil servants and more than a third of those unionized, it was entitled to more than the single seat it then held out of the twelve union seats on the High Council of the Civil Service.[33] Two years later the FEN received two regular seats,[34] but

28 *Documentation Administrative*, Brochure No. 98, par. 4/A2, pp. 1–3.
29 *E.P.*, 5e année, No. 1 (September-October, 1949), p. 4.
30 *Documentation Administrative*, Brochure No. 98, par. 4/B1, pp. 3–4.
31 *Le Monde*, April 5, 1960.
32 *E.P.*, 5e année, No. 1 (September-October, 1949), p. 4.
33 *E.P.*, Nouvelle série, No. 6 (March, 1949), p. 6.
34 *E.P.*, 6e année, No. 7 (April, 1951), p. 6.

when union representation on the Council was increased from twelve to fourteen in 1958, their request for an additional seat was rejected.[35]

Relations with other unions. In its dealings with the government and administration the FEN is surrounded by unions and labor confederations which engage in common, or at least parallel, action with it. Particularly important are the civil service unions which share the interest of the FEN in pressing for salary increases.

The French labor movement emerged from the Resistance and the Liberation with a high degree of moral and organizational unity. The FEN (then the FGE) was organizationally linked to both the CGT and the Union Générale des Fédérations de Fonctionnaires (UGFF), a broad civil service federation organized as an industrial federation of the CGT. However, after the schism of the CGT in 1947, the FEN avoided all permanent organizational links with other unions and labor confederations. It joined other teachers' and civil service unions in taking action to support common demands but limited organization to committees of coordination and loosely united cartels; sometimes informal contacts between leaders sufficed. At various times it cooperated with the UGFF-CGT (about 100,000 members); the Fédération Générale des Fonctionnaires affiliated with the CGT-FO (FGF-FO); the Fédération Générale des Syndicats Chrétiens de Fonctionnaires (CFTC) (87,000 members in 1958); the independent Fédération Générale Autonome des Fonctionnaires (FGAF); the Cartel Interfédéral Force Ouvrière (about 350,000 members, including the FGF-FO); and the Cartel des Services Publics.[36]

The character of the relations of the FEN with each of these organizations varies. Relations are cordial with the FGAF, an independent federation much like the FEN but without its ideological tendencies.[37] Relations with the CGT fluctuate between amicable cooperation and suspicious disdain. In the late 1940's the FEN was careful to avoid joint action committees with the CGT on the local level, for these could be easily captured and manipulated.[38] On October

[35] One seat was given to the Confédération Générale des Cadres, the other to the CFTC. *E.P.*, 13e année, No. 5 (March-April, 1958), p. 14. The civil service unions object vociferously when the government fails to call the High Council into session. The time between its last meeting of 1958 (on February 14) and its first meeting of 1959 (on October 27) was condemned as "eighteen months of silence." A minister promised that henceforth the Council would be convened every three months. *E.P.*, 5e année, No. 3 (December, 1959), p. 5.

[36] *Supplément à E.P.* [No. 16 (1947)], p. 3; *E.P.*, Nouvelle série, No. 2 (November, 1948), p. 2; *Le Monde*, July 24–25, 1949; June 9, 1960; and Tiano, *Les Traitements des Fonctionnaires*, pp. 253–80.

[37] Pierre Dhombres, interview, April 25, 1960.

[38] *E.P.*, 5e année, No. 2 (November, 1949), p. 1.

27, 1960, a demonstration for peace in Algeria was sponsored by the Union Nationale des Etudiants de France (UNEF), the FEN, the CFTC, and some FO unions. The CGT refused to support the demonstration on the grounds it had not been consulted during the planning stages. M. Lauré condemned this attitude of the CGT as a "stab in the back."[39] In 1961 relations with the CGT reached a low point as FEN leaders grew impatient with CGT tactics and policy.[40] On the other hand, during the 1950's the recognized strength and security of both the FEN and the CGT had built mutual respect and encouraged frank relations. Common attitudes on programs of higher salaries and laïcité had further encouraged cooperation.

Largely because of its profoundly anticlerical sentiments, the FEN has infrequent contacts with the CFTC. In 1951 the two worked together with other organizations in a Comité d'Action Universitaire; in the 1960–61 campaign for higher salaries they worked with other civil service unions to present a single counterplan to the government.[41] But often direct contacts between the FEN and the CFTC are impossible, and arrangements necessary for common action must be made by using leaders of the CGT or FO unions as intermediaries.

The relations of the FEN with the FO unions have not been good. After considerable post-schism bitterness, there soon developed a workable relationship in which FO supporters were recognized as an ideological tendency within the FEN. But the FO decision to refuse members the right of double affiliation restored relations to their former poor condition. The high-handed manner in which the FO called a strike for December 2, 1959, without consulting the FEN even indirectly, and the FO's attempts to breathe life into its own teachers' union, the FEN-FO, have not helped matters.[42]

The FEN has occasionally served as an intermediary for the CGT and FO unions which, manifesting hostility stemming from the 1947 schism, refuse direct contact with each other.[43] In the 1960–61 struggle between the government and the civil service workers, union delegations were received in two groups, first the FEN-CFTC-FO leaders

[39] Le Monde, October 28; and November 3, 1960.
[40] Cf. p. 74.
[41] Minutes of the 1951 Congress, in E.P., 7e année, No. 3 (December, 1951), p. 18; and Le Monde, December 3, 1960. For FEN relations with the CFTC and the FO, see Tiano, Les Traitements des Fonctionnaires, pp. 343–45.
[42] Syndicalisme Universitaire, Nouvelle série, No. 224 (February 17, 1960), p. 115/7; and E.P., 15e année, No. 3 (December, 1959), pp. 2–4. Syndicalisme Universitaire is the bulletin of the Syndicat General de l'Education Nationale (SGEN-CFTC).
[43] Pierre Dhombres, interview, April 25, 1960.

and then the representatives of the FEN-CFTC-CGT.[44] M. Lauré has explained that "for ten years, each time that we judged it useful and possible, we tried on all levels to be the necessary bridge between organizations equally interested in a common objective."[45]

The FEN also cooperates with other mass organizations in dealing with the government and administration, but these bodies have their greatest impact on public opinion and must be considered separately.

Tenor of FEN-administration relations. Factors of time, personality, political context, and issue importance so condition the tenor of relations between the FEN and the Ministry of Education that generalizations purporting to describe the effective influence of the teachers' unions must be treated with due skepticism. For example, it is impossible to accept as objective description the statement that "the departmental secretary of the Union [SNI] is invested with a *de facto* authority with which the Academy Inspector and the Prefect must contend; as for the national leaders, the ephemeral Minister who would engage in open conflict with them would not have the upper hand."[46] While the administration must always take into consideration the reaction of the teachers' unions, in the final analysis they do not have the upper hand. In a more felicitous statement, M. Lavergne said in 1946 that the teachers had an organization "capable of weighing on governmental decisions."[47] This phrase is a good description of the position of the FEN, for while it suggests that the organization has leaders, numbers, channels, and techniques for exerting pressure, it says nothing about the varying effectiveness of its pressures.

The FEN enjoys a number of advantages in its relations with the administration. First, the civil servants of the central administration are usually favorably disposed towards the teachers, their representatives, and their demands. They share the same outlook (republican and *laïque*), and often they are products of the same celebrated Normal Schools.[48] The administrators understand the problems of teachers, because most of them have been teachers themselves.[49] When they were teachers, they were usually members of the FEN; it is not sur-

---

[44] *Le Monde,* December 3, 1960; and May 6, 1961.
[45] *E.P.,* 16ᵉ année, No. 8 (August-September, 1961), p. 26.
[46] Ferré, *L'Instituteur,* p. 49.
[47] *E.P.,* No. 6 (February, 1946), p. 3.
[48] Interview, February 24, 1960.
[49] "All those who have authority over pupils, students, or teachers have themselves taught and know from within, so to speak, the nature of the problems they have to solve." P. Henry, "Les Enseignants dans les Postes Administratifs du Ministère de l'Education Nationale," *Avenirs,* p. 53.

prising that they should maintain sentimental attachments and personal friendships.

Secondly, the Minister of Education himself is often sympathetic to the FEN position and surrounds himself with like-minded aides.[50] He has almost always been a "convinced laïque," the minimum FEN requirement.[51] More important, like most ministers, he tends to identify with his employees and to support their demands against the Minister of Finance. On November 28, 1946, for example, M. Lavergne wrote to the Minister of Finance requesting the continuation of temporary salary supplements until the establishment of new pay scales and sent a copy of the Minister of Education. The latter replied, "I have the honor to inform you that . . . I am contacting the Minister of Finance to support your request most heartily." On December 16 the Minister of Finance granted the request.[52] In a more recent epoch, when relations between the government and the Federation were particularly strained, the FEN was nevertheless successful in getting two different Ministers of Education to send letters of support to the Minister of Finance.[53]

Thirdly, the FEN is usually successful in having its views accepted by the various councils consulted by the administration. M. Lavergne, noting that the councils facilitated agreements between the administration and the personnel, reported in 1950 that "the Federation's delegation . . . almost always had its proposals prevail" in the councils.[54] In fact, FEN success in these councils has resulted in complaints that the unions are usurping functions that belong to the administration. A deputy complained in Parliament that the unions sent out forms on which members were asked to list their preferences for transfers and promotions so the union could use its influence to bring them about. He also said the unions informed their members of promotions and transfers before word reached them through official channels. The Minister weakly replied that the proceedings of the consultative councils are confidential and the unions are not supposed to reveal them, a reply which promised no diminution of the Federation's influence in the councils.[55]

[50] In 1950 two members of the Minister of Education's cabinet belonged to the FEN and defended the Federation's point of view whenever possible. E.P., 5ᵉ année, No. 8 (April-May, 1950), p. 2.

[51] E.P., No. 1 [1945], p. 6.

[52] E.P., No. 15 (January, 1947), p. 3.

[53] According to the FEN, however, the Minister neither answered the letters nor replied to FEN requests for an audience. E.P., 14ᵉ année, No. 7 (August-September, 1959), p. 10.

[54] E.P., 6ᵉ année, No. 1 (October, 1950), p. 1.

[55] J.O., Assemblée Nationale, October 3, 1959, p. 1673; and October 6, 1959, p. 1715.

While these advantages confer on the FEN a clear "capability of weighing" on governmental decisions, union complaints make clear that the teachers are not always successful. The complaint most commonly reiterated is that the government either fails to consult the unions or, if it does consult them, it fails to heed their advice.[56] It is noteworthy that this conclusion is consistent with generalizations made by authorities on foreign pressure groups. LaPalombara has cautioned that common educational backgrounds and outlooks of administrators and pressure-group leaders do not show that the former are prey to the latter. Furthermore, LaPalombara and Ehrmann both question the view that consultative councils mean control by pressure groups.[57] Several examples support the conclusion that, while the unions may be consulted, the government has the last word in every case.

Although the FEN has long demanded the unification of all state educational services under the Ministry of Education, it has been eminently unsuccessful in bringing it about. Various ministries continue to operate their own schools in a relatively independent fashion, despite FEN warnings that this educational fragmentation creates "a particularistic spirit prejudicial to French unity and the higher interests of the country."[58] In fact, a 1955 law placed agricultural education exclusively under the Ministry of Agriculture, a major defeat for the FEN.[59] On the other hand, the FEN has been successful in opposing

---

[56] "The government aspires to impose its decisions unilaterally without previous consultation of the interested representative union organizations." *Combat*, October 4, 1956. Under the Fifth Republic the government's delay in convening the High Council of the Civil Service and its alleged circumvention of the High Council of National Education for the School Bill of 1959 irritated union leaders. One spokesman charged that "the will to ignore . . . the union organizations, the various assemblies, organs, or councils which the government is legally obliged to consult, seems indeed to be one of the characteristics of governmental action." *E.L.*, 26e année, No. 17 (January 23, 1959), p. 567; 27e année, No. 9 (November 6, 1959), p. 459; and also Chap. VII.

[57] Joseph LaPalombara, "The Utility and Limitations of Interest Group Theory in Non-American Field Situations," *Journal of Politics*, Vol. XXII (February, 1960), 46–47; and Henry W. Ehrmann, "French Bureaucracy and Organized Interests," *Administrative Science Quarterly*, Vol. V (March, 1961), 541–43. However, in view of the high degree of FEN activity in contacts with the Ministry of Education, one may question the generalization of Meynaud that pressure groups are most active in the newer ministries, as both Ehrmann and LaPalombara have already done. Cf. Meynaud, *Les Groupes de Pression*, p. 207; LaPalombara, *loc. cit.*, p. 44; and Ehrmann, *loc. cit.*, pp. 538–41. Meynaud stresses the greater success of groups in the "vertical ministries" in his revised version, *Nouvelles Etudes sur les Groupes de Pression en France*, p. 272.

[58] *E.P.*, No. 3 (November, 1945), p. 15; *E.P.*, No. 10 (July, 1946), p. 2; and *Combat*, November 3, 1954. Another unarticulated objection rises from the fact that teachers who are active or potential union members are scattered among ministries where the FEN has less influence than in the Ministry of Education.

[59] The law also provided funds for private schools. The FEN helped to delay the opening of debate on the bill and supported the obstructionist tactics of the

the removal of services from the jurisdiction of the Ministry of Education. The School and University Health Service was not transferred to the Ministry of Health as had been proposed, and the High Commission for Youth and Sports did not become an independent service; both remained under the Minister of Education.[60] On another organizational question facing the Ministry, that of reforming the High Council of National Education, the FEN met with notable failure. The FEN wanted one-third of the High Council's members to be directly appointed by the teachers' unions, but its plan was rejected by a combination of administration and non-union representatives on the High Council.[61]

The problem of setting the summer vacation dates has often brought the teachers' unions into conflict with the Minister of Education. Sometimes union influence has succeeded in altering a Minister's decision, but other times the unions have been ignored, particularly when disagreements between them furnished the Minister with the opportunity. In 1953, when the government disregarded the advice of the Ministerial Joint Technical Committee and the desires of the organized teachers, the FEN arranged to have the Minister interpellated in the National Assembly; certain adjustments in examination dates were soon made in the direction of greater conformity with FEN demands for uniform vacations for all teachers.[62] In 1954, the Minister promised that vacations would be of practically the same duration for all teachers, but he rejected the dates proposed by the FEN and the High Council of National Education.[63] In 1955, the Minister satisfied union demands so that M. Lavergne was able to report to the FEN Congress that the FEN had "intervened successfully to set the vacation and examination dates in 1955."[64] In 1959, disagreements between the primary and

Socialist and Communist parties. A special issue of E.P. gave reasons for opposing the bill: E.P., 10e année, No. 2 (October, 1954). Also see No. 3 (December, 1954), p. 1; and André Siegfried, Edouard Bonnefous, and J. B. Duroselle (eds.), L'Année Politique: 1955 (Paris: Presses Universitaires de France, 1956), pp. 60–61.

[60] L'Organisation de l'Enseignement en France, p. 75; G. Loriaux, "L'Education Physique et Sportive," Avenirs, p. 160; Minutes of the Administrative Commission for October 16, 1958, in E.P., 14e année, No. 2 (November-December, 1958), p. 23; and 9e année, No. 2 (November, 1953), p. 17.

[61] E.P., 5e année, No. 7 (March, 1950), p. 8; No. 9 (June, 1950), p. 7; and 6e année, No. 1 (October, 1950), pp. 1–2.

[62] Le Populaire de Paris, March 13, 1953; and E.P., 9e année, No. 1 (September-October, 1953), p. 8.

[63] E.P., 9e année, No. 4 (January-February, 1954), pp. 5–6; No. 5 (March-April, 1954), p. 15; No. 8 (August-September, 1954), p. 7; and J. O., Lois et Decrets, February 23, 1954, p. 1821.

[64] E.P., 10e année, No. 5 (February, 1955), p. 10; and No. 9 (August-September, 1955), p. 9.

secondary teachers made it impossible for the High Council of National Education to give its advice on proposed vacation dates; the Minister chose the dates approved by the SNI and made certain adjustments only after the SNES threatened a strike.[65] In short, on the question of vacations, the FEN proposes with a voice sometimes enfeebled by internal dissent, but the Minister disposes.

Educational reform is a fundamental FEN goal, but its record of influence and accomplishment on this count is not distinguished. It prepared its own plan based upon the report of the Langevin Commission but could not get it accepted by the government.[66] In 1955, when Minister of Education Berthoin appointed a Study Committee for Educational Reform on which the teachers' unions were not represented, the FEN protested and finally opposed "with all its force" the bill which emerged from the Committee's work. The FEN sought to oppose the government's position in the High Council of National Education but failed to obtain the Council's support because the secondary teachers could not agree with the others on the "common trunk" orientation period.[67] After the 1956 elections the new Minister of Education, M. René Billères, appointed a "Commission for the Democratization of Secondary, Technical, and Higher Education" to develop further the Berthoin reform, and included the secretaries general of the FEN, the SNES, the SNI, and the SNET among its members; the FEN reluctantly approved the resulting reform bill as a "minimum program," but before the National Assembly could pass it, the events of May 13, 1958, and their sequel pre-empted the agenda, truncated the Parliamentary session, and toppled the Fourth Republic.[68] When it was learned that the de Gaulle government was preparing

65 See Chap. IV, pp. 00–00.
66 E.P., Nouvelle série, No. 3 (December, 1948), p. 11; 5e année, No. 5 (January, 1950), p. 11; No. 6 (February, 1950), pp. 2, 7; 6e année, No. 1 (October, 1950), p. 15; 10e année, No. 5 (February, 1955), p. 7; and Miles, Recent Reform in French Secondary Education, p. 70.
67 E.P., 10e année, No. 5 (February, 1955), p. 7; No. 7 (April-May, 1955), p. 7; No. 8 (June, 1955), p. 3; No. 9 (August-September, 1955), p. 9; and 11e année, No. 2 (November, 1955), p. 6. Senator Berthoin felt later that the differences between the FEN and himself had been exaggerated. He stated that his plan represented the possible as opposed to the ideal; the two plans only differed in degree. Interview, June 1, 1960. An official of the Ministry of Education referred to the Langevin plan as an ideal which practical reforms could only aim for. Interview, February 24, 1960.
68 J.O., Lois et Decrets, March 20, 1956, p. 2678; J.O., Assemblée Nationale, July 25–27, 1957, pp. 3933–4025; E.P., 11e année, No. 8 (August-September, 1956), p. 2; and 13e année, No. 2 (November-December, 1957), pp. 18, 20. The SNES voted against the resolution supporting the Billères bill on the grounds that all the points of disagreement had been decided in its disfavor. Minutes of the 1957 FEN Congress, in E.P., 13e année, No. 3 (January, 1958), p. 29. A thorough

its own reform plan, the FEN, which had not been invited to participate in its formulation, denounced "the unwonted conditions under
which the Minister of Education put in final form what he abusively
considers a reform of education."[69] Put into effect by decree in
January, 1959, the reform was attacked by union leaders as "minor and
conservative," "profoundly reactionary," and "a caricature."[70] It is
instructive to note that the FEN helped formulate the Langevin and
Billères plans and approved of both; it was not invited to participate
in the preparation of the 1955 and 1959 schemes and condemned
both. It should not be concluded, however, that union participation
made the only difference in the Federation's attitude. The 1959 reform
clearly marked a retreat from the earlier proposals; it reduced the cycle
of orientation, for example, from two years to three months, to the
consternation of the SNI which claimed paternity for the idea.[71] Nor
should it be concluded that FEN influence was insignificant on educational reform; the inclusion of even a minimal cycle of observation was
a modest victory for the Federation.

These three case studies reveal that the tenor of FEN relations with
the administration is a variable quality. Amicable and mutually helpful
at the inception of the Fourth Republic, relations became strained and
even hostile at the beginning of the Fifth. In the interim the FEN
enjoyed limited success in its proposals on the structure of the Ministry
of Education; sometimes it had its views on the summer vacation dates
accepted and sometimes rejected; and it generally was disappointed
on the question of educational reform. Internal discord reduced the
potential impact of the organization, a common occurrence with large

---

case study of the reaction of the teachers' unions to the Billères reform is F.-G.
Dreyfus, "Un Groupe de Pression en Action," *Revue Française de Science Politique*, Vol. XV (April, 1965), 213–50.

[69] The Minister answered in a letter to the FEN: "It has always been my
habit to associate your group with studies concerning the situation of civil servants.
That it should be so is quite normal and in conformity with customs which, for
my part, I have always respected.

"But, in truth, the problem of educational reform is of quite another nature. My
intentions as well as texts were submitted to the regular procedures of the Ministry
of Education and communicated to the different councils and the representatives
of the unions. In application of its constitutional powers, the government has a
perfect right to modify these texts and, as long as they are not definitive, certainly
has the duty to do so in secrecy." *E.P.*, 14e année, No. 3 (January, 1959), pp. 5,
8; and *E.L.*, 26e année, No. 15 (January 9, 1959), p. 460; and No. 16 (January
16, 1959), p. 509.

[70] They agreed, however, that the reform was better than nothing at all. *E.P.*,
14e année, No. 3 (January, 1959), p. 8; No. 7 (August-September, 1959), p. 5;
and *Le Monde*, July 10, 1959, April 7, 1960, and April 8, 1960.

[71] *Le Monde*, July 20, 1956.

confederations according to Ehrmann.[72] But the disappointment on educational reform was part of a general decline in the influence of the FEN under the Fifth Republic. The strengthening of the executive achieved by the new Constitution contributed to the decline. Although the highest civil servants in the Ministry of Education remained practically the same men,[73] the augmented authority of the government permitted them to operate with a greater degree of independence. One former deputy declared that the FEN relations with the administration had changed "radically."[74] The FEN Congress of 1959 voted a resolution declaring that "the majority of the statutory or contractual [consultative] organs have been put to sleep and the unions are less and less consulted or even informed of the government's intentions."[75] M. Lauré claimed in 1961 that because the government was ignoring the consultative organs "the demands of the country have no other way of manifesting themselves except through threat and violence. . . ."[76] While similar complaints had been registered from time to time under the Fourth Republic, the frequency and consistency of statements since 1958 show that the union leaders believe that their influence has been diminished under the Fifth Republic. Personal relations between FEN leaders and administrative officials remain warm and cordial. But political relations between the government and all groups have been so altered that the effective impact of the FEN on the administration has been reduced. Eckstein's view, therefore, that the real structure of governmental power affects the targets and channels of pressure group activity appears to be borne out by the information on relations with administration.[77] Changes in FEN relations with Parliament and the parties give support as well to this view.

PARLIAMENT AND PARTIES

If the efforts of the FEN to influence governmental decisions were limited to the contacts with the government and administration already

[72] Henry W. Ehrmann, "French Bureaucracy and Organized Interests," *Administrative Science Quarterly*, Vol. V (March, 1961), p. 547.

[73] Of the fifty-three highest officials in the Directions and Services of the Ministry of Education in 1956, forty-six retained their posts in 1957. Including the occupants of newly created posts, nine new men appeared that year. There were only two new names in 1958 and nine in 1959. *Répertoire Permanent de l'Administration Française* (Paris: La Documentation Française, 1957–60).

[74] A member of the Independent Socialist party (Parti Socialiste Autonome), he said that just as the government wants a pseudo-Parliament, it also would have pseudo-unions. Interview, March 22, 1960.

[75] *E.P.*, 15e année, No. 2 (November, 1959), p. 14.

[76] *E.P.*, 16e année, No. 8 (August-September, 1961), p. 2.

[77] Eckstein, *Pressure Group Politics*, p. 16.

described, it could be argued that the FEN is not a pressure group but only a labor union bargaining with its "boss," the state. That argument crumbles when the organization's relations with political parties and Parliament are considered. It is in this realm that the behavior of the FEN is most typically characteristic of pressure groups.

Relations with parties. Loyal to its syndicalist tradition of non-political unionism, the FEN disdains organizational links with any political party. Members of the Administrative Commission who run for Parliament must resign their union posts if elected. Union officers may not make use of their titles for political purposes.[78] M. Lavergne warned in 1946 that "there can be no question of linking the lot of unionism with that of such-and-such a political party."[79] While the FEN avoids affiliation with any one party, it does not abstain from all contacts with parties; it claims to seek support from as many parties as possible. The former secretary general of the SNI, M. Henri Aigueperse explained: "There is no party which has a monopoly of the defense of the *laïque* school."[80]

It is evident, however, that the successes of the FEN are largely limited to the parties of the left. These parties have a common secular outlook which is hospitable to the teachers' attitudes and proposals. The Communists, Socialists, and many Radical Socialists regularly support the teachers in their defense of *laïcité*. But the FEN is closest ideologically to the Socialist party. It rejects the social and economic conservatism of the Radical Socialists and looks with favor on social leveling.[81] Although supporters of the Communist party are numerous, the majority of members and union leaders oppose the authoritarian habits of that party. Of the thirty-one primary school teachers elected to the National Assembly in 1951, two-thirds were Socialists and only one-third Communists. Of the eighty-four educators of all kinds elected, almost half belonged to the Socialist party and only a fifth to the Communist party. In fact, 40 per cent of the Socialist deputies had been educators.[82]

---

[78] Constitution, art. 9.

[79] *E.P.*, No. 13 (November, 1946), p. 1. M. Lavergne was not a member of any political party. *E.P.*, No. 2 (October, 1945), p. 10.

[80] *Le Monde*, July 19, 1951. Jean Meynaud has noted this practice as one of the several possible patterns of party-interest group relations. He notes, however, that since the groups know in advance what parties will support their aims, the claim of neutrality is "pure artifice or . . . propaganda." *Nouvelles Etudes sur les Groupes de Pression en France*, p. 124. In Italy with few exceptions groups tend to work with parties which can give aid that is consistent with their own ideologies. LaPalombara, *Interest Groups in Italian Politics*, pp. 218–20.

[81] *E.P.*, 12e année, No. 3 (January, 1957), p. 11.

[82] Duverger, *Partis Politiques*, pp. 305–308. According to a former Socialist Minister of Education, the "communion of ideas" existing between the Socialists

While closest to the Socialist party, the FEN still seeks to maximize its influence by working through all the parties. In his activity report to the 1951 Congress, M. Lavergne claimed at least a partial victory. "Although we could not obtain a sharp increase in the appropriations of the 1951 budget over those of 1950, we got all the political parties to admit the impossibility of reducing the funds for education."[83] The FEN is particularly active at election time. The National Council of 1945 mandated the bureau to submit the Federation's program to the various parties "to obtain the necessary engagements" before the elections of 1946.[84] In the 1951 elections the FEN supported an attempt to obtain pledges from candidates to oppose state aid to private schools.[85] In 1956 the FEN with its allies sought similar pledges from candidates supporting a "minimum program" of laïcité. The FEN consistently maintains, however, that this electoral activity does not make it a political group.[86]

Relations with Parliament. Under the system of parliamentary dominance of the Fourth Republic, good relations with Parliament were essential for any pressure group seeking implementation of its aims. The two main targets of the FEN were the members of the Education Committees of the two houses and the leaders of the parliamentary groups. Trying to influence action, it sent messages, obtained interviews, testified, and urged interpellations of the government.[87] Its activities reached a peak during the annual discussion of the budget of the Ministry of Education. Under the 1958 Constitution the Parliament is still a target of FEN activity but a less important one.

Under the system of specialized committees utilized by the Parliament of the Fourth Republic, not only was contact between committee members and pressure groups facilitated, but friends of particular groups also gravitated to the appropriate committee.[88] It was natural

and the SNI is not surprising. "Men animated by the same love of liberty and justice are destined to meet. They aim at the same goal. They have the same adversaries. They necessarily take part in the same combat." *Le Populaire de Paris,* July 22, 1953.

[83] *E.P.,* 7e année, No. 1 (October, 1951), p. 5.

[84] *E.P.,* No. 2 (October, 1945), p. 17.

[85] Brown, "Religious Schools and Politics in France," *Midwest Journal of Political Science,* Vol. II (May, 1958), 170–71.

[86] See M. Lauré's statement on the political action of unions in *Combat,* November 12, 1958.

[87] The FEN is represented in the Economic and Social Council, a constitutional body with advisory functions on legislation, by one nonvoting member of the FEN Administrative Commission. The FEN would like to have this representation increased. *E.L.,* 26e année, No. 36 (June 19, 1959), p. 1635; and *E.P.,* 15e année, No. 3 (December, 1959), p. 27.

[88] Meynaud, *Les Groupes de Pression,* pp. 198–99; and Williams, *Politics in Post-War France,* pp. 239–40.

for the FEN to concentrate its efforts on the specialists found on the Education Committees of the National Assembly and the Council of the Republic. The FEN supplied members of these committees with innumerable reports, messages, and declarations. Its leaders offered testimony before meetings of the committees and their chairmen. For example, in 1952, the FEN bureau had an audience with the chairman of the Education Committee on the question of restoring the salary parities established by the 1948 Reclassification. A report was then submitted to each member of the two Education Committees.[89] On the question of the vacation dates in 1952, the FEN secretary general sent to each member of the two committees copies of the recommendations of the consultative councils which had been ignored by the administration; the committees adopted positions along the lines of the FEN recommendations.[90] The bureau also testified before the Education Committee of the National Assembly on the question of educational reform.[91] The confidence of the FEN in the Education Committee was not misplaced: in both 1950 and 1951 the committee unanimously protested against cuts in the education budget demanded by the Finance Ministry.[92]

Support of the Education Committees was not enough; measures still had to pass the full assemblies. Besides working with individual deputies, the FEN maintained contacts with the parliamentary groups. In 1955, for example, the FEN sent a letter on civil service salaries to the chairmen of all the groups. It received replies from the head of the Documentation Service of the MRP group and from the chairmen of the Communist, Socialist, Peasant and Democratic Center, Independent Republican, and Independent Peasant groups. The correspondent for the last took the trouble to note that he had brought the letter to the attention of the members of his group.[93] The SNI suggested in 1955 the creation of a special parliamentary "inter-group" to oppose the Association Parlementaire pour la Liberté de l'Enseignement (APLE), an organization of deputies who favored aid to church schools, but this was not done.[94]

The annual parliamentary debates on the budget brought pressure group activity to a peak and demonstrated the most important and most effective means of action used in influencing Parliament.[95] No

89 E.P., 8e année, No. 4 (January, 1953), pp. 2–3.
90 E.P., 8e année, No. 1 (October, 1952), p. 6.
91 E.P., 12e année, No. 5 (April, 1957), p. 6.
92 Williams, Politics in Post-War France, pp. 246–47.
93 E.P., 11e année, No. 2 (November, 1955), pp. 2–3.
94 Le Monde, July 23, 1955.
95 Meynaud, Les Groupes de Pression, pp. 195–97.

exception to the rule, the FEN concentrated its efforts on securing an increase in the funds allocated to the Ministry of Education. In 1950, the FEN contacted all the Parliamentary groups and obtained letters of support from spokesmen of the Socialist and Communist groups. The FEN managed to obtain a letter from the Minister of Education opposing the proposed cuts in the education budget and, as already noted, received the unanimous support of the Education Committee. In the end, the teachers were successful, for the Finance Committee accepted a Communist motion that the proposed reductions in the national budget were not to be applied to the Ministry of Education. A spokesman of the SNI gave credit for this triumph to "the campaign waged by the teachers' unions and by the friends of the school."[96]

The teachers in 1954 used every possible tactic including the strike in order to obtain increased appropriations for education. On November 9, 1953, the teachers held a one-day strike to underline their demands for a 10 per cent increase in salaries. On November 20 the Council of the Republic passed a resolution supporting increases for education. On November 27, Chairman René Billères of the Assembly's Education Committee wrote to Minister of Finance Edgar Faure that his committee would not pass the education budget if substantial increases and, in particular, a 10 per cent increase in salaries, were not granted. On November 30 and twice more in December the Assembly, at the request of the chairman of the Education Committee and in opposition to the Ministers of Finance and Education, voted to postpone discussion of the education budget until the government agreed to allocate more funds. M. Lavergne wrote to M. Faure on December 1 advocating a return to the "golden rule" of Jules Ferry which stipulated that one-sixth of the national budget should be devoted to education. The Minister replied that while the national budget had been cut by 100 billion francs, the education budget had been increased by 25 billion. Since the budget was not ready at the start of the new fiscal year, the Assembly had to vote a month's provisional funds. The FEN continued to apply pressure. On December 20–21 documentation of the FEN position was sent to all the members of the Education and Finance Committees of the two Houses. The students demonstrated for more funds for education. A "day of protest" on January 19 was followed one week later by a "Fortnight for the Defense of National Education" supported by the FEN, the SNI, and allied groups. The announcement by the Prime Minister on February 22 of an increase of

[96] E.P., 5e année, No. 8 (April-May, 1950), pp. 3–4; and Minutes of the SNI National Congress of 1950, in E.L., 17e année, Nouvelle série, No. 39 (September 21, 1950), p. 701.

ten billion francs in the education budget was followed by more FEN demonstrations of dissatisfaction; on February 26 the SNES and the SNET held a one-day strike supported by the FEN. After an FEN delegation failed to obtain satisfaction from the Prime Minister, the protest movement culminated on March 31 in a strike organized by the FEN and announced in a special number of *L'Enseignement Public*. Finally, on April 1, 1954, after the government had agreed to a small increase, the National Assembly adopted the education budget by a vote of 355 to 249.[97]

It is undebatable that the resistance of the Parliament to the government's education budget in 1954 resulted in a larger slice for education; it is clear as well that the teachers' unions helped arouse and maintain that resistance. The opening debate indicated that the FEN had been unsuccessful in its direct contacts with the government, for the government was intent on holding the line at the 1953 level for education. Often a spokesman for the teachers, the Minister of Education in this case supported his government's budget while recognizing its shortcomings. On the other side was the Education Committee of the Assembly, in almost every vote unanimously against the government's budget. The Socialist and Communist members were closest to the unions, and most frequently mentioned the union demands and activities in debate. The majority of the Assembly supported the Education Committee in voting three times to postpone debate. Although the government granted only a moderate increase, the Assembly finally adopted the budget because the practice of voting provisional monthly funds had the effect of continuing the previous year's budget, and because the moderates recognized that they had obtained all they practically could through tactical maneuvers.

As a corollary to the strengthening of the executive under the Fifth Republic, the Parliament has been weakened, making it a less useful target for pressure group activity. In the words of an FEN resolution, "The workers have been deprived of the recourse to Parliament and to public opinion which they normally have in any democratic regime. The former is today stripped of all real power and the latter is mystified and chloroformed by systematic propaganda."[98]

[97] *E.P.*, 9e année, No. 3 (December, 1953), pp. 2–3; No. 4 (January-February, 1954), pp. 7–10; No. 5 (March-April, 1954), p. 1; No. 6 (May, 1954), p. 2; No. 8 (August-September, 1954), pp. 4–6; and *J.O., Assemblée Nationale*, December 8, 1953, pp. 6266–72; December 14, 1953, pp. 6796–6804; February 25, 1954, pp. 525–28; March 30, 1954, pp. 1503–15; March 31, 1954, pp. 1530–43; April 1, 1954, pp. 1567–1725.
[98] *E.P.*, 15e année, No. 2 (November, 1959), p. 14.

PUBLIC OPINION

The third target of FEN action is public opinion. As the meetings, petitions, and demonstrations held to dramatize the teachers' plight in the struggle over the 1954 budget indicate, the teachers seek to arouse public opinion to promote parliamentary action. This is not a new development; the prospectus of an abortive teachers' union of 1845 urged the teachers to alert the press in order to put pressure on the legislators through the action of opinion.[99] This prospectus remains a historical curiosity; several decades passed before the organization of teachers had progressed to a point where they could effectively wage a public opinion campaign. In modern France the teachers' unions skilfully seek public support through widely varied means: teacher-parent contacts, meetings, mass media, broad ideological organizations, and ultimately strikes. They also keep their own fences mended by trying to keep members informed of union activities through internal communications.

Union publications. The union press is the major means of internal communication. Besides the organs of the Federation and the major national unions, there are bulletins published by the small member unions. Some sixty-five of the SNI and the FEN departmental sections publish their own bulletins. There is some evidence that their reading public is smaller than their circulation.

Published under the direction of the FEN bureau, *L'Enseignement Public* is distributed monthly to the members of all the national unions in the Federation. It is the subject of criticism at almost every Congress. In 1957, for example, one departmental section announced that the expenditure of twelve million francs was too much for a publication that is not read. Another speaker called it "unreadable"; another thought it should have a more attractive appearance.[100] *L'Ecole Libératrice* is the weekly publication of the SNI. Begun in 1929, it includes pedagogical advice and practical lesson plans as well as union news. It is distinctly anticlerical.[101] The bimonthly *L'Université Syndicaliste* is published by the SNES and has a circulation of 38,000. The union leaders try to avoid duplication of stories in *L'Enseignement Public* and the bulletins of the national unions.[102]

Enlisting public opinion. Probably the most frequent means employed in order to enlist the support of public opinion on an issue is

---

99 Ferré, *Mouvement Syndicaliste Revolutionnaire*, p. 15.
100 *E.P.*, 13e année, No. 3 (January, 1958), p. 18.
101 For an example, see *E.L.*, 26e année, No. 25 (April 3, 1959), p. 1063.
102 *E.P.*, 9e année, No. 1 (September-October, 1953), p. 11.

the press conference. The FEN officers, usually including the heads of the large national unions, call in reporters to announce their positions and answer questions. Usually the leaders justify their demands for an increased education budget and announce the steps they plan to take.[103] Sometimes the secretary general of a national union, accompanied by some fellow officers, holds a press conference.[104] He is not always successful. A spokesman for the research workers' union complained, for example, that his union could only intermittently obtain the audience of the press. Even if reported, coverage may be minimal.[105]

On occasion the FEN distributes petitions to the teachers with the request that they circulate them and send them on to the Prime Minister or Parliament. In 1950, for example, the FEN distributed a special issue of *L'Enseignement Public* which included a "Petition to be addressed to the Prime Minister by way of the Prefect." The most ambitious petition campaign in the history of the FEN was undertaken in opposition to the School Law of 1959.[106]

Protest marches and meetings are also utilized in order to mobilize public opinion. Sometimes these movements of protest are joined by representatives of the labor confederations.[107] Where the defense of *laïcité* is involved, the FEN has the support of several other militant organizations. The Ligue Française de l'Enseignement, founded in 1866 to promote literacy and *laïcité*, is linked with the FEN and other like-minded groups in the Comité National d'Action Laïque (CNAL), an umbrella organization which campaigns against public aid to Catholic schools. Representatives of the Union Nationale des Etudiants de France (UNEF), which included a majority of the 258,000 students in French higher education in 1961–62, often express their support of the FEN. Spokesmen from these and similar groups have participated in mass demonstrations with the teachers to influence public opinion.

Occasionally these demonstrations receive wide publicity. A demonstration on October 27, 1960, for peace in Algeria, supported by the UNEF, the FEN, the CFTC, and FO departmental unions received front-page coverage; attracting about 10,000 participants, the demonstration ended with five hundred arrests and about one hundred injuries (including fifty-eight police officers).[108]

---

103 For reports on typical conferences, see *Le Monde,* September 20–21, 1953; and June 14, 1956.
104 *Le Monde,* January 23, 1959; and October 9, 1959.
105 *La Vie de la Recherche Scientifique,* No. 17 (January, 1959), p. 7.
106 *E.P.,* 5ᵉ année (May, 1950); and also Chap. VII.
107 *Combat,* October 21, 1959.
108 *Le Monde,* October 19, 21, 26–31, 1960.

STRIKES

The final weapon in the arsenal of the FEN is the strike. Aimed at all three of the action targets just described—the administration, the Parliament, and public opinion—the strike is judiciously used as a weapon of last resort. Primarily employed to support the teachers' material demands, it has occasionally served political ends. Since the teachers' employer is the government, there are legal questions about the teachers' right to resort to it.

The General Civil Service *Statut* of 1946 officially recognized the right of civil servants to organize, but it said nothing about their right to strike. The parties in power at the time preferred to avoid this delicate problem. The Constitution of 1946 guaranteed all workers the right to strike, but the promised regulatory legislation was never passed, except for the laws of 1947 and 1948 which denied the right to policemen. In the absence of permissive legislation, the Council of State has ruled that civil service employees may be disciplined through normal channels for striking, provided they have been warned ahead of time. It has apparently been considered politically unwise to apply such sanctions to the teachers, for they strike on an average of once a year—not only with impunity, but usually with success.[109]

In negotiations with the government and in announcements to the public, the teachers' unions effectively employ the weapon of the strike threat. They declare to the press that they are resolved to employ "all union means, including the strike."[110] As M. Lauré explained, "The strike . . . is a weapon if the threat is permitted to exercise its power."[111] The threat alone is sometimes sufficient. Strikes scheduled for July 1, 1955, and May 25, 1962, among many others, were canceled when the government satisfied the teachers' demands. It is true that these strike threats sometimes came on the heels of strikes actually carried out, as in the round of 1960–61; the combination of strikes and strike threats is particularly effective.[112]

The strike weapon is used sparingly and, according to former Minister of Education Jean Berthoin, responsibly.[113] One union official

[109] Lorwin, *Labor Movement*, pp. 244–49; Duverger, *Partis Politiques*, p. 145; Grégoire, *La Fonction Politique*, pp. 67, 320-23; and Tiano, *Les Traitements des Fonctionnaires*, pp. 391–413. For an FEN analysis of the teachers' right to strike, see *E.P.*, 16e année, No. 6 (April, 1961) pp. 11–12.

[110] *Combat*, May 2, 1956; also *Le Populaire de Paris*, March 29, 1956.

[111] Minutes of the 1957 FEN Congress, in *E.P.*, 13e année, No. 3 (January, 1958), p. 22.

[112] *Le Populaire de Paris*, July 1, 1955; *Le Monde*, May 31, 1961; and *E.P.*, 17e année, No. 8 (June-July, 1962), pp. 8, 17.

[113] Interview, June 1, 1960.

wrote that the right to strike creates "responsibilities which the teachers' unions are proud of and which they assume with the greatest awareness of the public interest."[114] M. Lauré reminded the FEN that, particularly where a strike is involved, there can be conflict between union rights and the duties of teachers to the youth of the nation.[115] The facts that FEN strikes are infrequent, that long periods of negotiation and agitation precede them, and that they are normally of brief duration attest to the responsible fashion in which the teachers have employed this weapon. They also demonstrate an awareness that too frequent strikes can arouse public resentment instead of public sympathy. The teachers' sense of responsibility and their awareness of public reaction both illustrate Eckstein's point that attitudes sharply influence the choice of pressure group action technique.[116]

Strikes are usually called in such a way as to minimize losses of class time while maximizing their effect. One effective technique is known as the "examination strike." Teachers continue to conduct their classes, but they refuse to grade the important examinations marking the termination of elementary or secondary studies. While class time is not lost, parental pressure on the government becomes intense. In 1951 the teachers even refused to proctor the examinations.[117] The technique of the broad administrative strike introduced in 1961 was an effective extension of the principle of the examination strike.[118] Using another technique on May 21, 1951, the teachers extended the recess period by thirty minutes. Little class time was lost, yet the teachers' plight was called to the attention of parents.[119]

If the examination strike or brief work stoppage fails, then a full day's strike may be necessary. Strikes of unlimited duration are rarely favored by the FEN. A meeting of the FEN Administrative Commission in 1946, for example, when authorizing an examination strike and, if necessary, a limited strike, decided that a National Council would have to be held to authorize an unlimited strike.[120] In this case, no strike was

---

114 *L'Enseignement Français à l'Etranger*, p. 247.

115 *E.P.*, 12e année, No. 8 (August-September, 1957), p. 2.

116 Eckstein, *Pressure Group Politics*, pp. 16–22. Lorwin argues that French unions are unable to finance long strikes, *Labor Movement*, pp. 241–44. It is relevant to point out that the FEN has no strike fund.

117 Although sympathetic to the teachers' demands, the parents were apparently more concerned about the welfare of their children, for they took over the task. *Le Monde*, September 13, September 30–October 1, and October 2, 1951. Lorwin also notes the "examination strike" as one of the several forms of the strike known in France, *ibid.*, pp. 236–41.

118 See p. 112.

119 *Le Monde*, May 19, 1951.

120 *E.P.*, No. 13 (November, 1946), p. 13.

finally held. Usually an attempt is made to coordinate a day-long strike with similar action on the part of the other civil service unions. Such common action had been rendered difficult by the 1947 schism; it was not until November 19, 1957, that all the civil service unions were once again able to coordinate their strike action.[121] Several times the FEN has refused to participate in common strike action. In June, 1949, it did not join a strike of civil servants but instead condemned "agitation for the sake of agitation"; it apparently felt that the time was inauspicious for the teachers.[122] Similarly the FEN refused to take part in a civil service strike on December 2, 1959, because it was engrossed in the struggle against the School Law of 1959 and opposed to premature use of the teachers' "last recourse."[123]

The teachers' strike, alone or in cooperation with the other civil service unions, has proved to be a powerful weapon. The round of strikes and negotiations in 1960–61 demonstrated both the skill of the FEN in planning and implementing its strike strategy and the success of the methods employed against the determined resistance of the leaders of the Fifth Republic. Teacher demands for a general upward revision of their salary schedule dated from 1957 when the government agreed to study the problem; in 1959 the government promised action within six months, but no funds were earmarked in the next national budget for this purpose.[124] After increases had been granted in the nationalized industries, the teachers joined with the other civil service unions to demand corresponding increases in a twenty-four-hour strike on June 10, 1960.[125] Discussions in October on a government plan for salary revision led to no agreement; a common counterplan prepared by the FEN, CGT, CFTC, and FO civil service unions was received by the government in December but not acted on.[126]

Beginning a separate action for the teachers that was to prove successful, the FEN scheduled a one-hour strike for December 13, 1960, as a "warning" to the government; the strike order was widely followed.[127] In January, 1961, the FEN announced two rounds of rotating strikes. During the period January 30–February 13 a half-day strike was to be held in each of seven academic regions at the rate of

---

[121] Le Monde, September 21, 1951; November 14, 1957; and Combat, November 15, 1957.
[122] E.P., 5e année, No. 1 (September-October, 1949), p. 5.
[123] E.P., 15e année, No. 3 (December, 1959), pp. 2–4.
[124] Le Monde, December 9, 1960; and March 10, 1961.
[125] E.P., 15e année, No. 9 (June-July, 1960), p. 3; and Le Monde, June 3, 10, 11, 1960.
[126] Le Monde, December 3, 1960.
[127] Le Monde, December 9, 14, 1960.

one every other day; the second round was to consist of full-day strikes
on the same pattern from February 24 to March 10. The press deemed
the strikes a success; in some regions over 90 per cent of the primary
and secondary teachers walked out, and many primary schools were
completely empty.[128]

In what Secretary General Lauré called a "trial of force" between
the union and the government, FEN action was broadened to include
an audacious "administrative strike" during the second round of rotating
strikes. Teachers refused to report grades to either students or the
administration, to submit examination questions to the administration
or keep secret those already submitted, to sit on any examination
boards, to transmit records needed for promotions to secondary schools,
or to accept any overtime work.[129] Several offers made by the government during February and March were rejected as inadequate. Pressure on the government was increased by extending the administrative
strike; the SNES announced a complete examination strike affecting
the nationwide *baccalauréat* examinations. After consultation on the
highest levels the government made its final offer on April 8; the FEN
accepted and lifted the strike order the following day. In the last days
of the struggle the government had raised its offer from a plan costing
180 million new francs to one costing 260 million, a significant measure
of the effectiveness of the FEN methods. It is interesting that professors
in higher education received almost nothing in the settlement, a point
their spokesmen were quick to deplore; it appears significant that only
a small percentage of them are FEN members and that these joined
neither the administrative nor the examination strikes.[130]

Immediately following this success the FEN resumed its joint
efforts with the other civil service unions to obtain a general increase
in salaries. It joined demonstrations and promised more rotating strikes
in a broad movement that was only temporarily interrupted by a
protest strike on April 24 against the rebellion led by four generals in
Algiers.[131] Numerous strikes in May throughout the nationalized industries and sectors of the civil service were followed, after rejection of
several government offers, by agreement among the FEN, FO, CGT,
and CFTC civil service unions upon a twenty-four-hour strike on

128 *E.P.*, 16e année, No. 4 (January, 1961), p. 3; and *Le Monde*, January 11,
29–31, February 10, 15, 1961.
129 *E.P.*, 16e année, No. 5 (March, 1961), pp. 2–3; and *Le Monde*, February
5–6, 17, 25, 1961.
130 *E.P.*, 16e année, No. 6 (April, 1961), pp. 2–3, 16; and *Le Monde*, March 23,
26–31, April 9–13, 1961.
131 *E.P.*, 16e année, No. 6 (April, 1961), pp. 8–9; and No. 7 (May-June, 1961),
p. 15; and *Le Monde*, April 16–17, 20–26, 1961.

June 6.[132] The strike order was lifted when the government raised the salaries of lower level employees and promised to study a total revision of civil service salaries.[133] On reflection M. Lauré concluded that while the teachers had regained, relative to other civil servants, the favorable salary position accorded them in the 1948 reclassification, the civil service as a whole was still underpaid.[134]

A listing in Table 2 of the strikes called by the FEN since World War II demonstrates two facts. First, the strike weapon is used with restraint. There were twenty-one FEN strikes between 1945 and 1962, but nine of these were either examination strikes or strikes of short duration. Only the 1947 strike caused a loss of more than one school day.[135] There were five years with no FEN strikes at all, although demonstrations and strike threats continued. Second, most strikes are called to support salary demands, not to promote FEN ideological aims.[136] Only seven were intended to protest political action, and five of these may be attributed to a single problem, the Algerian war. The strikes of November 9, 1951, and March 23, 1955, were called in support of laïcité and the public schools. The strike of May 30, 1958, was called to demonstrate support for the Fourth Republic, then collapsing because of pressures rising from the Algerian War. Strikes on February 1, 1960, and April 24, 1961, protested uprisings in Algiers directed against the government's liberal Algerian policy. The actions on December 19, 1961, and February 13, 1962, called for a negotiated peace and condemned the extremist OAS.

It is a fact that political strikes have, on a yearly average, quadrupled in frequency since the advent of the Fifth Republic. It would be incorrect to conclude, however, that this increase reflects the known hostility of the FEN to the Fifth Republic or that it shows that the blocking of traditional channels of influence has forced resort to strike action. It seems more logical to attribute the increase to the stubborn persistence of the Algerian problem and the complexities of its evolution. There is no reason to believe that any of the last four political strikes mentioned would not have occurred under the Fourth Republic, given the same cause.

[132] Le Monde, May 5, 6, 14–15, 17, 21–22, 1961.

[133] E.P., 16e année, No. 7 (May-June, 1961), p. 7; and Le Monde, May 31, 1961.

[134] E.P., 16e année, No. 8 (August-September, 1961), p. 23.

[135] Not listed is a peculiar form of limited strike which occurred when primary school teachers, on the instructions of the FEN Administrative Commission, reduced the size of their classes to forty by sending home the surplus pupils. Le Monde, October 20, 1957.

[136] For a treatment of political strikes in Italy, see LaPalombara, The Italian Labor Movement, pp. 20–21, 80–91.

TABLE 2
TEACHERS' STRIKES CALLED BY THE FEN, 1945–62

Date	Nature	Aims
Fourth Republic		
1945 December 12	Brief work stoppage	Higher civil service salaries
1947 December 5, 6, 8, 9	Wide support in Paris, scattered elsewhere	Protest civil service reclassification scheme
1948 June 14–July 3	Examination strike	Reclassification of teachers
September 24	Two hours	Higher civil service salaries
1949 November 25	One day	Higher civil service salaries
1951 May 21	30-minute extension of recess	Protest low education budget
September 21– October 25	Examination strike	Higher salaries
November 9	One day	*Protest Marie and Barangé laws
1953 November 9	One day	10 per cent increase in teachers' salaries
1954 March 31	One day	For increased education budget
1955 March 23	One day	*Protest bill on agricultural education
1957 November 19	One day	Higher civil service salaries
Fifth Republic		
1958 May 30	One day	*Protest end of Fourth Republic
1960 February 1	One hour	*Protest Algerian uprising of January 24, 1960
1960 June 10	One day	Higher civil service salaries
December 13	One hour	Higher salaries
1961 January 30	Rotating strikes by academic region; one-half day in each	Higher salaries
1961 February 24–March 10	Rotating strikes by academic region; one day in each. Administrative strike	Higher salaries
1961 April 24	One hour	*Protest rebellion of four generals
December 19	Fifteen minutes	*Protest OAS; support negotiated peace in Algeria
1962 February 13	One day	*Protest OAS; support negotiated peace in Algeria

* Asterisk indicates political strikes.

Information gathered from *L'Enseignement Public*. Strikes called by FEN national unions but not supported by the whole FEN membership are omitted; FEN leaders normally aid in the negotiations resulting from them, however. For examples, see *E.P.*, 6ᵉ année, No. 8 (May, 1951), p. 3; and 15ᵉ année, No. 9 (June–July, 1960), pp. 21–22.

The emphasis in this chapter has been on the relations of the FEN with the administration. Contacts with the administration are friendly; teachers and administrators share similar educational outlooks. Contacts are regular because they are institutionalized. Most of the time the FEN obtains satisfaction from these contacts. But as Eckstein points out, the type of decision influences the targets and methods of action.[137] When satisfaction is not obtained from the administration, the FEN turns to Parliament and public opinion, especially for the defense of *laïcité* and questions of salaries, as the debate on the 1954 budget illustrates. Resort to public opinion seems less suited to educational reform, as this subject raises technical and professional questions which may not always be readily understood. The question of *laïcité* is particularly appropriate for popularization because of its simplicity and its traditional role in French local politics. On the question of salaries, the FEN often works with the other civil service unions; on *laïcité* it enjoys the cooperation of the other *laïque* organizations, and on educational reform it largely works alone. The teachers' strike and its variations have proved to be most effective weapons for pursuing material demands. As a comparison of the 1954 and 1961 salary struggles shows, the strike and related direct action methods have become more important under the Fifth Republic. The efficacy of these methods in promoting other political ends is more debatable. In fact, it appears that the farther the organization goes afield from its basic material and educational objectives, the less effective it is regardless of the action techniques used.

[137] *Pressure Group Politics*, pp. 16–17.

VI

The School Laws of 1951

The problem of the church schools in France may be traced back to the time of the French Revolution; a review of the milestones in French school legislation since that cataclysm gives perspective to the 1951 struggle. The preliminary skirmishes, the parliamentary battle, and the sharp reaction of the teachers in 1951 are an episode in the enduring conflict that the French aptly call the School War.

EVOLUTION OF THE SCHOOL WAR

The roots of the School War stretch deep into the past, but they are neither buried nor forgotten. Politicians and clergymen regularly expose and revive them, reinforcing the ideological quarrels which divide Frenchmen. The living omnipresence of these historical roots informs the contemporary political battles of the School War. To understand the role of the teachers' unions in the legislation of 1951, it is imperative to know the origins and development of the school question.

Like so many problems of contemporary France, the school question was raised by the French Revolution and its post-revolutionary adjustments. The triumph of the *laïque* forces under the Third Republic seemed to settle the question once and for all, but the action of the Vichy regime in aiding church schools showed that the issue was far from dead. The Vichy legislation was quickly repealed, but new skirmishes between the organized church school forces and their *laïque* opponents, particularly the organized teachers, proved to be a prelude to the battle over the School Laws of 1951.

The origins of the school question may be found in the intellectual movements that heralded and abetted the French Revolution. Protestantism favored individualism and fostered anticlericalism. Cartesianism of the seventeenth century and rationalism of the eighteenth century dichotomized faith and reason and exposed accepted ideas and practices to corrosive questioning. These movements eroded established

116

beliefs and institutions and bred a new faith in progress and in man; they proclaimed confidence in education, freed of all prejudice and superstition and organized according to the concept of *laïcité*. Seeking to realize this ideal, the Convention voted in 1794 to secularize primary education.[1]

Napoleon created a monopoly of education in his Imperial University but mollified the church forces by providing for religious education in the state school program. Soon after Napoleon's period cracks appeared in the state monopoly. The Guizot Law of 1833 provided for liberty of education on the primary level. Any lay or clerical teacher possessing certificates of capacity and morality henceforth had the right to open a primary school without prior permission.[2] The Falloux Law of 1850 extended liberty of education to the secondary level. Any teacher with either a *baccalauréat* or a certificate of capacity awarded by an examining board was granted the right to open a secondary school. This law also provided that a *commune* could choose to support a private elementary school in lieu of a public one, but this provision was effectively nullified by later administrative interpretations.[3]

Schools under the Third Republic. The early years of the Third Republic witnessed the triumph of *laïcité* in the public schools under the celebrated Minister of Education Jules Ferry. In pursuing his goal of free, compulsory, and religiously neutral primary education, Ferry carried out a thoroughgoing policy of secularization. The law of 1882 secularized the school programs by replacing religious training with "moral and civic instruction"; it secularized the school buildings by closing the schools on Thursdays so religious training could be given on church property; and it secularized school surveillance by denying clergymen the right to inspect public schools. Laws in 1880 and 1886 secularized the consultative councils by removing clergymen from them, and a law of 1886 secularized the personnel by forbidding clergymen to teach in the public schools. A resurgence of republican strength following the Dreyfus Affair led to the laws of 1901 and 1904 which made it illegal for members of religious orders to teach in any schools, public or private. This work of secularization was capped symbolically by the law of 1905 on the separation of church and state, although efforts at secularization continued sporadically until World

[1] For an unsympathetic account of this development, see Redmond, *Laicism in the Schools*, pp. 1–15.

[2] Emile Faguet, *Problèmes Politiques du Temps Présent* (Paris: Colin, 1907), pp. 200–203; and M. Hébert and A. Carnec, *La Loi Falloux et la Liberté de l'Enseignement* (La Rochelle, France: Rupella, 1953), p. 19.

[3] Faguet, *ibid.*, pp. 204–205; and Hébert and Carnec, *ibid.*, pp. 193, 200, 236–40.

War I.[4] Primary and secondary church schools continued as purely private organizations; religion had been effectively separated from government.

The supporters of the church schools could perhaps claim two accomplishments under the Third Republic: the law of 1875 which allowed the establishment of private institutions of higher education; and the Astier Law of 1919 which permitted recipients of state scholarships to attend private technical schools.[5] But on the whole the church schools were threatened by the increasing competition of the public schools and the militant secularism of the teachers. Indeed, a pastoral letter of 1909 required parents to withdraw their children from school if they "learn there is a danger of moral perversion and consequently of eternal damnation."[6] To the church school supporters, the early Vichy legislation restored justice in education.

Vichy and the schools. The Vichy government laid much of the blame for the defeat of 1940 on the secularized public schools. As part of Marshal Pétain's National Revolution, reforms were undertaken to restore religion and patriotism to the schools. State scholarships were declared valid for either public or private schools; subsidies were granted to private schools; tuition was restored for public secondary schools; religious instruction was given during class hours (but at the request of parents and outside of the school buildings); and crucifixes reappeared in the classrooms.[7]

Most of the Vichy legislation was declared null and void after the war. After a stormy debate which resurrected the old arguments and bitternesses, the Provisional Consultative Assembly voted on March 28, 1945, to end subsidies to private schools immediately. The Education Committee had recommended ending them at the end of the school year, but the Assembly rejected transitional measures designed to soften the shock to private schools.[8] The provisional government, however, decided that the subsidies would be terminated at the end of the school year.[9] Other measures abolished tuition for secondary schools and limited state scholarships to public school students.

[4] Hébert and Carnec, *ibid.*, pp. 253–83; Redmond, *Laicism in the Schools,* pp. 15–33; and Duveau, *Les Instituteurs,* pp. 111–21.

[5] Hébert and Carnec, *ibid.*, p. 231.

[6] Redmond, *Laicism in the Schools,* pp. 29–30.

[7] Other measures abolished the laws of 1901 and 1904 which had outlawed the teaching orders. These had not been applied since World War I, however, and were not re-enacted after the end of the Vichy government. Hébert and Carnec, *La Loi Falloux,* pp. 285–87.

[8] *L'Année Politique. . . . de la Libération de Paris au 31 Décembre 1945,* pp. 156–57; and *J.O., Assemblée Consultative Provisoire,* March 28, 1945, pp. 836–67.

[9] *J.O., Lois et Decrets,* April 18, 1945, pp. 2163–64. The FEN National Council

Renewal of the School War. Although many Frenchmen felt that the struggle over the schools had been laid to rest along with the other celebrated but bypassed causes of the Third Republic, a series of minor conflicts beginning in 1947 reminded them that a question on which Frenchmen were evenly split could not be settled with any degree of finality.[10] Skirmishes between the supporters of the church schools on the one hand and the FEN with its allied groups on the other broke out over three issues: the affair of the *kermesses,* the schools of the nationalized coal mines, and the Poinso-Chapuis decrees. "Tax strikes" declared by the church school partisans underlined the weak financial position of the religious schools. The two sides emerged from these skirmishes with improved and broadened battle organizations which were tested in the struggle over the School Laws of 1951.[11]

In France as elsewhere the Roman Catholic church raises funds for its schools and charities through social functions. The *kermesses* are church carnivals or fairs of this type. In 1947, however, some organizers of *kermesses* refused to pay the tax levied on them on the grounds that charitable activities should not be taxed. Although the law was ultimately upheld, the incident provoked the *laïques* and dramatized the persistence of the church school problem.

Another conflict resulted from the decision of the government to absorb into the public school system the church schools located on the property of the nationalized coal mines. A decree of November 2, 1945, brought the teachers in some of these schools into the civil service.[12] However, parents and church authorities resisted vigorously and prevented the application of the decree until a 1948 Assembly debate, which very nearly toppled the government, ended with a vote supporting nationalization of the schools.

A few days later another skirmish engaged public attention. Madame Poinso-Chapuis, the MRP Minister of Public Health, issued a decree granting public assistance to needy families for the purpose of educating their children. A second decree specified that the children could attend public *or* private schools. The *laïque* forces raised such a storm of protest that the decrees were never enforced.

In the spring of 1950 the defenders of the church schools took direct action, motivated by the deteriorating financial condition of the schools. About one in every five pupils in France goes to a private

---

of July, 1945, insisted that this termination date be observed. It was. *E.P.,* No. 2 (October, 1945), p. 19.

[10] Jacques Fauvet, *La France Déchirée* (Paris: Fayard, 1957), pp. 68–70.

[11] This section is based largely on Brown, "Religious Schools and Politics in France," *Midwest Journal of Political Science,* Vol. II (May, 1958), pp. 162–66.

[12] *J.O., Assemblée Nationale,* November 22, 1955, p. 2789.

school (usually Catholic), a total of about 1,500,000 pupils. The percentage attending private schools is higher for secondary and technical students: 40 per cent for the former, 45 per cent for the latter. Classes are taught by some 75,000 teachers, more than half of whom are lay persons. But in 1949 the salaries of these lay teachers averaged 11,000 francs a month (about $31.00). Buildings were deteriorating, and equipment was poor.[13] Although a section of the Falloux Law of 1850 still in force permitted local governments to subsidize secondary church schools (a practice condemned by the FEN),[14] few local governments did. However, the gravest need existed on the primary level where enrollments were large and tuition income was low. In the heavily Catholic West an aggressive Comité d'Action pour la Liberté Scolaire organized giant rallies to dramatize Catholic demands for state aid to private schools. Finally, the Bishop of Vendée recommended that citizens withhold 10 per cent of their tax payments until the demands of the church schools were met. The laïque forces jumped to their battle stations. They sent an open letter to the President of the Republic on May 9, 1950, condemning the "tax strike." They obtained an audience with the Prime Minister on May 12 to demand enforcement of the tax laws. The laïques were again successful; the ill-advised "tax strike" was postponed.[15]

The opponents organize. But the School War had only begun. The issue mushroomed, engulfing more persons and groups, and impelling each camp to seek allies and improve its organization. In April, 1948, organizations representing the parents, teachers, and alumni of the church schools created a Secrétariat d'Etude pour la Liberté de l'Enseignement. This Secretariat took the offensive in the School War and effectively coordinated the church school forces. A number of groups were represented on the Board of Directors of the Secretariat; included were the alumni group (Fédération Nationale des Amicales de l'Enseignement Libre), claiming a membership of 1,500,000, and the particularly active parents' organization (Union Nationale des Associations de Parents d'Elèves de l'Enseignement Libre or APEL), numbering some 400,000 members.[16]

[13] Brown, "Religious Schools and Politics in France," *loc. cit.*, pp. 160–61; *J.O., Assemblée Nationale,* December 24, 1959, p. 3599; and *E.L.,* 26e année, No. 24 (March 13, 1959), p. 961. Figures on private education are for 1957–58.

[14] *E.P.,* 6e année, No. 4 (January, 1951), p. 10.

[15] Brown, "Religious Schools and Politics in France," *loc. cit.*, pp. 168–69; *E.P.,* 5e année, No. 9 (June, 1950), p. 3; and 6e année, No. 1 (October, 1950), p. 7.

[16] *Le Monde,* July 20, October 4, 1951. Brown, *ibid.*, p. 163, gives the figure of 800,000 for the APEL. The Secrétariat d'Etude pour la Liberté de l'Enseignement is hereafter called simply the Secretariat.

The teachers helped create a counter-organization for mobilizing and coordinating the laïque forces. As early as 1946 the FEN established a center for studying and promoting laïcité and for maintaining contact with sympathetic organizations.[17] In 1948 the FEN joined in organizing a national rally known as the "Estates General of Laïque France." It was attended by twelve hundred representatives of the teachers' unions, the laïque parties (Communist, Socialist, and Radical Socialist), the laïque trade union confederations (CGT and CGT-FO), and other laïque organizations. Repeated in 1949, this method was abandoned in 1950 because the Socialists and Communists could no longer tolerate each other. M. Lavergne thought it would be regrettable if a meeting of laïques should become a "confrontation of the theses of certain proletarian parties."[18] In May, 1949, four laïque organizations formed a Centre Laïque d'Etudes et de Propagande.[19] Shortly thereafter the same four established a coordinating committee which was to bear the brunt of the battle in both 1951 and 1959. Known as the Comité National de Défense Laïque (CNDL) in 1951 and as the Comité National d'Action Laïque (CNAL) in 1959, this committee conducted a vigorous campaign of defense by drawing on the resources of its member organizations: the FEN with its broad membership; the homogeneous and militantly laïque SNI; the Parents' Federation (Fédération Nationale des Conseils de Parents d'Elèves des Ecoles Publiques) with its 700,000 parents of children in public primary schools; and the venerable and aggressively laïque Ligue Française de l'Enseignement (the League hereafter). The League is a broad confederation of some 25,000 groups interested in popular education, including physical education, travel, cinema, camping, and similar societies. It includes teachers, parents, politicians, and about one million children in its total membership of 2,700,000. Some of the technical services of the League are supported by the state; in 1959 the League received 640,000 new francs in subsidies.[20]

[17] E.P., No. 13 (November, 1946), p. 3.
[18] E.P., Nouvelle série, No. 1 (October, 1948), p. 6; No. 5 (February, 1949), p. 1; and 6e année, No. 3 (December, 1950), p. 4.
[19] E.P., Nouvelle série, No. 8 (June-July, 1949), p. 15.
[20] For membership figures, see UNESCO, An International Directory of Education Associations (Educational Studies and Documents No. 34) (ED/59/XII/34.A) ([Paris, 1959]), p. 18. For information on the League, see Carlton J. H. Hayes, France: A Nation of Patriots (New York: Columbia University Press, 1930), p. 400; Duveau, Les Instituteurs, pp. 102–105; Brown, "Religious Schools and Politics in France," loc. cit., p. 162; and Le Monde, July 13, 19, 1960. Originally associated with Freemasonry and the Radical Socialist party, the League is now close to the Socialist party. See Daniel Bardonnet, Evolution de la Structure du Parti Radical (Paris: Monchrestien, 1960), pp. 242–44.

The teachers appear to dominate the Comité National d'Action Laïque. While the exact relationship between the constituent members of the CNAL (or CNDL) cannot be sharply delineated, a certain overlapping of personnel and certain identities of policy suggest that the teachers' unions control the Committee. First, two of the four member organizations represent teachers. In a sense, the SNI is represented twice on the Committee since the FEN also represents it. In all likelihood, the SNI has separate representation because it can muster greater militance than the more broadly based FEN. Secondly, the teachers have great influence in the League. The president of the League (and of the CNAL) in 1959 was M. Albert Bayet, once a secondary school teacher, later a professor at the Sorbonne, and a life-long devotee of *laïcité*; and the secretary general was M. J. A. Senèze, a member of the FEN Administrative Commission from 1945 to 1948. Also, some five hundred teachers on the state payroll are regularly placed at the disposition of the League for its extra-curricular activities. M. Bayet once said that the League would take "no initiative whatsoever without the agreement of the three other organizations of the CNAL."

Thirdly, the Parents' Federation has close ties with the teachers. While M. Jean Cornec was president of the Parents' Federation in 1959, its secretary general was M. Clément Durand, a long-time member of the SNI and for fourteen years a member of the FEN Administrative Commission. In 1959 he was both a member of the FEN bureau and the head of its Committee on *Laïque* Action.[21] The attitude of the teachers toward the Parents' Federation is suggested by the remark of a member of the SNI bureau that "We must multiply the parents' associations and profit from their next regional meetings," and by the resolution of the 1961 SNES Congress inviting its members to create parents' organizations without delay.[22] The League and the Parents' Federation have the same address in Paris (3, rue Recamier). The directing board (Conseil d'Administration) of the Parents' Federation includes among its eighteen members three persons selected by the FEN (including two SNI representatives) and three chosen by the League.[23] According to a critic complaining of the "intolerable pres-

[21] *E.L.*, 23e année, No. 39 (September 21, 1956), p. 961; 26e année, No. 32 (May 22, 1959), p. 1405; No. 33 (May 29, 1959), p. 1469; *E.P.*, 15e année, No. 3 (December, 1959), p. 31; and Brown, *ibid.*

[22] *E.L.*, 26e année, No. 22 (February 27, 1959), p. 855; and *Le Monde*, October 3, 1961.

[23] In 1960 the Parents' Federation sought to extend its recruitment efforts to parents of secondary and technical school students. The head of the already existing Fédération des Associations de Parents d'Elèves des Lycées et Collèges warned: "If the operation waged against us should succeed, the Federation of National

sure" exerted on politics by the SNI, the CNAL is only an extension of the primary teachers' union since the League and the Parents' Federation are "colonized" by the SNI.[24] However that may be, there is no doubt about the unity of view between the CNAL and the teachers' unions. In 1951 M. Lavergne reported: "Since the FEN linked its *laïque* action to that of the Comité National de Défense Laïque, to give the report of this Committee is to give the report of the FEN at the same time." In 1959 the FEN worked almost exclusively through the CNAL, with the advance approval of both the FEN and the SNI congresses.[25]

In 1950 the FEN Congress directed the bureau to cooperate with the CNDL in submitting the FEN program to the political parties and public opinion. The program not only condemned the "tax strike" and subsidies for religious schools; it also took the offensive by demanding the repeal of the Falloux Law, the removal of crucifixes from schoolroom walls, and the termination of the special concessions made to religious instruction in Alsace-Lorraine.[26] The SNI also took the offensive in the hope of intimidating the church school forces. It proposed the nationalization of all private schools. M. Durand, the SNI expert on *laïcité*, was instructed to draw up "a concrete project" to oppose to the eventual schemes of the church school supporters; his plan was adopted by an SNI National Council on March 19, 1951. Since nationalization was not a new idea—it had been blessed in principle by the SNI and the CGT in 1927, the League in 1928, and the FEN in 1945—its reappearance at this time indicates that the SNI considered it to be a tactical weapon for use in the school battle.[27] Hoping to garner support on the widest possible front and aware that the *cégétistes* and certain other groups opposed nationalization as a radical, divisive measure,[28] the FEN and the CNDL did not emphasize M. Durand's plan in their propaganda. Only after the *laïque* forces had

Education (where three out of four members are elementary school teachers) would have at its disposal a maneuverable mass of 1,300,000 families, receiving their directives from the National Teachers Union [SNI] and [its] satellite organizations. . . . Is it in the last analysis an important political reorganization which they are seeking?" *Le Monde,* October 3, 1961.

[24] *Combat,* August 17–18, 1957.

[25] *E.P.,* 7e année, No. 1 (October, 1951), p. 13; 14e année, No. 7 (August-September, 1959), p. 6; and *E.L.,* 26e année, No. 30 (May 8, 1959), p. 1297.

[26] *E.P.,* 6e année, No. 3 (December, 1950), p. 3. The last demand has been part of the SNI program since 1922 and was again revived in 1959. Hayes, *France,* p. 401. For an explanation of the school arrangements in Alsace-Lorraine, see Duveau, *Les Instituteurs,* pp. 168–71.

[27] *E.L.,* 18e année, Nouvelle série, No. 16 (January 18, 1951), p. 273; No. 26 (April 12, 1951), pp. 466–68; and *J.O., Assemblée Nationale,* September 7, 1951, p. 7018.

[28] *Le Monde,* July 22–23, 1951.

failed did the CNDL resolve to struggle not only for the restoration of
the school laws of the Third Republic but also for the creation of a
single national system of laïque schools.[29]

The Paul-Boncour Commission. After a series of ministerial crises
aggravated by the divisive effect of the school question on cooperation
between the Socialists and the MRP, a compromise made possible the
investiture of M. René Pleven as Prime Minister on July 11, 1950. As
part of this compromise M. Pleven promised that he would appoint a
commission to study the problem of the schools. One week later the
SNI Congress expressed its indignation and announced its opposition
to the very principle of such a commission. Nonetheless, on September
28, 1950, the Council of Ministers approved the appointment of a
twenty-five-member "Commission for the Overall Study of School
Problems," divided evenly between supporters of public and private
schools and presided over by a distinguished lawyer and former Prime
Minister, M. Joseph Paul-Boncour.[30]

Having failed to prevent the creation of the Commission, the laïque
forces proceeded to hinder its operations as much as possible.[31] The
CNDL and its four constituent organizations notified the Prime Minister that they refused to take any part whatsoever in the activities of
the Commission.[32] The government repeated its invitation to participate, but in vain.[33] Members of the FEN, even primary inspectors, normal school directors, and academy inspectors, refused to testify before
the Commission.[34] On December 10, 1950, the laïque forces organized
a national demonstration at Rennes, in the heart of Catholic Brittany,
to alert the political parties and to arouse public opinion against the
Commission. Shortly thereafter, four members of the Commission resigned. The teachers in the High Council of National Education protested that the Commission was encroaching on its prerogatives[35] and
frequent resolutions of the teachers' unions demanded the dissolution
of the Commission.[36] Supporting the teachers, the Socialist party

29 *E.P.*, 7e année, No. 4 (January, 1952), p. 11.

30 *Le Monde*, June 7, 1951; *E.P.*, 6e année, No. 2 (November, 1950), p. 6; and
J.O., *Lois et Decrets*, October 5, 1950, p. 10372.

31 *E.L.*, 18e année, Nouvelle série, No. 33 (June 7, 1951), p. 595.

32 *E.P.*, 6e année, No. 1 (October, 1950), p. 21; and No. 2 (November, 1950),
p. 6.

33 *E.P.*, 6e anneé, No. 3 (December, 1950), p. 4.

34 *E.L.*, 18e année, Nouvelle série, No. 18 (February 1, 1951), p. 313.

35 *E.P.*, 6e année, No. 3 (December, 1950), p. 4; *E.L.*, 18e année, Nouvelle
série, No. 17 (January 25, 1951), p. 296; *J.O.*, *Lois et Decrets*, January 19, 1951,
p. 725; and *Le Monde*, June 7, 1951.

36 For the FEN Congress in November, 1950, see *E.P.*, 6e année, No. 3 (December, 1950), p. 16; for the SNI National Councils in December, 1950, and March,
1951, see *E.L.*, 18e année, Nouvelle série, No. 18 (February 1, 1951), p. 313; and

ordered its members to quit the Commission. To the express satisfaction of the CNDL, a number of resignations took place in the early months of 1951. Finally, M. Paul-Boncour himself resigned, announcing that further objective discussion was impossible. In his letter of resignation he sadly wrote: "Alas, a battle which takes us back to anachronistic divisions has begun."[37]

Legislative initiatives. With the situation of the church schools becoming more desperate, two attempts were made to provide financial relief by amending the budget in the National Assembly. Both attempts met with failure.

At its 1950 Congress the MRP took the position that the private schools render a social service and that every social service has the right to state support.[38] While not wishing to prejudice the findings of the Paul-Boncour Commission, the president of the MRP, M. Pierre-Henri Teitgen, introduced in March, 1951, an amendment to the labor budget requiring the state to pay lay teachers in the church schools. The deputy explained that aid was urgently needed in order to raise teachers' salaries to the level of the national minimum wage. The amendment was referred to the Finance and Education committees and rejected by both. The National Assembly supported its committees by a vote of 303 to 277.[39]

Two months later another MRP deputy, M. de Tinguy de Pouët, tried a similar parliamentary maneuver. He introduced an amendment to the Finance bill which would have granted tax privileges to the church schools and their teachers. Although only twenty deputies were in the Chamber on the night of May 18, the amendment passed by a vote, mostly by proxy, of 290 to 282. The CPDL met the next day and protested sharply against this "inadmissible attack on the principle of *laïcité.*" M. Albert Bayet expressed his Committee's indignation in letters to the Prime Minister and the Minister of Education. An SNI delegation met with Vice Prime Minister Guy Mollet in the presence of Minister of Education Pierre-Olivier Lapie. Another delegation prevailed on M. Edouard Herriot, the Radical Socialist President of the

No. 26 (April 12, 1951), pp. 466–68; and for the FEN Administrative Commission in February, 1951, see *E.P.,* 6e année, No. 6 (March, 1951), p. 4.

[37] Brown, "Religious Schools and Politics in France," *loc. cit.,* p. 166; and *Le Monde,* June 29, September 19, 1951.

[38] Anthony T. Bouscaren, "The MRP in French Governments, 1948–1951," *Journal of Politics,* Vol. XIV (February, 1952), 116–22. The Rassemblement du Peuple Francais (RPF) had adopted a similar position in 1949. *Le Monde,* July 8–9, 1951.

[39] *J.O., Assemblée Nationale,* March 20, 1951, pp. 2216–19, 2233–38; March 21, 1951, pp. 2271–72; *E.P.,* 6e année, No. 7 (April, 1951), p. 5; and *Le Monde,* March 22, 1951.

National Assembly, to use his influence on the Radical members of the cabinet with the result that one threatened to resign if the government would not repudiate the amendment. The government finally withdrew its support for the amendment, which was then dropped from the budget. The SNI was proud of its rapid action which "bore fruit."[40]

These two incidents demonstrated that the church school forces were determined to obtain state aid by one means or another, and that the *laïque* forces were just as intent on denying it to them. No atmosphere of moderation or conciliation existed, and no compromise seemed possible. In this situation it was clear that triumph or failure for the church school forces would depend upon the political composition of the legislature elected on June 17, 1951.

TRIUMPH OF THE CHURCH SCHOOL FORCES

After an aggressively waged campaign, the *laïques* were dismayed to discover that the elections delivered a parliamentary majority to the church school forces. The latter lost little time in transforming their parliamentary advantage into legislation favorable to their side, the Marie and Barangé laws, over the vociferous protests of the *laïque* organizations.

The election of 1951. Although the electoral campaign did not officially begin until May 28, the two sides began to marshal their forces weeks before. Two meetings in April underlined the determination of the church school forces to obtain relief. Both sides resorted to the tactic of obtaining pledges from candidates.

On April 1, 1951, thirty thousand representatives of church school parents and alumni met in the first "National Congress of Free Education" at Toulouse. Claiming to speak for four million voters, they pledged their honor to vote for candidates who would promise to join the Parliamentary Association for the Liberty of Education (APLE), the church school intergroup in Parliament. They also made explicit their demands: tax privileges for private schools, state scholarships for private school students, and state aid to raise teachers' salaries to the national minimum wage. Two days later the first general meeting since 1906 of the French higher clergy (bishops, archbishops, and cardinals) published a moderate declaration holding that many parents found it financially impossible to exercise their legal right of giving their children a religious education.[41] A few days before the election

---

40 Brown, "Religious Schools and Politics in France," *loc. cit.*, pp. 167–68; *E.L.*, 18e année, Nouvelle série, No. 31 (May 24, 1951), p. 555; *E.P.*, 7e année, No. 1 (October, 1951), p. 5; and *Le Monde*, May 23, 24, 25, 1951.

41 *Le Monde*, April 3, 6, 1951; and *É.L.*, 18e année, Nouvelle série, No. 26 (April 12, 1951), p. 463.

the Secretariat was able to announce that more than 2,000 candidates had agreed to join the APLE. Most of these were members of the MRP, the RPF, and the Independent and Peasant parties, with a few from the Rassemblement des Gauches Républicains (RGR).[42]

Towards the end of May the CPDL put its election strategy into effect. It sought pledges of support from candidates with the question: "Do you pledge yourself, if elected, . . . to refuse all public subsidies, direct or indirect, to private schools and their activities?" In a manifesto it asked all citizens "to vote only for candidates who, whatever their party, formally pledge themselves to refuse all direct or indirect subsidies to private schools." The manifesto was signed by the FEN, the SNI, the League, and the Parents' Federation. A copy was circulated in the union press accompanied by a subscription form entitled "Reply to the Congress of Free Education and to the Bishops' Manifesto." The FEN published a special, newspaper-size issue carrying the manifesto, an appeal for funds, and an editorial by M. Lavergne; the reverse side opened into a large red-and-black poster proclaiming: "Vote laïque!"[43] During the campaign the CPDL organized rallies of laïques to keep the issue before the public; 20,000 gathered at Lille on June 3 to hear the president of the Parents' Federation and MM. Durand, Lavergne, and Bayet. It also pursued its poster campaign despite harassment which moved the Committee to complain to the Prime Minister and the Minister of the Interior.[44]

The results of the election disappointed and dismayed the laïque forces. In terms of popular votes, the nation was about evenly divided (although the laïque voters had a slight edge).[45] But in terms of voting strength in the Assembly the laïques had lost, for a new electoral law had operated to the disadvantage of the parties of the left. The Communists lost seventy-four seats, and the Socialists gained only five. While the moderate RGR gained thirty-four, many of these deputies had joined the APLE. Indeed, by the middle of July, the APLE counted 296 members, close to a majority of the Assembly, and a number of overseas deputies had not yet had time to join. The APLE

[42] Brown, "Religious Schools and Politics in France," loc. cit., p. 171; and Le Monde, June 14, 1951.

[43] E.L., 18e année, Nouvelle série, No. 31 (May 24, 1951), pp. 561–62; and E.P., 6e année, No. 10 (June, 1951), pp. 1–4.

[44] Le Monde, June 3–4, 1951; E.L., 18e année, Nouvelle série, No. 33 (June 7, 1951), p. 600; and E.P., 7e année, No. 1 (October, 1951), p. 6.

[45] The CNDL claimed that 60 per cent of the voters had cast their ballots for supporters of laïcité. Another source estimated nine million votes for the clerical parties, ten million for the laïques, if the two million RGR votes are counted. But this group was split on the school question. E.L., 18e année, Nouvelle série, No. 36 (June 28, 1951), p. 672; and L'Année Politique, 1951, p. 156.

included: all the MRP deputies; all but two of the Peasant and Independent deputies; all but seven of the RPF deputies; nine Radicals, and sixteen others. The church school forces could smell victory.[46]

Formation of the Pleven government. After the resignation of the former government on July 10 following the elections, there ensued the longest governmental crisis of the Fourth Republic to that time. While the anti-republican extremes had not been greatly increased (total Communist and RPF seats increased from 213 to 221),[47] differences on the school question among the other parties made a Center coalition difficult to organize. In the face of increasing pressure from the APLE and increasingly bitter warnings from the *laïques,* M. René Pleven was finally able to form a government only by promising to leave the solution of the school problem, within limits, to the initiative of the legislature.

In spite of M. Guy Mollet's comment to the Socialist Congress that "in the present circumstances, it would be folly to reopen the school conflict,"[48] the positions assumed by the parties and groups made clear that the school question would dominate negotiations for a new government. The MRP and the Independent and Peasant parties had adopted programs promising state aid to private schools, and many RGR deputies had made similar promises to their constituents.[49] The RPF had a specific plan for making grants to education committees made up of parents of children in both public and private schools.[50] The Socialists warned that while they were presently accepting the status quo out of a spirit of conciliation, they would return to their traditional goal of nationalization of all schools and termination of the special arrangements in Alsace-Lorraine if the church school forces should continue to demand subsidies.[51]

The position of the teachers' unions was practically identical with that of the Socialists. The SNI continued to advocate nationalization and joined the FEN in denouncing church privileges in Alsace-Lorraine. On July 16 the FEN released a press communiqué declaring that the clericals would have to assume responsibility for a resumption of the School War if they attacked *laïcité.* The FEN declared that the public schools could "not be the stakes of a political compromise." The SNI Congress on July 21 approved a resolution stating that the teachers would not hesitate to strike on behalf of the public schools. The FEN

46 *L'Année Politique, 1951,* pp. 154, 179; and *Le Monde,* July 18, 1951.
47 *L'Année Politique, 1951,* p. 157.
48 *Le Monde,* June 6, 1951.
49 *Le Monde,* June 30, 1951.
50 *Le Monde,* July 18–19, 1951.
51 *Le Monde,* June 30, 1951.

departmental section of Algiers emphasized that subsidies would result in separate Catholic, Protestant, Jewish, and Moslem schools. After circulating a letter to the members of the National Assembly explaining its position, the FEN met with the CNDL to draft a letter to President of the Republic Vincent Auriol. The letter asked him to use his authority to make "a supreme effort on behalf of school peace." It also blamed the MRP implicitly for prolonging the government crisis. In interviews on three different dates the CNDL communicated the *laïque* point of view to parliamentary groups including the Communists, Socialists, Radicals, and Independents. On August 1 the CNDL announced to the press that it was asking all "republican" deputies to vote against the investiture of any Prime Minister supporting tax privileges, scholarships, or teachers' salary supplements for private schools.[52]

Undaunted by these moves, the church school forces acted confidently, with full awareness of their strength in the Assembly. Secretary General Edouard Lizop of the Secretariat convened the members of APLE in mid-July and reminded them: "You pledged yourselves to introduce bills permitting private schools to survive. The country follows you with great hope and also great severity." A few days later he sent a letter to the members of the APLE asking them to participate in and vote only for a government which would promise to support the APLE program. Besides scholarships, tax privileges, and aid to teachers' salaries, the APLE program also demanded the right for local governments to subsidize private schools. The Secretariat requested deputies to refrain from taking any "isolated initiative" in the struggle; in other words, they were to accept the direction of the Secretariat.[53]

During the cabinet crisis which lasted from July 10 to August 8, President Auriol called on eight different persons to form a government. Five refused to try. M. Maurice Petsche, Minister of Finance in the preceding government and not a member of any parliamentary group,

---

[52] *Le Monde,* July 18, 22–23, 31, August 1, 1951. For summaries of the action taken by the SNI and the FEN in July, August, and September of 1951, see *E.L.,* 18e année, Nouvelle série, No. 38 (September 15, 1951), pp. 710–16; and *E.P.,* 7e année, No. 1 (October, 1951), pp. 13–15, 18–19.

[53] *Le Monde,* July 13, 18–19, 1951. It should be noted that the Catholic camp was not united. The leader of the Fédération Française des Syndicats Chrétiens de l'Enseignement Libre (CFTC), the union of lay teachers employed in private schools, resigned from the Secretariat in protest over its aims and methods. Also differing from the Secretariat was the SGEN (CFTC) which, representing some 18,000 Catholic teachers in the public schools, favored having the state rent private school buildings and hire their qualified teachers, while still permitting optional religious instruction in them. *Le Monde,* June 14, July 1–2, 22–23, September 7, 1951.

was asked twice: consultations with party leaders convinced him the first time that he could not reconcile the differences between the MRP and the SFIO, and so he declined the offer; he tried a second time on July 27 but failed to obtain the necessary majority of the National Assembly, in part because the Socialists would not support his fairly conservative economic program. Similarly, the MRP refused to support M. René Mayer (Radical Socialist) on July 19 because he would not promise government neutrality on the school question. Both MM. Mayer and Petsche had proposed temporary solutions to the school question, pending the report of the Paul-Boncour Commission. M. Mayer suggested a supplementary family allotment to parents with children in elementary schools and the extension of state scholarships to pupils in private schools. M. Petsche proposed a fund for guaranteeing private school teachers the national minimum wage and apparently agreed with M. Mayer on scholarships. ("It does not appear impossible to revise the regulatory conditions for awarding state scholarships"). M. Mayer received 241 favorable votes, and M. Petsche received 281, but neither total was sufficient. On August 4, M. René Pleven of the Union Démocratique et Socialiste de la Résistance (UDSR), identified with neither side on the school question, was asked to form a government. His formula on the school question satisfied the MRP and permitted the Socialists to vote grudging support. M. Pleven declared in his speech to the Assembly that, although he personally would prefer to wait for the report of the Paul-Boncour Commission before acting, he would agree to provisional measures. First, his government would increase scholarship funds and make them available to students in both public and private secondary schools; and secondly, his government would not oppose bills along the lines of either the Mayer or the Petsche proposals for aiding private elementary education. Since the Socialists had voted for M. Mayer's investiture and the MRP for that of M. Petsche, this formula presumably achieved the necessary balance. On August 8, 1951, the investiture of M. Pleven was approved by a vote of 391 to 102, with the Communists opposing and the RPF abstaining.[54]

Preparing the bills. The compromise formula which made possible the Pleven government worried the *laïque* forces. The Socialists decided not to accept any cabinet seats in order to retain their freedom of action. The teachers' unions, although it was the middle of the vacation month of August, stepped up their efforts to block the legislation

[54] Brown, "Religious Schools and Politics in France," *loc. cit.*, pp. 172–73; *L'Année Politique, 1951*, pp. 179–81, 198–99, 369–76; and *Le Monde,* July 20, 28, August 3, 6, 7, 10, 1951.

which now seemed inevitable. Despite an energetic campaign which even included the attempt of the SNI to provoke a ministerial crisis by getting the Radical ministers to resign,[55] the *laïques* could not prevent the passage in September of what were to be called the Marie and Barangé laws.

While the government prepared its scholarship plan and the APLE proceeded with its program for state aid to private schools, the *laïques* issued a barrage of protests and warnings. The CNDL warned of the divisive effect of reopening the School War and asked citizens to urge their deputies to maintain the status quo. It was pointed out that neither the Mayer nor the Petsche proposals had been approved by a majority of the Assembly. The head of the Socialist parliamentary group let it be known that his party would not remain silent. The SNI told the government that it would oppose any violation of the principles of *laïcité* "by all means within its power."[56] However, on August 17 the Council of Ministers approved plans for increasing state scholarship funds and making them available to both public and private secondary school students. Known eventually as the Marie bill after the new Minister of Education, M. André Marie, this proposal impelled the *laïques* to action. The FEN immediately protested against the division of scholarship funds between public and private schools. A few days later the CNDL obtained audiences with the Prime Minister and the Minister of Education to state its opposition to the Marie bill. It sent out 50,000 printed appeals to the mayors of France suggesting that they raise "the very voice of France" by having their municipal councils protest to the prefects. It sent a letter to all the members of Parliament, warning them that if they were going to revive the school arrangements of Vichy, "the order to all *laïques* would be that of ten years ago: Resistance." It met again with Minister of Education Marie who assured the Committee that he would concede no more than scholarships to the private school forces. It contacted the RPF, Radical, Communist, and Socialist parties. Bracing itself for a national effort, the CNDL also notified its departmental committees to stand by for action.[57]

Five days after the blow of the Marie bill, the teachers' unions suffered the shock of the Barangé bill. Named after M. Charles Barangé, vice president of the APLE, the bill followed the lines of the Mayer proposal. It provided for an allotment of 3,000 francs a year for each

[55] *E.L.*, 18e année, Nouvelle série, No. 39 (September 24, 1951), p. 719.
[56] *Le Monde*, August 11, 17, 18, 1951.
[57] *Le Monde*, August 19–20, 1951; and *E.L.*, 18e année, Nouvelle série, No. 38 (September 15, 1951), p. 711.

child attending either public or private schools. There were, however, two deviations from the Mayer proposal. First, the funds were not to be granted to the head of the family but allocated directly either to the parents' associations of the private schools or to the departmental General Councils for maintaining and equipping public school buildings; and secondly, local government units were to be given the right to subsidize local private schools.[58] When the APLE proposal was published, M. Aigueperse of the SNI warned that the Barangé bill would abolish the laïque status of education and was certain to arouse "a considerable emotion," an unaccustomed understatement. In letters to MM. Pleven and Marie the CNDL claimed that the proposal not only went far beyond the Marie bill, which the Minister of Education had promised would be the limit of his concessions to the church schools, but also exceeded the limits set by the Mayer plan. The Pleven government had decided earlier that if the cabinet agreed that the bills proposed by Parliament went beyond the Mayer-Petsche formulas, the government would oppose them; if the cabinet felt that they were within the Mayer-Petsche framework, the ministers would vote for them; and if the cabinet was split, they would abstain. The CNDL therefore asked the Prime Minister and the Minister of Education to oppose the Barangé bill. The CNDL pursued this same line of argument in meetings with leading Radicals, including members of the cabinet. It sent letters to the members of Parliament and to all the mayors of France. On August 26 it drew up and published an appeal to all Frenchmen. The FEN requested all its militants to bring the CNDL appeal to the attention of their mayors; to urge all laïque organizations to send their protests against the Marie and Barangé bills to members of Parliament, to the Prime Minister, and to the Minister of Education; and to complain to the MRP. The FEN and the SNI again contacted MM. Pleven and Marie to emphasize their opposition. The FEN's Parisian departmental section declared that the plans for subsidizing private schools would encounter the "irreducible opposition of all laïques."[59]

Passing the bills. The Marie bill in the Parliament provided a dress rehearsal for debates on the Barangé bill. The Marie bill was shorter, simpler, and a little less controversial than the Barangé bill, but its passage first demonstrated what the Barangé bill corroborated a few days later: the laïque deputies were in the minority, and neither the pressure tactics of the teachers' unions nor the obstructionist methods

[58] *Le Monde*, August 22, 1951.
[59] *Le Monde*, August 23, 24, 25, 28, 29, 1951; and *L'Année Politique, 1951*, p. 201.

of their Communist and Socialist allies could long delay the offensive of the church school forces.

The Education Committee of the Assembly decided to let the Finance Committee handle the bills. The first parliamentary victory for the church school forces, this decision demonstrated that the *laïques* were in the minority even on the Education Committee, where the greatest concentration of former teachers and militant *laïques* is usually found. The Finance Committee quickly approved both bills, although it did not decide how the Barangé funds were to be distributed because the MRP and RPF could not come to an agreement.[60]

The battle over the Marie bill opened in the midst of parliamentary maneuvers and delaying tactics attempted by the Communists and Socialists, who sorely tried the patience of members and even of Assembly President Edouard Herriot. Objections that the High Council of National Education had not been consulted, that the Marie bill was unconstitutional, that the debate was untimely, and numerous others, were interposed to delay the opening of discussion, but with no lasting effect.[61] The Assembly deliberated four days on the Marie bill, with the Socialists and Communists leading the opposition when they were not opposing each other. MM. Jean Binot and Maurice Deixonne presented the Socialist arguments which coincided with those proffered by the FEN and its allies. Only one amendment, stipulating that the government could issue regulations setting standards for private schools attended by holders of state scholarships, was finally accepted from the veritable shower of amendments proposed by the opposition. On September 4 the Assembly approved the Marie bill 370 to 238. The Communists and Socialists voted as a bloc against the bill; and the Radicals split (33 for, 29 against, and 12 abstentions).[62] After a relatively mild debate, the Council of the Republic also approved a slightly amended version of the bill by a vote of 202 to 97. The original version of the bill was passed once again on September 21, 1951, by the National Assembly with a final vote of 378 to 236.[63]

[60] *Le Monde,* August 24, 25, 26–27, 1951.

[61] *Le Monde,* August 26–27, September 1, 1951; *J.O., Assemblée Nationale,* August 24, 1951, pp. 6505–11; August 28, 1951, pp. 6536–42; August 29, 1951, pp. 6576–81; August 30, 1951, pp. 6675–77; and August 31, 1951, pp. 6696–6705, 6711–19.

[62] *J.O., Assemblée Nationale,* August 31, September 1, 3, 4, 1951, pp. 6720–6844; and *Le Monde,* September 2–3, 4, 6, 1951. The split in the Radical votes, repeated later on the Barangé bill, marks a decline in Radical anticlericalism. See Nathan Leites, *On the Game of Politics in France* (Stanford: Stanford University Press, 1959), pp. 31–32.

[63] *J.O., Conseil de la République,* September 11, 12, 1951, pp. 2344–2411; *J.O., Assemblée Nationale,* September 21, 1951, pp. 7531–69; and *Le Monde,* September 14, 16–17, 22, 1951.

The Assembly took up the Barangé bill immediately after its first passage of the Marie bill.[64] The Socialists and Communists again led the opposition in seeking to block or at least delay action. The Assembly majority had to fight its way through a barrage of dilatory motions, quarrels over the rules, numerous interruptions, two motions of censure, and a welter of amendments. Practically all the amendments were voted down, including a Socialist motion to rename the bill an act "to reestablish the subsidies to religious elementary schools in force under the Vichy regime." A journalist described one sitting as a "debauchery of incidents . . . where inanity disputed with burlesque."

The action on the Barangé bill in the Assembly reinforced two observations. First, the APLE majority had even overwhelmed the traditional stronghold of laïcité, the Education Committee, for the Committee, consulted only for an opinion, reported favorably on the Barangé bill. Its report reflected a successful MRP-RPF compromise on the disposition of Barangé funds: the departmental General Councils were to be empowered to spend 10 per cent of the funds for "educational works" (extracurricular activities, vacation camps, etc.), a provision retained in the final law. Secondly, the Socialists apparently spoke for the teachers' unions, since their views and actions coincided. M. Deixonne, seeking to carry out the threat of the SNI and the Socialist party, introduced an amendment calling for the nationalization of private schools; it was quickly rejected. Another Socialist spokesman announced at one point in the debate that his party would "take the initiative of a vast national petition, a kind of popular referendum," requesting the President of the Repubic to seek a ruling on the constitutionality of the Barangé bill from the Constitutional Committee. It was no coincidence that on the same day the CNDL announced its decision to circulate such a petition. The FEN quickly called on its members to gather millions of signatures and to bring the appeal of the CNDL to the attention of all municipalities. The SNI sent explanatory circulars to all of its sections and printed a copy of the CNDL petition in L'Ecole Libératrice. The action of the laïque forces was well coordinated.

While working hand-in-hand with the Socialists, the CNDL did not neglect the Radicals. In fact, since the Communists and Socialists were already well committed to laïcité, the Radicals were favored targets. The CNDL continued its appeals to the Presidents of the two houses and to the chairmen of the laïque parliamentary groups, but it

---

[64] The following account of the Assembly debate is based upon the J.O., Assemblée Nationale, September 4–10, 1951, pp. 6854–7283; Le Monde, September 4–11, 1951; and union summaries already cited.

tried in particular to obtain the resignation of the Radical ministers in the cabinet: "No elected *laïque* will continue to work with a government which will not frankly reject" the Barangé bill. However, a meeting of the cabinet on September 8 decided on a policy which permitted the Radical ministers to stay. The government decided to abstain on the article delegating the funds directly to parents' associations and General Councils, since the Radicals felt this violated the Mayer-Petsche framework; and the government, for the same reason, would demand elimination of the clause which allowed local governments to advance funds to private schools. The Assembly removed the latter clause, but the Radical ministers were apparently still opposed to the direct delegation of funds, for in the final vote the whole cabinet abstained. Forty-six of the seventy-five Radicals in the Assembly joined with the Communists, Socialists, and six others in voting against the bill in the early morning hours of September 10, 1951. The Barangé bill passed by a vote of 313 to 255.

The Council of the Republic made some changes in the Barangé bill, but the only two of any importance finally retained by the Assembly were: the extension to private school parents' associations of the right to devote 10 per cent of their Barangé funds to "educational works"; and a Socialist amendment demanding first priority for raising private school teachers' salaries. In accordance with the directions of the APLE, many senators abstained in the final vote (123 to 119) in order to avoid an absolute majority which, under the Constitution, would have required repassage by an absolute majority in the Assembly. Finally, on September 21, 1951, the National Assembly repassed the bill in its final form, by a vote of 315 to 253.[65]

REACTION OF THE TEACHERS

The FEN, still operating through the CNDL, reacted with quick hostility to the Marie and Barangé laws. The CNDL intensified its campaign of demonstrations and petitions; the teachers' representatives refused to approve the decrees of application in the consultative councils; and the FEN called a day-long protest strike.

Petitions and demonstrations. On September 10, the day the Assembly passed the Barangé bill, the CNDL announced that it was taking immediate measures "to give an irresistible force to the protests which are rising from the depths of the country." Two days later at a press conference attended by MM. Senèze and Bayet of the League and

[65] *J.O., Conseil de la République,* September 18–20, 1951, pp. 2443–2565; *J.O., Assemblée Nationale,* September 21, 1951, pp. 7575–7598; and *Le Monde,* September 16–17, 19, 20, 22, 23–24, 1951.

four members of the FEN Administrative Commission (including MM. Aigueperse and Durand of the SNI), the CNDL released the text of its national petition. The petition attacked the two laws and called upon the Presidents of the National Assembly and the Council of the Republic to have them abrogated. A few days later the CNDL sent copies of its petition to the twenty-seven organizations belonging to the loose Cartel National d'Action Laïque; in June the FEN had been reluctant to resort to this group, fearing it would publicize divisions among the *laïques* rising from Socialist-Communist hostility.[66]

At its press conference the CNDL also announced a rally to be held on September 30 at the tomb of Jules Ferry, "the vanquished hero of the school battle." Here *laïque* supporters, estimated at twenty thousand by M. Durand and at five or six thousand by *Le Monde*, took an oath to pursue the struggle until the Republic should reestablish the "great *laïque* laws." Similar demonstrations were sponsored by the CNDL throughout France in the course of October and November. M. Bayet also mentioned at the press conference the possibility of a teachers' strike.[67]

The decrees of application. The law required the Minister of Education to consult the High Council of National Education for its advice on the decrees of application (administrative regulations) which would put the new laws into effect. This gave the teachers another opportunity to remind public opinion of their hostility to the Marie and Barangé laws.

The relations between the Minister of Education and the teachers' unions finally reached the breaking point. After a meeting of the SNI National Council on October 11, M. Aigueperse wrote to M. Marie informing him that further cooperation between them was impossible.

> Informed of the attitude that you chose to adopt in the course of the debates, of the flagrant disagreement between your acts and the numerous declarations you made to us between August 14 and September 22, of the ardor with which you are preparing the decrees of application of these laws . . . , the National Council feels obliged to recognize that [further] collaboration is impossible. . . .
>
> If one remembers that since . . . 1935, a constant collaboration has prevailed between the Ministers of Education and the National Teachers Union [SNI]—except for the period of Vichy—he will

[66] *Le Monde*, September 13, 14, 1951; *E.L.*, 18e année, Nouvelle série, No. 39 (September 24, 1951), p. 719; and *E.P.*, 7e année, No. 1 (October, 1951), p. 28.
[67] *Le Monde*, October 2, 1951; *E.L.*, 19e année, Nouvelle série, No. 2 (October 4, 1951), p. 27; and *E.P.*, 7e année, No. 1 (October, 1951), p. 19.

understand better the importance that the primary school teachers of the whole country attach to this decision.

The FEN Congress in November passed a resolution congratulating the SNI for having broken with the Minister.[68]

When the Marie decrees came before the High Council, M. Lauré, speaking on behalf of the FEN, read a statement condemning the government for not consulting the Council before introducing the Marie bill in the Assembly, and for giving its members too little time to study the decrees. The Council voted to send the decrees to the Secondary Education Council. Before the High Council met again on October 2 for final consideration of the decrees, the FEN assembled all of the elected members and persuaded them to support a resolution condemning the principle of state scholarships for private schools. The High Council formally approved the resolution but, apparently mollified by the mildness of the decrees or resigned to the inevitable, the majority of the Council voted to accept the decrees of application. However, changes which appeared in the final versions impelled the High Council to register a protest.[69]

When the High Council received the decrees of application for the Barangé Law, the reaction of the teachers' representatives was much more emphatic. In the Primary Education Council twenty-two of its thirty-two members signed a letter presented to the presiding officer of the Council by two SNI members and stating that they could "not participate in any manner whatsoever." The twenty-two signers then walked out, depriving the Council of a quorum. When the Barangé decrees reached the High Council on November 2, thirty-seven of its seventy-nine members declared it was absolutely impossible to consider them and walked out of the room. The remaining members decided unanimously to abstain from voting on the decrees. M. Aigueperse commented that there had probably never been as "complete a divorce between the policy of a Minister of Education and the opinion of all those under him."[70]

The teachers' strike. At the suggestion of the SNI, the CNDL organized on November 9, 1951, "a day of protest against the anti-*laïque* André Marie and Barangé laws." At the heart of this day of protest was a strike called by the FEN.

[68] E.L., 19e année, Nouvelle série, No. 4 (October 18, 1951), pp. 65–66; and E.P., 7e année, No. 3 (December, 1951), p. 9.

[69] E.P., 7e année, No. 1 (October, 1951), p. 6; and No. 3 (December, 1951), p. 3.

[70] E.L., 19e année, Nouvelle série, No. 5 (October 25, 1951), p. 92; No. 7 (November 8, 1951), p. 137; and E.P., 7e année, No. 3 (December, 1951), p. 3.

The July Congress of the SNI had approved a strike in principle, but the SNI bureau in September decided to postpone it. The moment was not auspicious for a general FEN strike. The teachers were caught up in the usual confusion of a new school year, and the secondary teachers and professors of higher education were engaged in an examination strike to obtain the restoration of a more highly graduated salary scale. This, of course, was never a popular cause with the SNI, which proceeded to plan its protest strike even before the collapse of the examination strike on October 25.

On October 11 an Extraordinary National Council of the SNI decided on a strike and asked all teachers to join in. The SNI also called on civil servants to demonstrate their solidarity with brief work stoppages, and on all workers to hold meetings at their place of work and sign the national petition. One week later the FEN Administrative Commission took up the call and asked all employees of the Ministry of Education to cease work on November 9 in order "to alert public opinion." The FEN circulated notice of the strike in *L'Enseignement Public* and also printed a "Letter to Parents" to explain its purpose. *L'Ecole Libératrice* printed the same letter along with a poster announcing a "National Day of Protest." The CNDL "warmly welcomed" the SNI initiative and invited all of the members of the Cartel National d'Action Laïque to join in protest demonstrations. Numerous labor unions and confederations replied with messages of support.

The strike was well observed, especially by the primary school teachers. The FEN Congress noted its pleasure at the "magnificent success of the strike and demonstrations." More demonstrations and a campaign to raise funds for support of the CNDL followed in the next few months, but the furor of the *laïque* organizations gradually diminished in intensity. They had lost the battle, and there was little that could be done until there was a shift in political forces.[71]

Some observations. The study by Bernard Brown on "Religious Schools and Politics in France" only briefly mentions the CNDL in its competent treatment of the struggle over the Barangé Law. It focuses on one member organization of the CNDL, the League, and treats it as the leader of the *laïque* forces in the struggle. It is true that the League is a powerful, venerable organization, having a long tradition of pressure techniques dating at least from 1872 when its founder deposited

71 *Le Monde,* September 20, October 20, 1951; *E.L.,* 19e année, Nouvelle série, No. 3 (October 11, 1951), p. 41; No. 4 (October 18, 1951), p. 65; No. 5 (October 25, 1951), p. 93; No. 6 (November 2, 1951), pp. 122–23; No. 8 (November 16, 1951), p. 152; *E.P.,* 7e année, No. 1 (October, 1951), p. 20; No. 2 (November, 1951), pp. 1, 5, 15; No. 3 (December, 1951), p. 9; and *L'Année Politique, 1951,* p. 289.

at the doors of the National Assembly a 440-pound petition for free, compulsory, and *laïque* schools.[72] It is also true that M. Bayet of the League headed the CNDL. Even without considering the view that the League has been "colonized" by the teachers, it appears that the teachers' unions had a much larger role in the struggle than Brown's otherwise excellent study attributes to them. At most of the press conferences, M. Bayet was seconded by FEN representatives. The union leaders took part in strategy conferences and provided funds, publications, and militant workers when the organization moved to action. And, of course, the teachers backed the Committee with one of their most effective weapons for influencing public opinion, a rather rare political strike.

While the teachers' role in the CNDL was important, it seems clear that it was not the whole FEN which provided the dynamic force of the CNDL's counter-offensive. M. Lavergne claimed that a report of CNDL activity was tantamount to a report on the FEN, but there are some facts which indicate that the SNI was more aggressive and enterprising in the CNDL's campaign than the FEN. The SNI first promoted the strike of November 9. The FEN, with its great diversity of membership and with some of its national unions already engaged in an examination strike for a goal not enthusiastically supported by other member unions, did not take the initiative. The SNET commented afterwards that it would have preferred a form of action other than the strike.[73] The SNI aggressively espoused nationalization of the private schools as a weapon of reprisal; the FEN belatedly acquiesced. The SNI regularly spends more on the defense of *laïcité* than does the less affluent FEN.[74] It is also significant that the SNI is represented separately in the CNDL. If the SNI is unwilling to let the Federation represent it exclusively, it must have reservations about the FEN's point of view, leadership, or militance. The government seems to have the same attitude, for it omitted the FEN when it repeated its invitation to the SNI, the League, and the Parents' Federation to participate in the Paul-Boncour Commission.[75]

The relations of the *laïque* forces with the *laïque* parties were cordial, as there was usually a congruence of views. Frequent contacts between the Socialist party and the FEN were not regarded as necessary, since both shared the same outlook.[76] Relations with the Com-

[72] Duveau, *Les Instituteurs*, p. 116.
[73] Minutes of the Administrative Commission of October 18, 1951, in *E.P.*, 7e année, No. 2 (November, 1951), p. 15.
[74] Cf. Chap. III, p. 51.
[75] *E.P.*, 6e année, No. 3 (December, 1950), p. 4.
[76] Interview, March 22, 1960.

munist party were quite different. The FEN seemed suspicious of the Communist party; it was reluctant to resort to the Cartel National d'Action *Laïque*, for example. The *laïque* forces were pleased to get the Communist votes in the Assembly, but the teachers, while claiming friendliness with all *laïque* parties, seemed to agree with the Socialists in their reservations about cooperating closely with Communists.

Besides illustrating some of the FEN's methods of action, the 1951 struggle also demonstrated that there are effective limits to what a pressure group can do. The sharp contrast between the action of the Education Committee in summarily rejecting the Teitgen amendment in March and approving the Barangé bill in September illustrates dramatically the effect of a change in parliamentary majorities. Whatever techniques the FEN could employ, it could not rescind the election results of June, 1951. It could perhaps influence some moderate deputies who were not totally committed to either camp; in fact, the Radical ministers were a crucial target because of their rather flexible position and, of course, because their continued presence was vital to the existence of the government. But with the election of a large majority of deputies committed to the APLE program, the defeat of the FEN was only a matter of time. The *laïque* forces took warning from similar portents seven years later.

VII

The School Law of 1959

Despite a continuous campaign of agitation against the Marie and Barangé laws of 1951, the FEN and its allies were unable to get them repealed. Disastrously worse in the eyes of the teachers was the fact that the Barangé aid proved insufficient, impelling the church school forces to seek increased financial help from the state. The decimation of the *laïque* members of Parliament in the elections of 1958 set the stage for a repeat performance of the drama of 1951.

The battle opened with a few preliminary skirmishes and verbal clashes reminiscent of the struggle seven years earlier. It reached its climax with the passage of the 1959 School Law by both houses of Parliament. And it subsided, temporarily at least, after the *laïque* forces had taken a series of counter-measures which, as in 1951, proved ineffective.

RESURGENCE OF THE PROBLEM

Rebuffed in its campaign against the 1951 laws, the FEN soon became apprehensive about further advances of the church school forces. This apprehension turned into open hostility when the triumph of the right in the 1958 elections was followed by Prime Minister Michel Debré's announcement that he would seek an early "definitive solution" of the school question. The antagonists in the school question girded themselves for the coming battle and engaged in such polemics that the Prime Minister was moved to intervene. Seeking a permanent solution acceptable to all sides, the Prime Minister appointed a commission to prepare recommendations for new legislation.

Despite continued agitation, the leaders of the FEN realized that the legislature which had passed the 1951 laws was not about to repeal them. In fact, there was some concern that the church school forces might press their advantage and have the state pay the salaries of private school teachers.[1] When the government of Prime Minister

[1] See the motion on *laïque* action of the 1954 SNI Congress in *E.L.*, 21ᵉ année, No. 38 (September 10, 1954), p. 859.

Edgar Faure dissolved Parliament and called for new elections on January 2, 1956, the FEN hoped for the return of a *laïque* majority which would repeal the Marie and Barangé laws. It worked for the election of such a majority through the Comité National d'Action Laïque (CNAL), as the CNDL had been rebaptized. The CNAL adopted a strategy proposed by the 1955 SNI Congress of restricting its immediate aims to a "minimum program" of restoration of the pre-1951 status quo in order to get the maximum number of commitments to it from parties and candidates. To the regret of M. Guy Mollet, as expressed in a letter to M. Lavergne, the CNAL omitted nationalization of private schools from the program for fear of alienating certain candidates and parties, "including the Communists." The Communist, Socialist, Radical Socialist, and UDSR parties accepted the "minimum program" as did other individuals and small groups. The church school forces, meanwhile, conducted a less vigorous campaign than the CNAL, the reverse of the situation in 1951.[2]

The election results heartened the leaders of the FEN, for the voters apparently returned a *laïque* majority. The electoral law operated to return to the Communists most of the seats they had lost in 1951, giving them a total (with affiliates) of 150 seats. The Republican Front, an election coalition formed by MM. Guy Mollet and Pierre Mendès-France, and supported by the Socialist party, Radicals of the left, some UDSR deputies, and some Social Republicans, enjoyed considerable success. However, the feud between MM. Mendès-France and Faure, which split the Radical party, and the Barangé Law, which separated the Center-Left from the Center-Right, made the formation of a new government very difficult. After lengthy negotiations, M. Mollet was invested as Prime Minister on February 1 at the head of a Republican Front government which, lacking a dependable majority, spurning Communist votes, and often relying on MRP support, was forced to leave certain knotty problems to parliamentary initiative. One of these was the question of the repeal of the 1951 laws. In his investiture speech M. Mollet promised that the government would not take a position in the debate on repeal; his ministers would be free to vote in accordance with their pledges to the voters.[3]

[2] Maurice Duverger, François Goguel, and Jean Touchard (eds.), *Les Elections du 2 Janvier 1956* ("Association Française de Science Politique: Cahiers de la Fondation Nationale des Sciences Politiques," No. 82; Paris: Colin, 1957), pp. 158–60; Meynaud, *Les Groupes de Pression*, p. 146; Brown, "Religious Schools and Politics in France," *Midwest Journal of Political Science*, Vol. II (May, 1958), pp. 175–76; *Combat*, July 23, 1955; *Le Monde*, July 24, 1955; and *L'Année Politique, 1955*, pp. 91–92, 98.

[3] Brown, *ibid.*, p. 176; and *L'Année Politique, 1956*, pp. 2–22.

M. Lavergne soon called upon those who had pledged their support to "accept their responsibilities" without delay. He warned: "The *laïques* can act directly on their deputies if it becomes necessary."[4] Several bills to repeal the 1951 laws were introduced and sent to the Education Committee of the National Assembly. This Committee, now having a *laïque* majority, approved the Cartier Report which recommended reserving public funds for public schools. But when the question of scheduling a debate on the Report came before the Assembly, it was twice rejected, 288 to 279 on February 17 and 301 to 276 a week later. Throughout the next few months, the SNI continued to put pressure on those who had pledged their support.[5] A debate on the Cartier Report, finally scheduled for November 6, 7, and 8, ended with the passage of a delaying motion (291 to 282) which indefinitely postponed a decision. The *laïque* majority had failed to materialize. The Radical members of the Education Committee made clear that while they might vote for repealing the 1951 laws, they would refuse to support the abrogation of the Falloux Law of 1850 or the Astier Law of 1919. Other Radicals in the Assembly did not wish to reopen the question, and a few UDSR deputies did not want to deepen the ditch between the Center-Left and the Center-Right. Some deputies were mindful of the fact that the Barangé Law also granted funds to the General Councils for school maintenance and equipment; terminating this aid would not have been popular on the local level.[6]

The *laïque* forces continued their campaign but without success. The League refused to put pressure on the Mollet government to make abrogation of the laws a question of confidence because it recognized that replacing a government of the left with one of the right would certainly not help its cause.[7] In March, 1957, the CNAL prepared two bills and had them introduced by the Communist group and a number of Radical Socialists. However, the bills were effectively killed by the Education Committee which refused to grant them legislative priority. Before they could be brought up for debate through normal parliamentary channels, the Fourth Republic expired.[8] M. Lauré complained

[4] *E.P.*, 11e année, No. 4 (February, 1956), p. 1.

[5] *Le Monde*, July 20, 1956.

[6] *L'Année Politique, 1956*, pp. 26–27, 105–106; and *E.L.*, 27e année, No. 2 (September 18, 1959), p. 63. M. Lauré later explained: "The Barangé law . . . created such an overlapping of interests and habits that when we wanted to abrogate it, we ran up against opposition or reticence which sometimes came from friends of the public schools." *E.P.*, 14e année, No. 7 (August-September, 1959), p. 7.

[7] *E.L.*, 23e année, No. 39 (September 21, 1956), p. 961.

[8] *L'Année Politique, 1957*, p. 25.

that the deputies had not kept their pledges, apparently preferring the status quo. The system of electoral pledges had failed.[9]

In the uncertainty that marked the transition from the Fourth Republic to the Fifth, the school question was largely lost from view. In June, 1958, the SNI reminded its members that the Gaullist RPF had voted for the Barangé Law, and in September it expressed apprehension over the implications of the new Constitution for the school question, but these warnings had little impact in the excitement of a near civil war and a change in regimes. Although the school question was little discussed in the electoral campaigns of November, 1958, the results of the election electrified the *laïque* forces. The Gaullist Union pour la Nouvelle République (UNR) alone won 206 seats, which, added to the 118 seats won by the Independents, presaged a church school majority even without the 64 votes of the MRP group. The SNI published an editorial entitled: *"Laïcité, a False Problem? Come Now, No Cheating!"* Summarized widely in the French press, the article predicted the policy of the new Assembly towards the schools. A meeting of the SNI National Council in December made preparations for countering the new onslaught of the church school forces. It decided to arouse public opinion, to encourage the reorganization of the Parents' Federation, and to prepare a "riposte on the political level" by helping the CNAL draw up a plan for nationalizing the private schools. The CNAL declared that it would refuse all dialogue with those who would segregate children, and warned them that they would have no scruples when the political forces were reversed.[10]

The storm heralded by the gathering clouds was not long in breaking. The month of January marked both the inauguration of the first regular government of the Fifth Republic under Prime Minister Michel Debré and the first incident in the School War of 1959. When M. Antoine Pinay, the Minister of Finance and Economic Affairs, visited the Pope and spent two hours with his Secretary of State, M. Durand of the SNI and FEN was certain that a program for state payment of Catholic teachers was discussed. A journalist interviewed the new Minister of Education, M. André Boulloche, and concluded that the resulting fears of the SNI were "little-founded or at least premature," for the Minister declared that for the moment it would be preferable to keep the status quo. But an incident in the Assembly

[9] Minutes of the 1957 FEN Congress, in *E.P.*, 13e année, No. 3 (January, 1958), p. 16.

[10] *L'Année Politique, 1958*, pp. 133–36; *L'Année Politique, 1959*, p. 13; *E.L.*, 26e année, No. 17 (January 23, 1959), p. 575; No. 23 (March 6, 1959), p. 902; and No. 30 (May 8, 1959), p. 1297.

convinced the *laïques* of the imminence of another school battle. When Prime Minister Debré presented his program to the Assembly on January 15, he made no reference to the school problem in his lengthy speech. In the ensuing discussion both an Independent and an MRP deputy brought this omission to his attention, the latter professing his astonishment at the program's silence on the poverty of the church schools. M. Debré replied:

> No one contests the existence of a problem. No one contests the necessity of resolving it in an atmosphere and in conditions such that the solution does not rekindle quarrels from which the public has only suffered too much.
>
> The government will work to create the conditions which will permit resolving the problem so that the solution is really definitive and considered as such by all men of good will.

Minister of Education Boulloche regretted the reopening of the question in the very first parliamentary debate. However, in a letter to the APLE the Prime Minister stated that legislation would be sought to settle the question before summer.[11]

As in 1951, the FEN worked almost exclusively through the CNAL in waging the struggle against a new law to aid the church schools. Now expanded to include the Fédération Nationale des Délégués Cantonaux, the CNAL set out to bring the implications of the government's declaration to the attention of the public. It drafted a letter to President de Gaulle pointing out that if further aid should be extended to private schools, there would have to be as many schools as there were "spiritual families in France." The letter declared that disturbing the equilibrium established by the Third Republic on this question would divide the country profoundly. Copies were sent to the Prime Minister and the Minister of Education, and it was released to the press. Articles on clericalism in *L'Ecole Libératrice* were multiplied. The SNI hoped to organize "a vast information campaign against the bills in preparation," to "demystify public opinion." However, since the government was preparing its plans in secret, the *laïque* forces had little information to distribute.[12]

In March the Association des Parents d'Elèves de l'Enseignement

[11] *E.L.*, 26e année, No. 16 (January 16, 1959), p. 558; No. 17 (January 23, 1959), p. 569; No. 18 (January 30, 1959), p. 623; No. 19 (February 6, 1959), p. 677; and *J.O., Assemblée Nationale*, January 15, 1959, pp. 44, 50, 78.

[12] *E.L.*, 26e année, No. 20 (February 13, 1959), p. 739; No. 22 (February 27, 1959), p. 855; No. 25 (April 3, 1959), p. 1021; and *E.P.*, 14e année, No. 7 (August-September, 1959), p. 6. For examples of anticlerical articles, see *E.L.*, 26e année, No. 21 (February 20, 1959), p. 840; and No. 33 (May 29, 1959), p. 1465.

Libre revealed its demands. (The APEL, with its approximately 600,000 members, is not to be confused with the parliamentary intergroup, the APLE.) The APEL maintained that teachers in private schools, both lay and religious, should receive the same salaries as public school teachers; state funds for this purpose should be allocated in proportion to the percentage of pupils attending private schools; funds under the Barangé, Marie, and Astier laws should be increased; and long-term, low-interest loans should be provided for building private schools. The government was under considerable pressure to satisfy these demands. On April 25, a delegation of the APLE, now 370 strong, called on the Prime Minister to impress him with the urgency of providing aid during the regular session of Parliament. They warned that their organization would be tempted to take the initiative in Parliament if relief were delayed.[13]

As expected, the CNAL reacted with vigor. After the announcement of the APEL demands, the CNAL issued a communiqué denouncing in violent language "the insensate character of such proposals, which not even Vichy dared to envisage, which openly violate the great school laws of 1886, the Law on the Separation of Church and State, and the Constitution, and which would consecrate through a brutal return of the forces of the past the outdated principle of school segregation." In an audience with the Minister of Education on April 15 the CNAL announced its will "not to leave unanswered the deliberate provocation of the APEL officers" and informed the Minister of its campaign to enlighten public opinion through the action of its members and its departmental committees. The CNAL campaign included contacts with prefects; a "poster day"; rallies which punctuated the months of May and especially June; and the organization of a "D-Day" of protest, prepared in advance to be triggered by a decision of the CNAL at the proper moment.[14]

On May 15, a few days after a giant APEL rally at Caen, a six-man CNAL delegation, which included M. Lauré of the FEN and M. Forestier of the SNI, had an audience with Prime Minister Debré. The Prime Minister told the delegation that he could "furnish no exact information on his intentions in the matter." One week later an FEN delegation met with Prime Minister Debré and informed him of the "painful impression" left by his declarations to the CNAL. The Prime

---

13 *L'Année Politique, 1959*, p. 76; Meynaud, *Les Groupes de Pression*, p. 83; E.L., 26e année, No. 24 (March 13, 1959), p. 961; and No. 29 (May 2, 1959), p. 1241.

14 E.L., 26e année, No. 24 (March 13, 1959), p. 957; No. 28 (April 24, 1959), p. 1182; and No. 30 (May 8, 1959), p. 1297.

Minister did not give the delegation any reason to modify their impression; remaining silent on the details of his plan, he stated his loyalty to his traditional principles on the question, thus implying that church schools would receive further aid. Meanwhile, on the occasion of the annual Congress of the Parents' Federation in Nancy, the CNAL issued a militant appeal to all *laïques*, marking "in history the point of departure for the riposte imposed on republicans by the insane demands of the APEL." The CNAL declared its intention to carry the debate beyond Parliament to the whole country. Its tactics could hardly be otherwise in view of the large APLE majority in Parliament. It also called for contacts with all groups to help in arousing public opinion through mass demonstrations in May and June. Organizations which pledged support were the Communist, Socialist, Independent Socialist, and Radical Socialist parties; the CGT and CGT-FO labor confederations; and the Ligue des Droits de l'Homme, Union Rationaliste, Libre Pensée, Masonic groups, and *laïque* youth movements. Rallies were organized on the departmental and regional level, especially in the middle two weeks of June. General Councils passed resolutions and mayors contacted prefects. The movement developed a certain resonance throughout the country.[15]

The *laïque* forces did not stop with arousing public opinion to defend the status quo. Following the pattern laid down in 1951, they adopted the tactic of threatening nationalization of private schools in order to intimidate the church school forces. Unlike 1951 when the SNI seemed to be the sole enthusiastic sponsor of nationalization, the CNAL took steps to prepare this "riposte" as early as November, 1958. M. Lauré of the FEN made the threat explicit. He said that if the state should begin to build religious schools and pay their teachers, it would be impossible for a new majority simply to cut off their funds and abandon them. He concluded:

> Our enemies themselves are creating the conditions for nationalization. They, not we, are setting in motion a process which will without fail turn against them, because the *laïques* returned to power will have no choice but immediate nationalization. By

[15] *E.L.*, 26e année, No. 32 (May 22, 1959), p. 1405–1406; No. 33 (May 29, 1959), pp. 1467, 1469; No. 34 (June 5, 1959), pp. 1519–22; and No. 35 (June 12, 1959), p. 1573. M. Forestier complained that the official radio was ignoring these demonstrations and chloroforming public opinion with its propaganda. *E.L.*, 26e année, No. 37 (September 4, 1959), p. 1692. "The crowded meetings denouncing the threat to *laïcité* were the only—and impressive—exceptions to the general public apathy about politics." Philip M. Williams and Martin Harrison, *De Gaulle's Republic* (London: Longmans, Green, 1960), p. 174.

warning them now, we furnish them with useful matter for reflection.

In May the CNAL repeated the threat. In July the SNI Congress adopted by acclamation the basic principles of its plan: nationalization of private school buildings as needed and integration of private school teachers on request into the public service; primary education to the age of eighteen to be exclusively given in free and laïque public schools under the supervision of tripartite boards composed of representatives of the Ministry of Education, the parents, and the teachers; and denial of state aid to all private schools.

Language and circumstances indicate that the teachers' espousal of nationalization was a tactical maneuver. At meetings of FEN officers it was openly discussed as a "tactic" or "riposte." A plan was prepared so as to have it ready to oppose to the scheme of the church school forces, but it was only to be published if the "clericals" actually introduced their bill. Although a traditional plank in the platforms of the teachers' unions, nationalization had long been a dormant issue. Not only did such an extreme measure have little chance of being approved by the National Assembly, but there was also resistance within the unions from those who feared the fascist potential of an educational monopoly and from the cégétistes who feared it would split the working class. In neither 1951 nor 1959 did this resistance keep the SNI from pushing its plan. Reluctant in 1951 because of its diverse and relatively conservative membership, the FEN gave its full support in 1959, perhaps aware in advance that its cause was lost. By adopting the nationalization proposal of the SNI as a threat to the church school forces, the FEN hoped to avert further encroachments on the school legislation of the Third Republic.[16]

The FEN and its allies could have no greater assurance that their campaign to arouse public opinion was having the desired effect than acknowledgment by the Prime Minister. M. Debré gave oblique recognition to the effectiveness of the laïque groups when he told them to keep quiet. Shortly after the League had held its seventieth Congress (at which M. Bayet had declared that the "Fourth Republic

16 L'Année Politique, 1959, pp. 56–57; E.P., No. 2 (October, 1945), p. 20; 14e année, No. 7 (August-September, 1959), p. 7; E.L., 26e année, No. 25 (April 3, 1959), p. 1021; No. 30 (May 8, 1959), pp. 1341–42; No. 37 (September 4, 1959), p. 1687; Combat, July 7, 1959, and Le Monde, July 10, 1959. The SGEN opposed nationalization which would give the public schools a legal monopoly. Syndicalisme Universitaire, Nouvelle série, No. 221 (January 13, 1960), p. 78/2. The tripartite boards were suggested in the SNI nationalization scheme of 1928. Jean-Albert Bédé, Le Problème de l'Ecole Unique en France ("Etudes Françaises," 24e cahier) (Paris: Belles Lettres, 1931), p. 87.

died in large part from the Barangé Law" and wondered if the "Fifth wants to die also for the same reasons, subsidies to private schools"), the Prime Minister made a declaration on the school question to the National Assembly in which he disparaged "noisy and passionate demonstrations." He said:

> If the interested organizations want to be wise, they will keep quiet: that is the advice I give them. But maybe they are not able to answer this appeal. I warn them then that they will influence in no way—I say, in no way—the behavior of the government.

In a press conference the following day the CNAL declared in no uncertain tones "that it [would] not keep quiet, that it [would] develop further the campaign which in the month of June had proved the deep attachment of the people to the school of the people."[17]

The Lapie Commission. Caught between the increasing pressure for action of the church school forces and the growing hostility of the *laïques,* the government, perhaps inspired by the example of M. Pleven in 1950, decided to appoint a study committee both in order to seek a compromise solution acceptable to all and to postpone action. On June 23, 1959, M. Pierre-Olivier Lapie, a former Socialist Minister of Education, was appointed to head a twelve-member "Commission for the Study of Relations between Private Education and the State."

In July, Prime Minister Debré told the National Assembly that the government would prepare its proposals in November after the Commission had made its report. Meanwhile, in order to provide the schools with temporary relief (and as a sop to the restive APLE majority) the government, with the approval of the Lapie Commission, would speed up the distribution of the Barangé funds. He also sought to appease the church school forces by promising them that their patience would be rewarded. At the opening of the fall session of Parliament in October, he repeated his government's commitment to prepare a law after the Commission had made its report. In view of the fact that the Prime Minister had promised at the beginning of the year to settle the school question before summer, there is some justification for M. Lauré's boast that with the support of crowds of demonstrators the FEN had warded off the offensive originally planned for July.[18]

In contrast with their policy towards the Paul-Boncour Commission

---

[17] *L'Année Politique, 1959,* pp. 85–86; *E.L.,* 27e année, No. 1 (September 11, 1959), p. 7; and *J.O., Assemblée Nationale,* July 24, 1959, p. 1458.

[18] *J.O., Assemblée Nationale,* July 23, 1959, pp. 1457–59; October 13, 1959, p. 1735; *J.O., Lois et Decrets,* June 24, 1959, pp. 6278–79; *E.L.,* 27e année, No. 1 (September 11, 1959), p. 7; *L'Année Politique, 1959,* p. 73; and *E.P.,* 14e année, No. 7 (August-September, 1959), p. 7.

in 1951, the members of the CNAL decided to testify before the Lapie Commission. M. Forestier explained that the CNAL organizations wanted to contribute to the government's avowed purpose of narrowing the gulf dividing opinion on the question. However, M. Forestier's testimony, which bore mostly on the nationalization scheme of the FEN, was reported fully in *L'Ecole Libératrice*, resulting in the only major incident of the Commission's investigations. On September 24 Chairman Lapie wrote to M. Forestier on behalf of the unanimous Commission complaining: "Alone of all the personalities heard by the Commission, you made public not only your testimony but also reported your version of the Commission's meeting." M. Forestier was particularly incensed by the fact that Chairman Lapie's letter appeared in *Le Monde* a few hours after he had received it. M. Forestier replied that he had not been informed by the Commission of any rules governing testimony; that as a union leader he was responsible to his comrades; and that, if doubt persisted about the accuracy of his report, he was willing to publish the stenographic record of the meeting in *L'Ecole Libératrice*. Apparently terminated at this point, the incident heightened the distrust of the teachers' unions for the Commission.[19]

After hearing thirty-three representatives of interested groups, the Lapie Commission decided to prepare a pragmatic report as free as possible of ideological passion. Finally made public in early December, after a long delay during which the government sought to reach agreement on a bill based on the Commission's findings, the report rejected direct aid of the Barangé type on the triple grounds that such aid would not discriminate between worthy and undeserving or superfluous institutions; it would increase the divisive competitiveness of the two systems; and it would exacerbate the school conflict, for the *laïques* could not accept it. Rather, the report suggested granting private schools four choices: nationalization with integration of the private school teachers into the civil service; *conventionnement* in which the schools would remain private, but public school teachers would take charge of classes under contract with the school;[20] *agrément* in which the state would supplement the salaries of private school teachers and impose certain financial, administrative, and pedagogical controls without interfering with the character of the education given (an alternative opposed by some *laïque* members of the Commission); and complete freedom with neither control nor state aid. This delicate

---

[19] *E.L.*, 27e année, No. 2 (September 18, 1959), pp. 62–63; and No. 4 (October 2, 1959), p. 181.

[20] Such an arrangement already existed exceptionally at the Collège Stanislas in Paris, where the author served a year as an English assistant.

compromise, painstakingly erected to avoid the total alienation of either camp in the struggle, could not withstand the unmitigated hostility of the *laïques* on the one side and the steam-roller pressure of the self-conscious APLE majority on the other. Chairman Lapie, meanwhile, was expelled from the Socialist party for his efforts.[21]

PASSAGE OF THE SCHOOL LAW

While the CNAL was bringing its campaign to a peak, the Debré government continued to work out a bill based on the report of the Lapie Commission. Despite the walk-out of a majority of the High Council of National Education and the resignation of the Minister of Education, the bill was passed by Parliament and promulgated on December 31, 1959.

The campaign of the CNAL. The November Congress of the FEN provided the theme and approved the means for the campaign of the *laïques* against the forthcoming school legislation. The theme of the campaign was to distinguish between the legal majority in Parliament intent on extending further aid to the church schools and the majority of the people determined to defend the public schools. The means of the campaign was a vast program of information and demonstrations to arouse public opinion.

The resolution on *laïque* action of the 1959 FEN Congress emphasized that "the school question was not at issue at the time of the last electoral consultations and that under these conditions it would be at least hazardous for the present parliamentary majority to claim that it represents on this very complex and very serious problem the point of view of the majority of the nation." Recognizing that they were clearly in the minority in Parliament where the APLE had enrolled more than 380 deputies, the teachers were led to oppose the "real country" to the "legal country," and in December the CNAL called for either a referendum or new elections. Reproached by M. Jacques Fauvet in *Le Monde* for reviving this old opposition associated with the discredited doctrines of Charles Maurras, M. Forestier denied the charge by claiming that the "legal country" includes voters as well as deputies and ministers, without abandoning his position that the voters must be consulted on such a fundamental national question.[22]

---

[21] France, Ministère de l'Education Nationale, de la Jeunesse et des Sports, *L'Education Nationale,* No. 36 (December 10, 1958 [1959]), pp. 1–2; No. 37 (December 17, 1959), pp. 1–2; and *L'Année Politique, 1959,* pp. 126, 150.

[22] *Le Monde,* December 2, 26, 1959; *E.P.,* 15e année, No. 2 (November, 1959), p. 11; *E.L.,* 27e année, No. 15bis (December 26, 1959), pp. 842–43; and *L'Année Politique, 1959,* pp. 149–50.

Aware that the church school forces had a solid majority in the National Assembly, the laïque forces concentrated their efforts on influencing public opinion. A resolution of the FEN Congress recommended continued cooperation with the CNAL in its efforts to get the support of all laïque organizations and to organize information campaigns and mass demonstrations. The FEN and the SNI both asked their members to contribute one day's pay in order to collect one-half billion francs to finance the campaign. The CNAL called on its departmental committees to organize demonstrations throughout the country.[23] These rallies and parades became frequent during the last week of November until they reached their peak on November 29 when one hundred meetings were scheduled in the department of the Seine; other rallies were planned in seventy departments, and some 700,000 laïques demonstrated throughout France. After a single rally in Paris, addressed by representatives of the teachers' unions, had assembled more than 100,000 people on December 6, M. Forestier was able to boast that one million demonstrators had participated in the campaign.[24]

While the government sought to reach agreement on a draft acceptable to ministers on both sides of the question, a task so difficult that numerous cabinet meetings were devoted to the problems and even the arbitration of President de Gaulle was solicited, the CNAL with limited hopes sought to make its influence felt on the government. On November 30 a delegation met with Minister of Education Boulloche and on December 4 with Prime Minister Debré. A press communiqué reported the Committee's disappointment at the end of each audience. A further audience with Minister Boulloche followed on December 15 with similar results. M. Forestier concluded: "Vichy triumphs over the spirit of the Liberation."[25] On the eve of the opening of debate in the Assembly the FEN accused the government of violating the law by failing to consult the High Council of National

[23] A directive of the APEL, purportedly intercepted by the laïque forces despite the enclosed warning that "it is indispensable that this note not be utilized by adverse propaganda," called on the APEL forces to make their demonstrations appear spontaneous, "coming from nearly everywhere and consequently diverse in expression." The CNAL openly organized the laïque demonstrations. E.L., 27e année, No. 7 (October 23, 1959), p. 343.

[24] E.P., 15e année, No. 2 (November, 1959), pp. 11–12; E.L., 27e année, No. 9 (November 6, 1959), p. 450; No. 11 (November 20, 1959), pp. 562–63; No. 12 (November 27, 1959), p. 623; No. 13 (December 4, 1959), pp. 674–75, 679; No. 14 (December 11, 1959), p. 730; and Le Monde, December 1, 8, 1959. The author can attest to the devotion of the assemblage in Paris, half of whom were obliged to stand outdoors in the cold.

[25] E.L., 27e année, No. 13 (December 4, 1959), pp. 674–75; No. 14 (December 11, 1959), p. 742; and No. 15 (December 18, 1959), p. 786.

Education on its bill.[26] The CNAL scheduled a "National Day of the *Laïque* School"; it was observed by ceremonies in the classroom and contacts with local government officials. Unlike 1951 no strike was called. In the classroom the teachers were asked to give:

a lesson of morality and civic instruction on the *laïque* ideal and the *laïque* school, the school of fraternity;

a French lesson on a text from one of our great authors on the subject of *laïcité* . . . ;

a history lesson on the educational accomplishments of the Third Republic;

a singing lesson, for example with the fifty-year-old song "Honor and Glory to the *Laïque* School."

Teaching materials for these lessons were printed in *L'Ecole Libératrice*. A second line of action called for the creation of broad CNAL delegations to contact mayors and prefects asking them to transmit their protests to the central government. Evening meetings in the communes and city wards concluded the day of protest. Even the SGEN (CFTC) took part in the demonstrations of December 22.[27]

The government's bill. On December 17 the President of the National Assembly announced the introduction of the long-awaited government bill on the relations between private schools and the state and sent it to the Committee on Cultural, Family, and Social Affairs.[28] Minister of Education Boulloche held a press conference to explain the bill to the public. As a bill of conciliation, it was designed to bring public and private schools closer together without sacrificing freedom of education for the private schools. The bill accepted the four options proposed by the Lapie Commission and now known as: integration, contract of association (formerly *conventionnement*), simple contract (formerly *agrément*), and total freedom without state aid. It also accepted the Lapie Commission recommendation to create local conciliation committees to iron out problems rising from the application of the law. Aid under the Barangé Law was to be temporarily continued.[29]

The government text was unsatisfactory to both sides. The CNAL labeled it "a veritable swindle," the League called it "a flagrant violation of the *laïque* character of the Republic," and M. Jean Cornec of

[26] *Le Monde,* December 17, 1959.
[27] *Le Monde,* December 22, 23, 24, 1959; *E.L.,* 27e année, No. 15 (December 18, 1959), p. 791; and *Syndicalisme Universitaire,* Nouvelle série, No. 221 (January 13, 1960), p. 87/11.
[28] *J.O., Assemblée Nationale,* December 17, 1959, p. 3449.
[29] *Le Monde,* December 19, 1959; and *L'Année Politique, 1959,* p. 151.

the Parents' Federation sent his objections in a letter to President de Gaulle. The FEN counterattacked through the High Council of National Education. When that body met in special session two days after M. Lauré had written to the President of the Constitutional Council complaining of the government's failure to consult the High Council (a complaint having no legal validity under the Constitution), its elected members resigned in protest, depriving it of a quorum and ending the meeting. As in 1951, the consultative councils had been used as a weapon by the teachers—and in vain.[30]

The church school forces opposed the government draft on the grounds that it would secularize private education. In committee the APLE representatives, backed by the overwhelming majority of committee members, wanted to alter Article I of the bill so as to emphasize that the existing character of private institutions would not be affected by the bill. At first the government resisted, hoping to maintain its precariously balanced text; but before debate opened in the National Assembly, the government acceded to the demands of the committee and the Independent and MRP ministers. As a result the Minister of Education resigned. M. Boulloche explained:

> I had given my consent to a bill which included a certain number of provisions of such a nature, I think, as to pacify and bring together public and private education.
>
> In view of the parliamentary situation, the government decided yesterday that it had to modify the text introduced in the Assembly. In so doing, it brought into question the agreement that we had so laboriously arrived at.
>
> Under these conditions, it was not possible for me to speak in the name of a unanimous government to defend the bill before the assemblies. . . . I believe that I could not present and defend the bill after it was decided to accept changes in its first article.[31]

Passing the bill. Called into special session on December 21 to take up the school question and the 1960 budget, the National Assembly began discussion of the government's school bill two days later.[32] In contrast with the long and frequently delayed debate of 1951, the school law was passed in one day and sent on to the Senate, which quickly passed it without change.

---

[30] *Le Monde,* December 20–21, 23, 1959; and *E.L.,* 27e année, No. 15bis (December 26, 1959), p. 844.

[31] *Le Monde,* December 24, 1959; *L'Education Nationale,* No. 38 (December 31, 1959), p. 5; and *L'Année Politique, 1959,* pp. 152–53.

[32] *J.O., Assemblée Nationale,* December 18, 1959, p. 3504; and December 22, 1959, p. 3582.

Provisionally fulfilling the duties of Minister of Education, Prime Minister Debré opened the debate with the presentation of his government's bill. Accepting the premise that private schools perform a public service, M. Debré granted that they deserve state aid but insisted that it must be accompanied by controls. He specifically rejected the solution of nationalization as "not acceptable," since such an "authoritarian transformation" would be an additional cause of division. He also rejected the idea of creating a vast independent and competing system of private schools. His reasoning led him to the conclusion that the state was obliged to aid private schools while controlling their educational standards and fostering their cooperation with the public schools. He said the law emphasized tolerance, since private schools under contract would have to be open to all; cooperation, since conciliation committees were to be set up; and experimentation, since two types of contract were to be offered and none imposed. He hoped that the bill would not be evaluated in terms of the "men, groups, and unions who . . . have been besieging the gates of power for so many weeks."[33]

In the discussion which followed, the Communists and Socialists spoke for the laïque forces as in 1951, although with many fewer voices. When the rapporteur for the Committee mentioned that two substitute bills introduced by the Socialists and Communists had been rejected, he noted that their content had been practically identical, "in spite of noteworthy differences in inspiration." It is possible to suspect identical inspiration as well, for the bills called for the nationalization of private schools under the control of tripartite boards composed of teachers, parents, and administrators, a plan identical with that adopted by the SNI at its last Congress. After delaying motions interposed by the Communists and Socialists had been voted down, M. Guy Mollet opened the general discussion. In the course of his speech he repeated the warning issued by M. Lauré the previous summer:

> New majorities will return. . . . On that day . . . all those schools and teachers who have solicited public funds will be considered ipso facto to have affirmed their desire to enter the public service. . . . This is neither blackmail nor a threat. . . . It will be the logical conclusion of the decisions taken today.

The Socialists failed in their attempt to have the bill returned to committee on the grounds that, contrary to law, no provision had been made for financing it and the High Council of National Education had not been properly consulted. The government accepted seven

[33] Ibid., December 23, 1959, pp. 3596–98.

amendments. One demanded by the church school forces changed the wording of the first article in order to give greater emphasis to the retention of full freedom for nonparticipating private schools and to clarify that the "particular character" of the contracting schools was to be fully protected. In the final vote, all ten Communists and forty-four Socialists voted as a bloc against the bill, supported by eight Radicals out of eighteen, and nine others. The final vote was 427 to 71.[34] One week later in the early morning hours of December 30, after a day's debate which resumed most of the arguments already heard in the Assembly, including the *laïque* threat of future nationalization, the Senate passed the bill by a vote of 173 to 99. Opposing the bill were all fourteen Communists, all fifty Socialists, thirty-four out of sixty-four members of the Democratic left, and one Senator affiliated with no party group. The law was promulgated on December 31, 1959.[35]

REACTION OF THE TEACHERS

In full congruence with the pattern established in 1951, the teachers' unions resorted to two main counter-measures: they had their representatives on the consultative councils reject the decrees of application, and they circulated a national petition demanding repeal. Their demonstrations and appeals proved ineffective, in the short run at least; a movement to bolster their forces for future battles could have long-range significance, however.

The decrees of application. The impact of the law of December 31, 1959, depended in large part on the decrees of application (administrative regulations) that were to put it into effect, for the law could be interpreted narrowly or broadly. Ignoring the hostility expressed by teachers' representatives in the consultative councils, the government finally approved decrees which were even more favorable for the church school forces than the original law had been.

In March the Ministry of Education sent its proposed decrees of application to Prime Minister Debré; the government announced that the consultative councils would be assembled to give their opinions on the proposals beginning on March 25. When each council met, the elected members refused to consider the decrees. M. Dhombres of the SNES spoke for the secondary teachers when he declared that they

---

34 *Ibid.*, pp. 3599–3649; *L'Année Politique*, 1959, pp. 153–54; and *E.L.*, 27e année, No. 16 (January 2, 1960), pp. 866–68.

35 *Le Monde*, December 31, 1959; *L'Année Politique*, 1959, pp. 154–55; *J.O., Lois et Decrets*, January 3, 1960, pp. 66–67; and *J.O., Sénat*, December 29, 1959, pp. 2014–54. In the course of the debate M. Jacques Duclos (Communist) referred to the action of the SNI and declared that "the 200,000 unionized primary school teachers consider themselves in a state of active resistance." *Ibid.*, p. 2037.

would not give an opinion because they had not been consulted while the law itself was being prepared; furthermore, the law violated both the Constitution and the Law on Separation of Church and State, a point reiterated by M. Durand of the SNI before he led his fellow primary teachers out of a meeting of the Primary Education Council. The High Council rejected the decrees by a vote of 43 to 16 with 2 abstentions.[36]

The teachers' unions were not only unable to block the decrees of application, but they were also appalled by further concessions to the church school forces made in the decrees before they were published on April 24 and later. The decrees as proposed in March were already fairly generous to the church schools. For example, instead of requiring directors and teachers in private schools under contract to have qualifications equivalent to those demanded in the public schools, three years' experience was made an acceptable substitute.[37] However, the MRP and several Catholic organizations called for even more favorable terms, and they received some satisfaction. For example, the final version of the decrees of April 24 omitted a clause which required that classes taught under a contract of association with the state should follow rules and programs established for the public schools by the Minister of Education.[38] Two more decrees were issued in July. Further changes in December establishing salary standards for private school teachers were regarded by Le Monde as "very generous."[39]

The APEL and other church school supporters continued to attack the omission in the decrees of any recognition of the "particular character" of each private institution. They regarded the inclusion by amendment of such a provision in the original law as an important and necessary victory protecting the Catholic orientation of their instruction. But the government had apparently felt that on this delicate subject it was best not to alter the careful language of the law.[40] Generally, however, the church school forces were satisfied with the

[36] Le Monde, March 20–21, 24, 26, 27–28, April 2, 6, 1960; and E.P., 15e année, No. 6 (March, 1960), p. 3.

[37] Le Monde, March 23, 1960.

[38] Le Monde, April 4, 12, 16–18, 24, 26, 1960; and E.P., 15e année, No. 7 (April-May, 1960), pp. 1–11. Changes also clarified the position of chaplains in the public schools. For example, they were to be provided only at the request of parents, not automatically, and costs were to be borne by the parents, not the state, although local governments could subsidize them if desired. Le Monde, April 17–18, 1960. The bishop of Arras declared these provisions to be in the "authentic republican tradition," and both he and the Cardinal of Lyons urged parents to make the necessary requests. Le Monde, September 6, 11–12, 1960.

[39] E.P., 16e année, No. 1 (October, 1960), pp. 6–8; and Le Monde, December 15, 1960.

[40] Le Monde, April 16–18, May 24, 1960.

law. The Plenary Assembly of Bishops promised a "loyal try" of the system despite some reservations.[41] The director of the Catholic publication *Etudes* stated that "A try must be attempted. . . . We must want it to succeed."[42]

The *laïque* reaction to the decrees was decidedly hostile. FEN Secretary General Lauré pointed out that the decrees of April were a long way from the Boulloche compromise of the previous December.[43] The FEN devoted an issue of *L'Enseignement Public* almost entirely to a critique of the decrees.[44] On September 23, 1960, the CNAL declared: "These texts go even beyond the letter of the law. All facilities have been granted to the church schools. . . ."[45]

The national petition. On December 26, 1959, MM. Durand, Forestier, and Lauré announced in a press conference that the CNAL would sponsor a nation-wide petition campaign in order to arouse public opinion and at the same time demonstrate that the parliamentary majority which had voted the law did not correspond to a majority in the country. In January members of the CNAL met with representatives of political, cultural, philosophical, and union groups to prepare for the campaign. Numbered signature sheets were printed for distribution in February. Delayed one week because of a rightist uprising in Algiers and roundly denounced by the MRP and members of the church hierarchy, the campaign got underway on February 13. Door-to-door solicitation, a method regarded as unpleasant by both campaigners and citizens in France, was used exclusively to get the maximum number of signatures without duplication. The petition demanded repeal of the law; it protested "solemnly against this anti-republican law which is going to impose on the taxpayers, to the sole profit of private and religious schools, a supplementary effort of nearly one hundred billion old francs annually." Within two days 500,000 signatures had been collected; after two months the total had risen to nine and one-half million. In each of forty-nine departments the number of signatures collected by then was greater than a majority of the voters in that department at the last election. M. Lauré pointed out that one of these departments was the Loire, all of whose seven deputies had voted for the law. The petition campaign continued until May 29. The CNAL received letters of support from numerous *laïque* organizations, including the Communist, Socialist, Independent So-

[41] *Le Monde*, April 29, 1960.
[42] *Le Monde*, October 6, 1960.
[43] Interview, May 11, 1960.
[44] *E.P.*, 15e année, No. 7 (April-May, 1960).
[45] *Le Monde*, September 25-26, 1960.

cialist, and Radical Socialist parties, the CGT and CGT-FO labor confederations, and the National Students Union of France (UNEF). Even the SGEN (CFTC) recommended that its members support the petition, noting that "unlike other documents of the same origin, the text of this petition contained nothing incompatible with the fundamental positions of the union"; according to a complaint at the SGEN Congress, however, the organizers of the campaign deliberately kept the SGEN on the sidelines.[46]

The petition campaign was brought to an end with a "National Day of *Laïque* Action" on June 19. In Paris on that day a rally attended by a crowd estimated at one to three hundred thousand persons received the report that a total of 10,813,697 signatures had been collected; in sixty-five departments a majority of voters had signed the petition. Members of the assemblage took an oath pledging to fight for abrogation of the law. A six-column headline on an inside page of *Le Monde* announced that the day had been "a great success."[47]

Besides the national petition and the demonstration of June 19, 1960, the teachers reacted in other ways. In several schools organizations of teachers and parents refused to participate with deputies who had voted for the Debré Law in the traditional ceremonies where honor students are awarded prizes.[48] Both the SNI and FEN congresses of 1960 promised active resistance to the Debré Law. M. Durand, representing the CNAL at the FEN Congress, urged members to remind local municipalities that they can refuse to vote funds for private schools.[49] The FEN requested its members to decline to sit on the conciliation committees provided for in the law; the Parents' Federation did the same. More than eighteen months after passage of the law several departments still did not have conciliation committees. Because of the difficulty of finding *laïques* willing to serve, the National Committee of Conciliation was unable to hold its first meeting

[46] *Le Monde,* December 26, 1959; January 20, February 9, 19, April 6, 26, 1960; *E.L.,* 27e année, No. 18 (January 15, 1960), p. 974; No. 21 (February 5, 1960), p. 1141; No. 22 (February 12, 1960), p. 1194, 1198–99; No. 24 (February 26, 1960), p. 1311; No. 25 (March 4, 1960), p. 1367; and *Syndicalisme Universitaire,* Nouvelle série, No. 222 (January 27, 1960), p. 89/1. The Archbishop of Rennes and head of an episcopal committee on education expressed his satisfaction that last-moment amendments had made the bill acceptable to the church school supporters. *Le Monde,* January 3–4, 1960.

[47] *Le Monde,* June 21, 1960. M. Lauré estimated attendance at 400,000 in addition to 25,000 delegates and declared that the demonstration "broke the wall of silence with which the press and radio had opposed us until then." *E.P.,* 15e année, No. 10 (August-September, 1960), p. 6.

[48] *Le Monde,* July 1, 1960.

[49] *Le Monde,* July 10–11, November 5, 1960; and *E.P.,* 15e année, No. 10 (August-September, 1960), p. 25.

until May, 1961.[50] In early 1961 the CNAL launched on the local level a campaign against the Debré Law that developed on the departmental level in the fall and then, as planned, terminated in a national demonstration on February 11, 1962. On that day in Paris, 4,200 delegates of departmental committees of *laïque* action met and declared their continuing devotion to the oath of June 19, 1960, and to the struggle against all "anti-*laïque*" laws.[51]

Finances for the campaign were covered by a special *laïque* fund. In 1960 the FEN felt it best not to publish details of the fund but instead communicated the information to the national unions and departmental unions by circular. In 1961 the financial report was given in detail to the FEN Congress with the request that the information not be passed outside the organization. In 1960 it was revealed that most of the funds had been forwarded by the SNI with the apportionment of charges still to be made among the members of the CNAL. In the first year of the campaign, to January, 1961, 75 million old francs were spent.[52]

By November, 1960, under the provisions of the new law seven schools had requested integration, 413 a contract of association, and 10,171 a simple contract.[53] By the beginning of the school year in 1961, 6,542 simple contracts had been signed, 1,500 requests rejected, and about 30 per cent of the applications for simple contracts were still pending.[54] The budgetary allocation for aid to private schools more than doubled to reach 487 million new francs in 1962.[55] The victory of the church school forces had begun to yield tangible results.

But there were other significant results as well. The failure of the teachers to prevent passage and application of the Debré Law had important repercussions on the parents' organizations. Before June, 1960, there were three large parents' groups: the Fédération des Conseils de Parents d'Elèves des Ecoles Publiques (called the Parents'

[50] *E.P.*, 16e année, No. 6 (April, 1961), p. 10; No. 8 (August-September, 1961), p. 7; and *Le Monde*, June 4, 1960, March 11, 1961.

[51] *Le Monde*, May 23, 1961; and *E.P.*, 17e année, No. 5 (February, 1962), p. 17. See the special CNAL supplement to *E.P.*, 17e année, No. 6 (March-April, 1962), for a report on the national demonstrations. In the midst of this campaign M. Lauré, then president of the CNAL, as well as secretary general of the FEN, received a proposal from the Communist party to organize action in common with the CNAL, the parties, the unions, and other *laïque* organizations. FEN reception of the letter was marked by the usual lack of enthusiasm shown for Communist initiatives. *Le Monde*, October 5, 1961.

[52] *E.P.*, 16e année, No. 3 (December, 1960), p. 25; No. 4 (January, 1961), p. 6; and 17e année, No. 3 (December, 1961), p. 22.

[53] *Le Monde*, November 27–28, 1960.

[54] *Le Monde*, November 11, 1961.

[55] *Le Monde*, October 11, 1961.

Federation in this work) with 800,000 parents of elementary school children; the Fédération des Associations de Parents d'Elèves des Lycées et Collèges with 400,000 parents of secondary school children; and the Fédération Nationale des Associations de Parents d'Elèves de l'Enseignement Public with 170,000 parents of secondary and technical school children. Because the Fédération des Associations refused to take a stand against state aid to private schools and because educational reform demanded greater cooperation and comprehension between branches and levels of education, the Parents' Federation decided in June, 1960, to seek to create a single parents' organization.[56] The Parents' Federation extended its recruitment activities to all levels of education and in 1961 established a conciliation committee to promote fusions with other organizations.[57]

The Fédération des Associations remained hostile to these initiatives. As a counterattack it considered accepting as members parents of elementary school children.[58] The head of the organization explained: "The attempt to create in every *lycée* a parents' council is almost always due to the initiative of the teachers' unions which, moreover, aim to be represented in these organizations by ex officio members. Such pressure betrays their fear of seeing the parents' associations take an orientation which the unions would not consider in conformity with their own plans." The Fédération Nationale des Associations was sympathetic to the idea of union with the Parents' Federation but suspicious of fusion and opposed to granting the teachers' unions the right to *de jure* representation. A Committee on Study and Action made up of representatives of the two federations, as well as teachers' union representatives, was appointed to study the question.[59] By November, 1961, the Parents' Federation had grown to represent 850,000 families; over 125 parents' councils had been established in secondary and technical schools.[60] At the next outbreak of the School War the teachers would have a formidable weapon of mass organization at their disposal.

Some observations. The two preceding case studies effectively illustrate FEN action techniques, point up some limitations on the effectiveness of pressure groups, and permit the comparison of FEN action

[56] *Le Monde,* June 4, 1960; and October 3, 1961. The latter issue reviews in detail the evolution of the parents' organizations.

[57] *E.P.,* 16e année, No. 3 (December, 1960), p. 13; and *Le Monde,* May 24, 1961.

[58] *Le Monde,* May 13, 1961.

[59] *Le Monde,* October 3, 1961; and *E.P.,* 16e année, No. 3 (December, 1960), p. 13; No. 6 (April, 1961), p. 10; and No. 7 (May-June, 1961), p. 10.

[60] *E.P.,* 17e année, No. 3 (December, 1961), p. 11.

under two different republics. The second case study confirms previous conclusions about FEN action techniques; it also demonstrates FEN reluctance to strike for political purposes: there was no protest strike against the School Law of 1959. It reemphasizes that a pressure group, when faced with a hostile parliamentary majority, will resort to a battery of action techniques outside of Parliament despite limited hope for success. But, most important, it permits a comparison of pressure group activity under the Fourth and Fifth Republics.

The differences in behavior of the FEN in 1951 and 1959 are due as much to political as to constitutional factors. Despite the fact that the government took upon itself the responsibility of preparing a final settlement of the school question, a task that no government of the Fourth Republic was strong enough to do, and which in 1951 was only deferred with a clearly labeled transitory measure, the FEN (with the CNAL) had fewer contacts with members of the cabinet than in the struggle eight years earlier. The reason was twofold. Not only was the government practically impregnable with its weighty constitutional powers, but it was also politically secure. In 1951 the cabinet included a number of Radical Socialists on whose presence the continued existence of the government depended; in 1959 there were only two or three laïque ministers in the cabinet, and their removal would not have threatened the government's hardy majority in the Assembly. So contacts with the cabinet were limited by the small number of potentially sympathetic ministers and, more importantly, pressure on them could not change the government's course of action, as the resignation of Boulloche showed.

Nor was the Assembly a good target for CNAL action, for both constitutional and political reasons. Constitutionally the power of the Assembly had been reduced, so there were fewer opportunities to deter the government from its intended action. The government set the date for the debate, opened the discussion based on its own text, accepted only the amendments it chose, and required a single vote on the whole bill. One day's session sufficed in each house, whereas it took the Assembly almost a week to pass the Barangé bill. More important than these changes, however, was the fact that the laïque bloc was much smaller than in 1951, a political fact which helps to explain why the CNAL focused its energies on public opinion. Without hope of blocking parliamentary action, the laïque forces sought to keep the issue alive until the next election could alter the balance of political forces.

In conclusion, it may be said that while it is difficult to separate the constitutional from the political influences on pressure group behavior, under the Fifth Republic a government with a secure parliamentary majority may resist group pressures with impunity if it so desires. The Parliament appears to be as permeable as ever, and, while a large majority may impel a sympathetic government to accommodate it, as the Debré government did in altering Article I to placate the APLE members, a determined government can apply its weighty constitutional powers to have its way. In the last analysis, however, since the government is ultimately responsible to the Assembly, the efficacy of pressure group activity depends mostly on the particular political mixture that emerges from popular elections.

VIII

Conclusion

Case studies never "prove" anything; their purpose is to illustrate generalizations which are established otherwise, or to direct
attention towards such generalizations.

With this pointed reminder of the limitations of the case study approach, Harry Eckstein introduced his recent pressure group study of
the British Medical Association.[1] Since the present work is essentially
three case studies—a pressure group analysis of the FEN and two detailed descriptions of its struggle against the School Laws of 1951 and
1959—Eckstein's reminder and, more importantly, his efforts to give his
case study a theoretical framework both heuristic and explanatory are
singularly relevant.

In the interests of comparability and the development of a genuinely cumulative political science, this chapter applies the scheme of
analysis developed by Eckstein for his study of the BMA to the FEN
and its activities. It would, of course, have been possible to create a
different format, perhaps better suited to the peculiarities of the
teachers' organization; but such theoretical construction would have
been at the expense of ready comparability. Therefore, after a brief
survey of recent developments in group theory, the findings of this
study and its relation to the literature in the field are summarized
under the headings of Eckstein: the determinants of the form, of the
scope and intensity, and of the effectiveness of pressure-group politics.

GROUP THEORY

Although the beginnings of modern group theory can be traced to
the early years of American political science in Arthur F. Bentley's
The Process of Government, published in 1908, after more than half a
century Bentley's book is still the subject of lively controversy in the

---

[1] *Pressure Group Politics,* p. 15.

discipline.[2] Bentley's work was at first largely ignored because it ran counter to the formal and legalistic bent of his contemporaries. In the interwar years a number of pressure group studies appeared, including landmark books by Peter H. Odegard, Pendleton Herring, and E. E. Schattschneider,[3] but it was not until the 1950's that further developments in group theory, largely inspired by a revival of interest in Bentley's work, gained considerable support among political scientists. In the most complete and logically consistent exposition of group theory to date, *The Governmental Process*, David Truman explicitly acknowledged his debt to Bentley.[4]

The fact that Truman's theoretical scheme was moderate and reasonable in making room for both individual action and "rules of the game" which put limits on struggle between groups did not spare it from attack. A number of critical articles appeared. Stanley Rothman claimed that Americans are not joiners, that an individual's attitudes are more than the sum of group influences on him, that the argument of the potential interest group which upholds the "rules of the game" is a *deus ex machina* which can be brought in for any purpose, that Truman's empirical work uses additional explanatory factors made necessary by the inadequacy of the theory, and that the theory does not give enough attention to "the patterns of normatively oriented political action which characterize a given social system."[5] R. E. Dowl-

[2] (Chicago: University of Chicago Press, 1908). A brief summary of the development of group theory and closely related concepts in the literature appeared recently in Harmon Zeigler, *Interest Groups in American Society* (Englewood Cliffs: Prentice-Hall, 1964), pp. 1–27.

[3] Odegard, *Pressure Politics: The Story of the Anti-Saloon League* (New York: Columbia University Press, 1928); Herring, *Group Representation Before Congress* (Baltimore: Johns Hopkins University Press, 1929); and Schattschneider, *Politics, Pressure and the Tariff* (Englewood Cliffs: Prentice-Hall, 1935).

[4] (New York: Knopf, 1951). Another important contribution to group theory was Earl Latham, *The Group Basis of Politics* (Ithaca: Cornell University Press, 1952). The person whose views come the closest to Bentley's all-inclusive position that "when the groups are adequately stated, everything is stated" is Charles B. Hagan, who holds that "a political science must reduce its problems to their simplest terms and the smallest number of explanatory principles. . . . The conception of the group that meets the requirements of the above rule is the one of the group as activity of human beings. I have shown that all the important qualities of ideas and institutions and individuals and interests meet on common ground in that conception. I have further shown that whatever qualities those words have that are not incorporated into the group activity are irrelevant for a political science." Charles B. Hagan, "The Group in Political Science," *Approaches to the Study of Politics,* ed. Roland Young (Evanston: Northwestern University Press, 1957), p. 51.

[5] "Systematic Political Theory: Observations on the Group Approach," *American Political Science Review,* Vol. LIV (March, 1960), 15–33. A brief but effective rejoinder from Truman appeared in the same journal, Vol. LIV (June, 1960), 494–95.

ing maintained that Truman neither elaborates Bentley's theory nor strictly applies it; in fact Truman's "method is just what you can find in almost any historian of the last hundred years."[6] The only thing new about modern group theory, according to Peter H. Odegard, is its pretension. Classical political philosophers had long recognized the importance of groups in the political process, but only the moderns insist that they explain everything. "Group theorists . . . have all but banished reason, knowledge, and intelligence from the governmental process. Public policy and administration are regarded as vectors of group pressures—a kind of resultant in a parallelogram of group forces." Besides, the basic concepts of the theory are excessively ambiguous.[7]

This on-going debate over the value of group theory is far from settled. But particularly germane to the present study is the fact that some students of foreign pressure groups have raised grave questions about the usefulness of group theory for research in the field.

This study of the FEN was inspired, it will be remembered, by the call for more empirical data on foreign pressure groups that emerged from the 1957 Round Table of the International Political Science Association and from a meeting, also in 1957, of the Committee on Comparative Politics of the Social Science Research Council. The rapporteur of the latter meeting, Gabriel A. Almond, pointed out that most of our present theories of political action groups are based upon American and to some degree European experience; more data is needed before significant advances can be made toward a general theory of politics.[8] The editor of the report of the former conference, Henry W. Ehrmann, emphasized the need for a conceptual framework to guide research and give it theoretical significance.[9] Samuel J. Eldersveld, in a paper prepared for the same IPSA conference, stated that "we have not yet satisfactorily solved the problem of conceptualization, and we have not met the need to develop proper categories for analysis."[10]

[6] "Pressure Group Theory: Its Methodological Range," American Political Science Review, Vol. LIV (December, 1960), 951–52.

[7] Odegard, "A Group Basis of Politics: A New Name for an Ancient Myth," Western Political Quarterly, Vol. XI (September, 1958), 689–702.

[8] "A Comparative Study of Interest Groups and the Political Process," American Political Science Review, Vol. LII (March, 1958), 270.

[9] Ehrmann (ed.), Pressure Groups on Four Continents, pp. 7–8. He reported some progress at the conference towards agreement on conceptualization. Ibid., p. 290.

[10] "American Interest Groups: A Survey of Research and Some Implications for Theory and Method," ibid., p. 179. This article includes a concise review of the landmarks in American pressure group literature.

It is clear that many researchers believe that group theory as developed by Bentley, Truman, and their followers has not met the requirements of adequate conceptualization. They find it incomplete, not very helpful, or even misleading.

Ehrmann agrees that American studies have helped make foreign political scientists aware of the importance of group activities for a realistic understanding of the political process, but he doubts that group theory yet provides an adequate conceptual framework for the analysis of politics in general.[11] Oliver Garceau has commented that "the search for such a complete theory of the group basis of politics may be stretching too far for theoretical elegance at the sacrifice of immediate convenience as an analytical tool."[12] Eckstein argues that overarching group theory which reduces all politics, from institutions to individuals, to aspects of groups embraces everything in the clutches of its "metaphysics" and illuminates nothing.[13] Similarly, in an incisive article highly critical of group theory Joseph LaPalombara goes so far as to declare that "except at a level of abstraction that renders it both useless and dangerous for empirical research, a general interest group theory does not exist."[14] Roy C. Macridis believes that explanations for differing patterns of political behavior cannot be found in interest group theory; rather "the best way to a theory of comparative politics is at this stage a comprehensive comparative look at the main features of a political system: political culture, social configuration, leadership and governmental institutions."[15]

Both Eckstein and LaPalombara then argue that nevertheless testable generalizations can and should be made about pressure groups and their behavior under given conditions. Eckstein recommends stating group theory "in a starker and less comprehensive form" than that used by the Bentleyites, and using it as "a powerful heuristic tool" for the analysis of certain kinds of policies and political systems.[16] La-Palombara believes political scientists must "examine comparatively some middle-range propositions about interest groups in order to

[11] Ehrmann, *Organized Business in France,* pp. ix–x. Ehrmann cites the critical article by W. J. M. Mackenzie, "Pressure Groups: The 'Conceptual Framework,'" *Political Studies,* Vol. III (October, 1955), 247–55.

[12] "Interest Group Theory in Political Research," *The Annals of the American Academy of Political and Social Science,* Vol. CCCXIX (September, 1958), 106.

[13] Eckstein, *Pressure Group Politics,* pp. 151–53.

[14] "The Utility and Limitations of Interest Group Theory in Non-American Field Situations," *Journal of Politics,* Vol. XXII (February, 1960), 30.

[15] Macridis, "Interest Groups in Comparative Analysis," *Journal of Politics,* Vol. XXIII (February, 1961), 30.

[16] *Pressure Group Politics,* pp. 153–56.

ascertain if the interest group focus has any utility at all for the construction of a general theory of politics."[17]

This tack of developing "middle-range propositions" and testing them against comparative empirical data is most likely to lead to findings of theoretical significance. It is a method explicitly recommended by LaPalombara and productive of felicitous results when applied by him in his article. It is a method which promotes the comparability of findings rightly valued by the participants in the IPSA and SSRC meetings which inspired this study. It is essentially the theoretical framework adopted by Eckstein for his study of the British Medical Association—which is, furthermore, the framework adopted for summarizing the theoretical implications of this study of the FEN.

FORM

The channels and targets of pressure group activity are profoundly influenced by three factors according to Eckstein: the structure of the decision-making process, the activities which result from governmental decisions, and attitudes toward groups and politics. While all three are significant in the case of the FEN, it is the first on which the evidence of this study bears most heavily.

Structure. It is axiomatic that pressure groups seek the centers of power in any political system. Consequently, the distribution of powers among governmental institutions and officials determines in large part the targets chosen and channels of action used by the pressure groups. It is not, however, the formal organization of powers which is determining; it is rather the realistic power structure which counts. In fact, as Eckstein acutely observes, the activities of pressure groups "are themselves one of the more reliable guides to the loci of effective power in any political system."[18] The shift in the loci of power which occurred with the creation of the Fifth Republic and the election of an anti-*laïque* majority in Parliament was clearly reflected in a corresponding shift in the action targets of the FEN.

Under the Fourth Republic the natural prime target of the FEN was the administration. As the employer of the Federation's members, the Ministry of Education had immediate and extensive authority over the professional lives of the teachers. It had considerable policy-making leeway, in part because of the natural devolution of powers from Parliament to bureaucracy necessary in a technically complex society and in part because of the instability and immobility of French govern-

---

[17] "The Utility and Limitations of Interest Group Theory in Non-American Field Situations," *loc. cit.*
[18] *Pressure Group Politics,* p. 16.

ments.[19] Normally relations between the teachers and the Ministry of Education were close and cordial, and the influence of the FEN significant.

However, the evidence of this study bears variously on certain generalizations that have been made about relations between groups and administration. For example, Meynaud has asserted that pressure groups are more active in the newer and more specialized ministries than in the older agencies. Yet, since the Ministry of Education is a traditional agency dating from the Revolution, the good access enjoyed by the teachers supports the skepticism expressed by LaPalombara and Ehrmann on this point. Ehrmann's hypothesis that "vertical" administrations, i.e., those concerned with a single interest, are most subject to influence seems best to fit the facts of this case.[20]

One obvious structural influence on the form of FEN activities is the existence of a multiplicity of consultative councils in the Ministry of Education. These councils have institutionalized the contacts between teachers and administrators and have improved the access of the teachers' unions to the decision makers. But LaPalombara's reminder that a group which shares in the making of governmental policy must also share responsibility for it is a sound one.[21] It is significant that of the four important schemes for educational reform since the war, the FEN has supported those two which it helped formulate.[22] And "administrative pluralism," to use Ehrmann's term for the system of consultative councils, does not mean that the interests have taken over administration.[23] This study shows numerous instances in which decisions made by the administration clearly went against FEN views. Indeed, decisions on the School Laws of 1951 and 1959 resulted in mass resignations of union representatives from the councils, a good publicity technique but ineffective in halting the decision. But for day-to-day questions of administration and for material questions vitally affecting teachers these councils have nevertheless added im-

[19] Ibid.; and Diamant, "The French Administrative System—The Republic Passes but the Administration Remains," in Toward the Comparative Study of Public Administration, ed. William J. Siffin, pp. 208–209.

[20] Cf. Meynaud, Les Groupes de Pression, p. 207; LaPalombara, "The Utility and Limitations of Interest Group Theory in Non-American Field Situations," loc. cit., p. 44; and Ehrmann, "French Bureaucracy and Organized Interests," Administrative Science Quarterly, Vol. V (March, 1961), 538–41. Meynaud's revision (Nouvelles Etudes sur les Groupes de Pression en France, p. 272) substantially agrees with Ehrmann.

[21] "The Utility and Limitations of Interest Group Theory in Non-American Field Situations," loc. cit., p. 46.

[22] See p. 100.

[23] Ehrmann, "French Bureaucracy and Organized Interests," loc. cit., pp. 541–43.

portant channels of communication between government and the teachers.

Eckstein has stated that "pressure groups tend somehow to resemble the organizations they seek to influence,"[24] and the evidence in this case supports him. The existence of departmental sections and national unions in the FEN reflects the administrative structure of the government on both its geographic and functional bases. Reorganization of the Ministry in 1960 and 1961 led to discussions on unification of the SNES and the SNET, whose reasons for separation had disappeared when secondary and technical education were united under a single director. Centralization of government decisions in Paris also has its counterpart in the FEN, a situation markedly similar to that prevailing in Great Britain and in contrast to that of the United States.[25]

Under the Fourth Republic with its system of parliamentary dominance and multiple parties FEN contacts with Parliament and the parties were second in significance only to its contacts with the administration. The structure of the party system and of Parliament influenced the channels and tactics of the FEN. Like most pressure groups the FEN abstained from permanent ties with any single political party and sought support for its objectives from all parties. In cooperation with like-minded organizations it sought "pledges" of support from candidates of all parties at election time; between elections it sent communications to sympathetic parties when the occasion demanded. However, the number and ideology of French parties meant that the FEN was naturally closer to some than to others. It would be impossible to overlook the close affinity between the FEN and the Socialist party and, to a lesser degree, the Communist party. On an appreciable number of questions, particularly those involving laïcité, the FEN enjoys cooperation from many Radical Socialists as well. While the strong cégétiste minority is markedly sympathetic to the Communist party, FEN leaders remain suspicious of Communist tactics and only cooperate with the party on limited programs of action while carefully guarding their independence. They are especially sensitive to charges of political "infeudation" and frequently feel it necessary to refute them.[26]

[24] Pressure Group Politics, p. 21.
[25] Ibid., p. 16.
[26] For example, cf. Le Populaire de Paris, July 21, 1953. An orator in the Assembly decried the excessive laïcité of the teachers and impugned their political neutrality when he said: "L'école qui s'affirme trop laïque est devenue une école partisane, une école de parti pris, parfois même une école de parti." J.O., Assemblée Nationale, December 23, 1959, p. 3618.

Under the Fourth Republic FEN influence on Parliament was focused on the Education Committee of the Assembly. Contacts with individual deputies and leaders of sympathetic parliamentary groups were not ignored, but it was natural for the Federation to cultivate relations with those bodies which specialized in the problems of education and where there was a high concentration of deputies friendly to the FEN, particularly former teachers. The Communist and Socialist members of the Education Committee could normally be counted on to defend the interests of the unionized teachers. Occasionally, members of the Committee from all parties rallied in unanimous support of the teachers, as in the 1954 budget debate. But the favorable report which the Committee made in 1951 on the Barangé Law showed that the FEN's influence could be effectively nullified by a hostile parliamentary majority. Hostility between the Communist and Socialist parties also undermined the influence of the FEN in Parliament; it proved impossible, for example, to create a parliamentary intergroup to defend *laïcité* in 1951 and 1959.

Public opinion was also an important target of FEN action under the Fourth Republic, particularly when the Federation was thwarted by the administration or Parliament. Press conferences, petitions, demonstrations, and communiqués were especially numerous in 1951 when FEN leaders realized that the *laïque* forces did not have enough votes in Parliament to block state aid to private schools. To put pressure on the administration and Parliament and to publicize their plight at the same time, the teachers' unions resorted to work stoppages in various forms: examination strikes, extended recesses, and one-day strikes. Lengthy strikes were normally avoided, not only because they were likely to incite stern counter-measures by the administration, always possible in view of the ambiguity surrounding the teachers' right to strike, but also because the sympathy of parents could be quickly eroded. Furthermore, teachers opposed excessive losses of class time. The threat of a strike was a fully exploited weapon for the same reasons.

In order to achieve the greatest penetration and breadth in campaigns aimed at public opinion, the FEN sought alliances with like-minded organizations such as the Parents' Federation and the militantly anticlerical Ligue Française de l'Enseignement. Close cooperation with these organizations was assured in part by the important if not dominant role that teachers play in them. Parties were also sought as allies, although the FEN remained wary of close organizational ties, particularly with the Communist party.

In short, under the Fourth Republic the FEN had excellent access to the decision-makers of the administration, good relations with the parties of the left, effective spokesmen in the Education Committees of Parliament, and a repertoire of tactics for influencing public opinion. Putting aside for the moment the question of how effective these action techniques were, one can conclude that certain fairly consistent patterns of action had developed. However, it appears that the creation of the Fifth Republic shifted these patterns, dramatically illustrating Eckstein's hypothesis of the close relationship between political structure and the form of pressure-group activities.

At Bayeux in 1946 and elsewhere General de Gaulle had made clear his preference for strong presidential rule; the events of 1958 gave him the opportunity to create a new government to his taste.[27] The principal author of the Constitution of the Fifth Republic and de Gaulle's first Prime Minister under it was M. Michel Debré whose published views on governmental authority corresponded to the General's. His 1957 book showed his concern over the extent to which unions and groups had penetrated the recesses of governmental power. He specifically cited the FEN, "a very powerful union in the heart of the educational system," and condemned its support for negotiating with the Algerian rebels. He continued:

> Such action on the part of the Federation is completely alien to its union mission. It is [also] illegal, for the charter of an organization of this type, as defined by the laws of the Republic, limits its action to professional matters. The Federation of National Education, nevertheless, abandons its role and violates the law in order to discourse on responsibilities which belong neither to it nor to its members. It can do so with impunity because there is no authority, not even to demand respect for the law. The princes of the Federation risk nothing; the princes in power are their friends or accomplices. The system which nourishes them both cannot be separated: the power of the former is based on the weakness of the latter, and vice versa.[28]

After his appointment as Prime Minister, M. Debré applied his policy of restoring executive authority. He explained in a speech to the National Assembly that some ministries had responded to cabinet weakness and instability by becoming nearly autonomous defenders of certain government functions and functionaries. "The Republic owes

    27 Roy C. Macridis and Bernard E. Brown, *The De Gaulle Republic: Quest for Unity* (Homewood, Illinois: Dorsey, 1960), pp. 148–52.
    28 Michel Debré, *Ces Princes Qui Nous Gouvernent* (Paris: Plon, 1957), pp. 108–109.

it to the nation to remount the slope and to reestablish the authority of the government over all administrations."[29]

The FEN vigorously opposed the new Constitution. The Federation was motivated not only by loyalty to the Fourth Republic and its liberties, but apparently also by fear of losing its ready access to authority. Some of the Federation's fears have been justified. M. Lauré has complained of the government's irregularity in convening the High Council of National Education, its tardy consultation of employee representatives after the decisions have already been made, and its habit of consulting union leaders as "personalities" rather than as mandated union officials.[30] At a meeting of the FEN Administrative Commission soon after the inception of the Fifth Republic, a member advocated new action techniques because "the parliamentary methods of the Fourth Republic are no longer valid."[31] M. Lauré stated in 1960 that the FEN maintained relations with Parliament largely out of habit, as Parliament has no power under the Fifth Republic.[32]

It is true that under the Fifth Republic the FEN is faced with an executive willing and able to resist its demands. The FEN retains the sympathy and good will of the high officials of the Ministry of Education, but the Prime Minister and cabinet are now constitutionally less susceptible to FEN pressures. Under the Fourth Republic FEN leaders managed to obtain interviews with the Prime Minister from time to time. The effectiveness of these contacts varied with the political situation of the moment, but their potential is illustrated by the promise of one Prime Minister to stake the life of his government on a measure favored by the teachers by making it a question of confidence.[33] Under the Fifth Republic the Prime Minister has felt secure enough not only to resist teacher demands but even to admonish them haughtily to hold their peace.[34] The cabinet can now put up a solid wall against group pressure since the Prime Minister can impose his will on a recalcitrant Minister, as the resignation of Minister of Education Boulloche in 1959 illustrated.

The net result of the increased resistance of the government to pressures has been a shift in FEN tactics to place more emphasis on influencing public opinion and on direct action techniques. The FEN has continued to utilize the full range of tactics for influencing public opinion developed under the Fourth Republic and has sought further

[29] *J.O., Assemblée Nationale*, December 24, 1959, p. 3596.
[30] *E.P.*, 15e année, No. 3 (December, 1959), p. 11.
[31] *E.P.*, 14e année, No. 5 (April, 1959), p. 12.
[32] Interview, May 11, 1960.
[33] Cf. p. 88.
[34] Cf. p. 149.

to intensify them. The vast petition campaign of 1960, the local, departmental, and national rallies of 1961–62 against the Debré Law, and the attempts to remold the parents' organizations all reveal the importance attached to reaching and mobilizing public opinion. Ingenious variations of the direct action techniques of the strike and strike threat have been utilized to arouse the public and apply direct pressure on the government where more restrained measures no longer work. The one-day strikes of 1960, the rotating strikes of the first three months of 1961, and particularly the broad scope of the accompanying administrative strike (when teachers refused to report grades, submit examination questions, transmit records, or accept paid overtime work) met with noteworthy success even against a government determined to resist. A comparison of the 1954 and 1961 salary struggles shows that strikes were important in both but much more so in 1961 when Parliament's role was insignificant.

These observations and the testimony of government and union leaders together provide support for the view that a strengthened executive has altered the pattern of pressure group politics. It has not, however, lessened pressure group activity; nor has it prevented pressure groups from achieving some of their goals. Bernard E. Brown has reached the same conclusion: "Political structure may well determine *how* groups press their claims and *which* groups are to be favored. But there is no simple equation between centralization of political power and subordination of pressure groups to that power."[35]

One further qualification needs to be recognized. The creation of the Fifth Republic coincided with the election of a parliamentary majority unsympathetic to many FEN aims. It is therefore impossible to tell which changes in FEN tactics were due to alterations in the constitutional structure of government alone and which were due to the new constellation of political forces. It is likely that the return of a *laïque* majority in Parliament would lead to increased FEN activity there; the degree of that activity would tell much about the importance of constitutional arrangements for the form of pressure group action.[36]

Activities. The decisions which emerge from the political structure

[35] "Pressure Politics in the Fifth Republic," *Journal of Politics,* Vol. XXV (August, 1963), 525. Roland Pennock argues similarly that the sharp differences in the political structures of America and Britain do not make the former any more susceptible than the latter to group pressures, at least as far as agricultural subsidies are concerned. J. Roland Pennock, " 'Responsible Government,' Separated Powers, and Special Interests: Agricultural Subsidies in Britain and America," *American Political Science Review,* Vol. LVI (September, 1962), 631.

[36] Meynaud reviews the impact of the Fifth Republic on pressure group activity in "Les Groupes de Pression sous la Vᵉ République," *Revue Française de Science Politique,* Vol. XII (September, 1962), 672–97.

also affect the channels of pressure group action. Obviously, some decisions affect structure and through it group action, such as legislative decisions to grant broad discretionary power to administrators or to create advisory councils for the direct representation of interest groups; other decisions directly affect the form of group activity. The type of decision sharply influences the targets and methods of action chosen by the reacting groups. For example, technical decisions affecting small groups of teachers through the alteration of recruitment, promotion, and transfer standards or procedures are likely to result in relatively quiet contacts between FEN leaders and the administration. In fact, it is usually through such quiet contacts that the FEN seeks benefits for the very small national union. However, these direct contacts with administrators would be quite useless for promoting broad policy positions, such as ending tests of atomic weapons, negotiation with the Algerian rebels, or general disarmament. For questions of this type it is quite natural for the FEN to resort to tactics designed to influence Parliament and public opinion, such as manifestoes, demonstrations, and political strikes. Questions of educational policy are both technical questions and matters of public policy; the Federation therefore communicates its views to Ministry officials and experts charged with preparing educational reform measures and encourages support for them through appeals to Parliament and public opinion.

Attitudes. The views of the public, of group leaders, and of government officials all affect the form of pressure group action. As expected in a nation with a highly fragmented political culture, attitudes towards pressure group activities are mixed. On the one hand, complaints about them are heard from many political sectors;[37] their very name has a negative connotation, as in the United States.[38] Largely absent in France is the lingering bias against individualism and the undercurrent of corporatist sentiment left over from the pre-liberal era which in England sanctions open and frank group activities;[39] in fact, the French tradition of Rousseau opposed intermediary bodies between the citizen and the state.[40] On the other hand, the picture is not all one-sided. For centuries groups in France have struggled to promote

[37] Henry W. Ehrmann, "Pressure Groups in France," *The Annals of the American Academy of Political and Social Science*, Vol. CCCXIX (September, 1958), 148.

[38] The author learned not to use the term in interviews in order to avoid lengthy denials that the teachers could be classified with the *bouilleurs de cru*.

[39] Eckstein, *Pressure Group Politics*, p. 24.

[40] George E. Lavau, "Political Pressures by Interest Groups in France," *Pressure Groups on Four Continents*, ed. Henry W. Ehrmann (Pittsburgh: University of Pittsburgh Press, 1958), p. 60.

their interests, regardless of the doctrines of Rousseau. Furthermore, groups whose activity is praiseworthy are not regarded by the public as pressure groups—although they of course are from the analytic point of view.[41] In addition, there is general acceptance of the system of consultative councils in the administration and considerable support for the idea that affected groups should be consulted before measures are enacted. When the government fails to consult the FEN, its leaders issue loud public protests in the belief their complaints will find resonance in the values of the people.

The consequence of this mixture of attitudes is that the channels of action available to each group vary. Approved groups, such as the teachers, may operate openly while big business must be more discreet.[42] Furthermore, the choice of action technique is clearly affected by public attitudes. A teachers' strike, widely disapproved and even illegal in many American states, may be used not only for material demands but even for demonstrating support for political policy goals, such as a cease-fire in Algeria. Limitations on the duration of strikes and resort to examination and administrative strikes which do not lose class time, however, show respect for the limits imposed by public attitudes on the use of this weapon.

The attitudes of the union leaders and of officials of the Ministry of Education encourage and facilitate regular contacts between them. It is no novelty to point out that the closeness and cordiality of their relations may be attributed partly to their common social and educational background. Former teachers themselves, usually graduates of the same highly respected Normal Schools, the high-level civil servants are deeply sympathetic to teacher needs. Often administrators and even the Minister himself have become spokesmen for their teacher "clientele," particularly in negotiations with the Ministry of Finance.

However, LaPalombara insists (and the varying fortunes of FEN proposals to the Ministry revealed by this study support him) that common attitudes do not make French administrators "prey to the demands of special interests."[43] Rather, the ethic of the administrator, his sense of loyalty to the demands of his office, his identification with the public interest, all of these "patterns of values and beliefs," to use the phraseology of Rothman,[44] prevent him from becoming merely a barometer registering the result of political pressures of varying

[41] *Ibid.*, pp. 61, 279–80.
[42] *Ibid.*, p. 77.
[43] "The Utility and Limitations of Interest Group Theory in Non-American Field Situations," *loc. cit.*, p. 47.
[44] Rothman, "Systematic Political Theory: Observations on the Group Approach," *loc. cit.*, p. 31.

directions and intensities.[45] Of course, a Ministry of Education official can easily identify support of the teachers with defense of the public interest so that there is no necessary conflict between duty to his office and sympathy for the teachers.

Structure, activities, and attitudes affect, then, the channels of group action; they also affect the nature of the relations between groups and government.[46] In the case of the FEN these relations have occasionally taken on the character of negotiations, where governmental action depends upon the consent of the group; they also have been in the form of consultations, where the government merely listens to the group before making a decision. Under the Fifth Republic negotiations appear to be limited to material questions; on questions of educational policy the unions may be consulted, but union leaders have complained that the government has increasingly failed even to consult them.

In Britain structure, activities, and attitudes together have tended to move relations toward the negotiations end of the range of possible relations; in France there are conflicting tendencies: structure and policies encourage negotiations, but attitudes engender a countermovement. FEN structure includes most teachers and empowers leaders to negotiate; likewise the present concentration of power in the executive branch of government puts it in a good position to negotiate. Policies of mass education for a modern society of course require the technical skills and full-hearted cooperation of the teachers; their indispensability places them in a good bargaining position. But public attitudes of hostility to pressure groups, even if not always applied to teachers, and a generalized suspicion of the state and its bureaucrats work against this tendency to negotiate. In addition, the determination of the leaders of the Fifth Republic to maintain governmental authority in the face of pressure group demands has strengthened this countertendency.[47] Consequently, the FEN has increasingly resorted to tactics outside the range of negotiation and consultation; there has been a greater emphasis on public protests, demonstrations, mass petitions, and variations of the strike, marking a change in the character of the FEN and its outside relations since the advent of the Fifth Republic.

[45] Cf. LaPalombara, "The Utility and Limitations of Interest Group Theory in Non-American Field Situations," *loc. cit.*, p. 48. Ehrmann adds that it is the younger administrators who are the most adamant in defending the public interest. Ehrmann, "French Bureaucracy and Organized Interests," *loc. cit.*, p. 552.

[46] Cf. Eckstein, *Pressure Group Politics*, pp. 22–25.

[47] President de Gaulle refused to summon Parliament in 1960, apparently contrary to constitutional provisions, partly because the demand had been initiated by agricultural pressure groups. Brown, "Pressure Politics in the Fifth Republic," *loc. cit.*, p. 511.

SCOPE AND INTENSITY

Governmental policy is the most important determinant of the scope and intensity of pressure group activity in a democracy; the history of the FEN bears witness to the validity of this generalization. Nevertheless, attitudes and structure are influential factors not to be overlooked.[48]

Policy. Often it is a government policy which transforms a private association uninterested in politics into a pressure group bent on protecting its interests threatened by the government's course of action; in the case of the French teachers it was governmental policy which created the group in the first place. The decision of the Third Republic to establish free and compulsory education necessitated a large teaching force. Since the teachers were employed by the government, they could not avoid being drawn into politics in the broad sense of the word; sooner or later they were bound to try to influence the decisions of government administrators, if only on questions of salary and conditions of work.

But the role of the teachers as intellectual leaders, particularly in the small towns, and their natural interest in educational and public policy questions quickly drew them into politics in the narrow sense. The primary school teacher was frequently the clerk of the commune and in the early days was often regarded by the local deputy as his electoral agent. But, more important for national politics, the teachers soon called upon their unions to represent them on matters that required legislative and executive action. They demanded expansion of the educational system to accommodate increasing numbers of pupils; they demanded modernization of schools and curriculums in order to provide adequately for the needs of an industrial society; and they demanded democratization to open up and expand the avenues of advancement to all social classes. Not limiting themselves to educational questions, and guided by ideologies of syndicalism and *laïcité* and attitudes of liberalism and socialism, the teachers' unions used the leverage of their weight and numbers to influence governments on questions of public policy. Governmental policy had created a potential interest group by establishing a national system of education. Given the conditions of free association and democratic government prevailing in France, the orientation and aims of the teachers virtually determined that their efforts would flow into the well-known channels of pressure group activity.

Attitudes. The effect of attitudes on the scope and intensity of group

[48] Eckstein, *Pressure Group Politics*, pp. 25–33.

activity is partly indirect in that they influence government policy and structure which in turn affect scope and intensity. For example, political attitudes may require the extension of government controls over business; these controls generate defensive organizations of businessmen, thus bringing more groups into the political arena. But attitudes also have a direct impact on scope and intensity.

Of prime importance historically was the fact that teachers in the early days identified with the working class and the union movement. It is well known that professional persons often are opposed not only to political action for their groups but even to organization of the very groups themselves; in France the small percentage of university professors belonging to the FEN reflects the persistence of this attitude.[49] But the economic condition of the elementary teachers and their ready intellectual acceptance of syndicalist and socialist ideas, as well as the social temper of the early twentieth century, favored the idea of organized solidarity with the working class. Ever broader federations of categories of teachers and workers developed until the period of the Popular Front and the spirit of the Resistance finally led to the realization of unity and solidarity. Political developments made it necessary in 1948 to sacrifice solidarity with the working class to protect the unity of the FEN, but the sentiment and goal remain.

The syndicalist ideology left a legacy of distrust of the state and politicians; the FEN still forbids its officers to hold public office. But changes in attitudes both on the part of the public and of union members have come to legitimize much pressure group action. Trade unions have become more acceptable in France as they have gradually put aside as operational goals revolution and the perfection of society on new foundations. With the decline of their syndicalist ideology to verbal irrelevancies, members of the FEN and other trade unions have come to accept political action and cooperation with the political parties which they no longer hope to supplant.[50]

The intensity of FEN activities is enhanced, as it has been for other groups, by a loss of faith in the impartiality of the state.[51] Pressure actions are deemed necessary to draw attention to the unfavorable position of the teachers compared to workers in the nationalized industries, to the civil service as a whole, or to some other category. Such attitudes reflect a loss of consensus on the moral and constitutional legitimacy of the state, a situation conducive to intense politicization of

[49] The history of British physicians is another case in point. *Ibid.*, pp. 28–29.

[50] Cf. Lavau, "Political Pressures by Interest Groups in France," in *Pressure Groups on Four Continents*, p. 66.

[51] *Ibid.*, p. 90.

groups according to Eckstein.[52] But the FEN does not become fully politicized and try to seize the government or withdraw as Eckstein hypothesizes. Remnants of syndicalist distrust of political action, the resistance of some categories of members, and particularly the divisions into the three major ideological tendencies that cohabit the Federation work against full politicization.

Structure. Governmental structure played a role in the political mobilization of the teachers. The centralization of decision making encouraged teachers to organize in order to resist what they considered to be distant and arbitrary authority. Consultative councils in the administration gave the teachers' unions access which promoted their expansion. The multiparty system and dominance of the legislative branch under the Third and Fourth Republics made possible effective contacts which attracted more members. Likelihood of success, in short, encouraged pressure group mobilization. The structural changes of the Fifth Republic have not led to demobilization but to a shift in tactics without noticeable reduction in scope or intensity.

EFFECTIVENESS

The crucial question of the political effectiveness of a pressure group depends upon many factors, all difficult to measure and some difficult to evaluate. These factors include attributes of the organization itself, attributes of governmental activities, and attributes of governmental structure.[53]

Attributes of the FEN. The size and physical resources of the FEN furnish its leaders a firm base from which to operate. Almost one-third of the total number of civilian government employees work in the Ministry of Education, and most of them belong to the Federation (281,000 members in 1961). Over 85 per cent of the elementary and secondary teachers belong to the Federation through their national unions, the SNI and the SNES. Union leaders make up most of the elected membership of the various consultative councils in the administration. With minor exceptions the FEN justifiably may claim to speak for the teaching profession.

The size of the organization is more impressive than its physical resources. As it depends upon dues collected by the national unions, its financial resources cannot compare with those of affluent business organizations.[54] Publication of the FEN bulletin, *L'Enseignement*

52 *Pressure Group Politics,* pp. 32–33.
53 *Ibid.,* pp. 33–38.
54 In 1958–59 its receipts totaled 39,390,000 old francs or roughly $79,000, 98 per cent of which came from dues. *E.P.,* 15e année, No. 1 (October, 1959), p. 9.

Public, consumes nearly half of the Federation's budgeted expenditures. FEN offices in Paris are modest. Offsetting factors exist, however. Member unions have budgets of their own which, often generously drawn as in the case of the massive SNI, may be utilized to further common action. It must be remembered, too, that in many campaigns the skilled leaders of the Federation are able to call upon sympathetic sister organizations with their additional resources, such as the labor confederations, parents' groups, and *laïque* organizations. In addition, a potent factor adding weight to the claims of the Federation is the high prestige accorded teachers in France. In a country whose traditional national ethic disdains material goods and worships intellectual values, teachers find a more receptive audience than big business or the *bouilleurs de cru.*

But whatever the size or physical resources of the organization, effective action must be predicated upon a high degree of cohesion. As groups expand with ever-growing membership rolls, thereby taking on the appearance of massive power, their internal tensions multiply. Heterogeneity of membership forces compromises on aims and methods and constitutes an internal limitation on effectiveness. It is certain, for example, that disagreements between the SNI and the SNES on summer vacation dates and the cycle of orientation weakened the Federation's position.[55] But by and large a high degree of cohesion has been maintained. The strike orders of early 1961, for example, were well observed as 90 per cent of the elementary and secondary teachers walked out.

Organizational ingenuity and skilled leadership have been utilized to overcome the disintegrative tendencies of so large a body. A federal structure reserves considerable autonomy to the member unions, allowing them to pursue their particular aims without hindrance, and, at the same time, permits the massing of members behind efforts of common concern. Formulas for representation are wisely designed to accommodate both large and small unions and reduce centrifugal tendencies. Careful adherence to democratic forms and the fair representation of minorities gives blocs of dissenting members who might otherwise be driven to schism a sense of belonging and participation, while the rule of ideological homogeneity for the bureau insures that effective action will not be thwarted by cross purposes in that executive body. Leaders

[55] Ehrmann comments that "sometimes the large confederation representing composite and diffuse interests is condemned to *immobilisme* in its own ranks and therefore proves a handicap against any measure involving a departure from the status quo." He adds that administrators may ignore the interests altogether where they are divided. Ehrmann, "French Bureaucracy and Organized Interests," *loc. cit.*, p. 547.

constantly emphasize the necessity of cohesion, cite the overarching common goals that all members share, exercise restraint in pushing for goals of their own national unions, and in general utilize full measures of tact and diplomacy to maintain unity.

A significant peculiarity of the problem of cohesion in the FEN is the existence of three ideological tendencies whose marked differences reflect in dramatic fashion France's fragmented political culture.[56] Revolutionary syndicalists, Communists and *cégétistes,* and the reformist majority coexist in a single Federation as factions; actually they may be likened to political parties with slates of candidates, programs, organizations, and proportional representation in the union councils. Confrontation of these diverse views at committee meetings and congresses, sharp criticism of leaders by the minority factions, and dissemination of dissenting views in the Federation's bulletin are all practices which differ sharply from those of most American unions.[57] Indeed, while calling attention to the internal stresses and strains of the Federation, these opportunities for criticism of the leaders and expression of minority views release tensions and help preserve unity. Of course, agreement on broad issues, such as *laïcité,* also helps to explain the organization's cohesion. In other words, consensus on certain limited fundamentals permits the coexistence of factions with diverse views in the same organization; the parallel with contemporary political theory needs no underlining.

Another attribute of the FEN determining effectiveness is of course the nature of its objectives. On this point the picture is clear: the farther the FEN goes afield from educational questions, the less effective it is.

The success of the FEN in winning material concessions from the government has provoked envy among other civil service unions.[58] It is beyond dispute that the Federation is singularly effective in bargaining for salary increases and fringe benefits for the teachers.[59] The successes

[56] Normally in France a left-wing trade unionist joins a left-wing veterans' group, etc. René Rémond, "Les Anciens Combattants et la Politique," *Revue Française de Science Politique,* Vol. V (April-June, 1944), 267–90, cited by Rothman, "Systematic Political Theory: Observations on the Group Approach," *loc. cit.,* p. 22.

[57] Oliver Garceau recently reviewed nine volumes on trade union government, an area of private government largely neglected by political scientists. See the *American Political Science Review,* Vol. LVII (December, 1963), 982–85.

[58] See excerpts from their bulletins in *E.P.,* 13e année, No. 6 (May, 1958), p. 7.

[59] A recent and reasonably successful attempt to relate the power of civil service unions to salary levels further substantiates this view. Tiano compared the disparities in salary of civil servants having identical coefficients but employed by different ministries with disparities in the power of unions representing those workers as estimated by various union leaders he interviewed. He discovered a

of 1961 in wringing important salary concessions from a reluctant government provide impressive recent evidence on this point, especially when it is noted that professors in higher education, only a few of whom belong to the FEN, received almost nothing.

However, the organization is less effective on questions of educational policy. It is true that the path of educational reform was partly shaped by FEN desires, but its influence would have been much greater if disagreements between the elementary and secondary teachers on the cycle of orientation had not prevented a united front. The FEN was absolutely unable to prevent passage of the School Laws of 1951 and 1959.

Although the FEN has won widespread recognition as the voice of the public school teachers on questions of public policy, its efforts to influence the resolution of such questions have been more often frustrated than rewarded. The Rosenbergs were executed, the Germans were rearmed, French atomic tests were continued, Red China was kept out of the United Nations, and the Fifth Republic was established, all contrary to the wishes of the FEN. In short, it appears that effectiveness decreases as operating goals stray farther from the essential purposes of the organization, those for which most members join.[60]

Attributes of governmental activities. How effective a group will be in translating its objectives into policy will depend in part on what policies the government is intent on pursuing. The success of the FEN

---

fairly close relationship. For example, at the coefficient of 185 (primary school teachers, public works technicians, administrative secretaries, etc.) the SNI was rated as the most powerful union, and the teachers' salaries were only exceeded by those of the administrative secretaries. Tiano suggested that this slight variation from the pattern might be because of the much greater total cost of an increase for the numerous teachers than the cost of an identical increase for the secretaries. Tiano, *Les Traitements des Fonctionnaires*, pp. 435–36, 533–34.

[60] In an interview on May 11, 1960, Secretary General Georges Lauré listed what he considered to be the four major accomplishments of the FEN since World War II: avoidance of schism in 1948; the Reclassification of 1948; the development of the Mutuelle Générale de l'Education Nationale; and unified opposition to the manner in which the Fifth Republic was born. The first of these, the FEN's success in maintaining its unity, was a precondition to its other successes. It is everywhere recognized as a large, significant, and powerful union. The Reclassification of 1948 was indeed a major union triumph; although its norms have not always been observed in determining salaries, it set a standard for teacher remuneration quite favorable compared to standards in other administrations. The Mutuelle Générale provides social services and insurance advantages to FEN members and their families; it has not been involved in FEN struggles with the government. M. Lauré considered the stand which the FEN took on the Fifth Republic to be a union accomplishment, a "victory over ourselves." It was a courageous and unpopular stand, but it really cannot be considered as an indication of the Federation's political effectiveness for it did not perceptibly alter the course of events.

in winning salary increases has been significant in view of the government's perennial efforts to hold down expenditures. On the question of educational reform the government was usually favorably predisposed but financially unable to undertake the thoroughgoing and expensive overhaul favored by the FEN. Nevertheless, population pressure has forced great increases in the education budget, thus improving the climate for teacher demands. In fact, the increasing size of the educational establishment has meant a burgeoning FEN membership and consequently an augmentation in its potential effectiveness.

Two major political defeats in a decade—passage of the School Laws of 1951 and 1959—have not harmed the Federation's cohesion but on the contrary seem to have enhanced it. Teachers of all categories and tendencies have drawn together to defend the principles of laïcité against what they consider violations by the government.

The irony of all this is that the Fifth Republic, known to be hostile to pressure groups, has pursued policies which have tended to strengthen the teachers' organization.

Attributes of governmental structure. It appears that the structure of government and its political composition largely decide whether a group succeeds or fails. A highly united FEN mobilized all its resources to oppose the School Laws of 1951 and 1959, but it was overwhelmed by superior and better-placed political forces.[61] Assuming that the issue is a major one, that it has been well publicized, and that it requires legislative action, it seems clear that even a militant, united, and powerful pressure group cannot block action in Parliament when the opposition has the votes.[62] Although there are grounds for questioning the representativeness of the two Parliaments responsible, it is nevertheless true that the nation's legally invested lawmakers decided as they did despite FEN pressures.

It has often been maintained that dispersal of power, such as in the American government or the Fourth Republic, favors groups defending the status quo while concentration of power favors innovators who have access.[63] The 1959 law fits the generalization. Concentration of legislative leadership in the executive of the Fifth Republic meant large concessions to the well-placed church school forces and significant alterations in the pattern of state aid to private schools. Passage of the

61 M. Lauré rightly considered these laws to be the major failures of the FEN since World War II. Interview, May 11, 1960.

62 In the words of an American lobbyist: "Ninety per cent of what goes on here during a session is decided on the previous election day." Donald R. Matthews, *U.S. Senators and Their World* (Caravelle ed.; New York: Random, 1960), p. 193.

63 Cf. Eckstein, *Pressure Group Politics*, p. 37.

1951 law under the Fourth Republic supports the generalization only in that the concessions to the church school forces were rather limited; nevertheless, the provision of even a limited amount of state aid was a break with the status quo, and to that extent the 1951 law was an exception to the generalization.

In relations with administrators on material questions and on many matters of educational policy the teachers' unions have access, sympathy, and often success. It is true that the administrators are not defenseless. Many develop skills to manipulate groups.[64] Unlike many agencies in France which must rely upon interest groups for data and documentation, the Ministry of Education has excellent research services.[65] Nevertheless, the effectiveness of FEN contacts with the administration appear to be greater than with the more political branches of the government. Their success in salary negotiations is widely recognized, and on the day-to-day questions of administration their effect is certain.

In conclusion, whatever final assessment may be made of the effectiveness of the FEN in accomplishing its goals, its very existence makes a significant contribution to French democracy. It speaks for French teachers, and it speaks with a moderate, reformist, and democratic voice. It promotes educational expansion and modernization, a vital ingredient for effective democracy. It practices internal democracy, demonstrating that trade union organization need not be authoritarian. It brings together persons of different ideological camps and professional levels, helping in a limited way to close the fissures of a fragmented political culture. It aggregates demands through internal compromise, easing the burden of government and promoting the stability of democracy. Whatever reservations may be justified with respect to certain policy decisions or techniques of action, promotion of the interests of the FEN has generally meant promotion of the interests of French democracy.

[64] LaPalombara, "The Utility and Limitations of Interest Group Theory in Non-American Field Situations," *loc. cit.*, p. 48. How U.S. Senators influence lobbyists is described by Matthews, *U.S. Senators and Their World*, pp. 188–90.

[65] Cf. Ehrmann, "French Bureaucracy and Organized Interests," *loc. cit.*, pp. 545–46.

Selected Bibliography

PUBLIC DOCUMENTS

France. *Journal Officiel.* All divisions.

France. Commissariat Général du Plan d'Equipement et de la Productivité. IVe *Plan de Développement Economique et Social 1962–65, Rapport Général de la Commission de l'Equipement Scolaire, Universitaire et Sportif.* Paris, 1961.

France. French Cultural Services. *The French System of Education.* Special issue of the quarterly *Education in France.* New York: French Embassy [1960].

France. Ministère de l'Education Nationale, de la Jeunesse et des Sports. Bulletin Officiel. Institut Pédagogique National. *Fascicules de Documentation Administrative.* Brochure Nos. 85 (1958), 97–99 (1959).

France. Ministère de l'Education Nationale, de la Jeunesse et des Sports. Bureau Universitaire de Statistique et de Documentation Scolaires et Professionnelles. *Avenirs.* No. 103–104 (May-June, 1959).

France. Ministère de l'Education Nationale, de la Jeunesse et des Sports. *L'Education Nationale.* Weekly bulletin.

France. Ministère de l'Education Nationale, de la Jeunesse et des Sports. Institut Pédagogique National. *L'Enseignement Française à l'Etranger.* Mémoires et Documents Scolaires, No. 11. Société d'Editions et de Vente des Publications de l'Education Nationale, 1959.

France. Ministère de l'Education Nationale, de la Jeunesse et des Sports. Institut Pédagogique National. *L'Organisation de l'Enseignement en France.* La Documentation Française, 1957.

France. [Ministère de l'Education Nationale, de la Jeunesse et des Sports]. *Le Problème Scolaire.* Société d'Editions et de Vente des Publications de l'Education Nationale, 1959.

France. *Répertoire Permanent de l'Administration Française.* Paris: La Documentation Française, 1957–60.

United Nations. Educational, Scientific, and Cultural Organization. International Bureau of Education. *Primary Teachers' Salaries.* Publication No. 147. Geneva, 1953.

United Nations. Educational, Scientific, and Cultural Organization. International Bureau of Education. *Secondary Teachers' Salaries,* Publication No. 157. Geneva, 1954.

United Nations. Educational, Scientific, and Cultural Organization. *An International Directory of Education Associations.* Educational Studies and Documents No. 34 (ED/59/XII/34.A) [Paris, 1959].

BOOKS

Almond, Gabriel A., and James S. Coleman (eds.). *The Politics of the Developing Areas.* Princeton: Princeton University Press, 1960.

Bardonnet, Daniel. *Evolution de la Structure du Parti Radical.* Paris: Monchrestien, 1960.

Bédé, Jean-Albert. *Le Problème de l'Ecole Unique en France.* ("Etudes Françaises," 24e cahier) Paris: Belles Lettres, 1931.

Bentley, Arthur F. *The Process of Government.* Chicago: University of Chicago Press, 1908.

Bernard, F., L. Bouet, M. Dommanget, and G. Serrat. *Le Syndicalisme dans l'Enseignement: Histoire de la Fédération de l'Enseignement et du Syndicalisme Universitaire.* Vol. I. Avignon: Edition de "L'Ecole Emancipée" [1924].

Bouet, Louis. *Les Pionniers du Syndicalisme Universitaire.* Bédarrides, Vaucluse: Edition de "L'Ecole Emancipée," n. d.

Cros, Louis. *"L'Explosion" Scolaire.* 2d ed. Paris: Société d'Editions et de Vente des Publications de l'Education Nationale, 1962.

Debré, Michel. *Ces Princes Qui Nous Gouvernent.* Paris: Plon, 1957.

Dolléans, Edouard. *Histoire du Mouvement Ouvrier.* 3 vols. 3d ed. Paris: Colin, 1947–53.

Duveau, Georges. *Les Instituteurs.* [Paris]: Editions du Seuil [1957].

Duverger, Maurice (ed.). *Partis Politiques et Classes Sociales en France.* ("Association Française de Science Politique: Cahiers de la Fondation Nationale des Sciences Politiques," No. 74) Paris: Colin, 1955.

Duverger, Maurice, François Goguel, and Jean Touchard (eds.). *Les Elections du 2 Janvier 1956.* ("Association Française de Science Politique: Cahiers de la Fondation Nationale des Sciences Politiques," No. 82) Paris: Colin, 1957.

Eckstein, Harry. *Pressure Group Politics: The Case of the British Medical Association.* Stanford: Stanford University Press, 1960.

Ehrmann, Henry W. *Pressure Groups on Four Continents.* Pittsburgh: University of Pittsburgh Press, 1958.

———. *Organized Business in France.* Princeton: Princeton University Press, 1957.

Faguet, Emile. *Problèmes Politiques du Temps Présent.* Paris: Colin, 1907.

Fauvet, Jacques. *La France Déchirée.* Paris: Fayard, 1957.

Ferré, André. *L'Instituteur.* Paris: La Table Ronde, 1954.

Ferré, Max. *Histoire du Mouvement Syndicaliste Révolutionnaire Chez les Instituteurs: Des Origines à 1922.* Paris: Société Universitaire d'Editions et de Librairie, 1955.

Grégoire, Roger. *La Fonction Publique.* Paris: Colin, 1954.

Hayes, Carlton J. H. *France: A Nation of Patriots.* New York: Columbia University Press, 1930.

Hébert, M., and A. Carnec. *La Loi Falloux et la Liberté de l'Enseignement.* La Rochelle, France: Rupella, 1953.

Horowitz, Daniel L. *The Italian Labor Movement.* Cambridge: Harvard University Press, 1963.

Kandel, I. L. *The Reform of Secondary Education in France.* New York: Teachers College, Columbia University, 1924.

LaPalombara, Joseph. *Interest Groups in Italian Politics.* Princeton: Princeton University Press, 1964.

Lefranc, Georges. *Le Syndicalisme en France.* ("Que Sais-je?" No. 585) Paris: Presses Universitaires de France, 1959.

Leites, Nathan. *On the Game of Politics in France.* Stanford: Stanford University Press, 1959.

Lorwin, Val R. *The French Labor Movement.* Cambridge: Harvard University Press, 1954.

Louis, Paul. *Histoire du Mouvement Syndical en France 1789–1910.* 2d ed. Paris: Alcan, 1911.

Maitron, Jean. *Le Syndicalisme Révolutionnaire: Paul Delesalle.* Paris: Editions Ouvrières, 1952.

Meynaud, Jean. *Les Groupes de Pression en France.* Paris: Colin, 1958.

————. *Nouvelles Etudes sur les Groupes de Pression en France.* ("Cahiers de la Fondation Nationale des Sciences Politiques," No. 118) Paris: Colin, 1962.

Miles, Donald W. *Recent Reforms in French Secondary Education.* New York: Teachers College, Columbia University, 1953.

Montreuil, Jean. *Histoire du Mouvement Ouvrier en France: Des Origines à Nos Jours.* Paris: Montaigne, 1946.

Naville, Pierre (ed.) *Ecole et Société.* Paris: Rivière, 1959.

Redmond, Sister M. Justine. *Laicism in the Schools of France.* Washington: Catholic University of America, 1932.

Shryock, Richard H. (ed.). *The Status of University Teachers.* Ghent: International Association of University Professors and Lecturers, 1961.

Siegfried, André, Edouard Bonnefous, and J. B. Duroselle (eds.). *L'Année Politique.* Paris: Presses Universitaires de France, 1944–59.

Tiano, André. *Les Traitements des Fonctionnaires et Leur Détermination, 1930–1957.* Paris: Génin, 1957.

Truman, David B. *The Governmental Process.* New York: Knopf, 1951.

Williams, Philip M. *Politics in Post-War France.* 2d ed. London: Longmans, Green, 1958.

Williams, Philip M., and Martin Harrison. *De Gaulle's Republic.* London: Longmans, Green, 1960.

Zeigler, Harmon. *Interest Groups in American Society.* Englewood Cliffs: Prentice-Hall, 1964.

ARTICLES

Almond, Gabriel A. "Comparative Political Systems," *Journal of Politics,* Vol. XVIII (August, 1956), 391–409.

————. "A Comparative Study of Interest Groups and the Political Process," *American Political Science Review,* Vol. LII (March, 1958), 270–82.

Bianconi, André. "Condition de l'Instituteur: Du Maître d'Autrefois à l'Enseignant d'Aujourd'hui," *L'Instituteur,* No. 22 (February, 1960), pp. 5–6.

————. "Les Instituteurs," *Revue Française de Science Politique,* Vol. IX (December, 1959), 935–50.

Blaisdell, Donald C. (ed.). "Unofficial Government: Pressure Groups and Lobbies," *The Annals of the American Academy of Political and Social Science,* Vol. CCCXIX (September, 1958).

Bouscaren, Anthony T. "The MRP in French Governments, 1948–1951," *Journal of Politics,* Vol. XIV (February, 1952), 104–31.

Brown, Bernard E. "Alcohol and Politics in France," *American Political Science Review,* Vol. LI (December, 1957), 976–94.

————. "The Army and Politics in France," *Journal of Politics*, Vol. XXIII (May, 1961), 262–78.

————. "Pressure Politics in the Fifth Republic," *Journal of Politics*, Vol. XXV (August, 1963), 509–25.

————. "Religious Schools and Politics in France," *Midwest Journal of Political Science*, Vol. II (May, 1958), 160–78.

Chabaut, Roger. "Situation du Syndicalisme Enseignant," *Esprit* (January, 1952), pp. 137–44.

Coutrot, Aline. "La Loi Scolaire de Décembre 1959," *Revue Française de Science Politique*, Vol. XIII (June, 1963).

Diamant, Alfred. "The French Administrative System—The Republic Passes but the Administration Remains," in *Toward the Comparative Study of Public Administration*, ed. William J. Siffin (Bloomington: Indiana University Press, 1959), 182–209.

Dowling, R. E. "Pressure Group Theory: Its Methodological Range," *American Political Science Review*, Vol. LIV (December, 1960), 944–54.

Dreyfus, F.-G. "Un Groupe de Pression en Action," *Revue Française de Science Politique*, Vol. XV (April, 1965), 213–50.

Ehrmann, Henry W. "French Bureaucracy and Organized Interests," *Administrative Science Quarterly*, Vol. V (March, 1961), 534–55.

Hagan, Charles B. "The Group in Political Science," in *Approaches to the Study of Politics*, ed. Roland Young (Evanston: Northwestern University Press, 1957), 38–51.

LaPalombara, Joseph. "The Political Role of Organized Labor in Western Europe," *Journal of Politics*, Vol. XVII (February, 1955), 59–81.

————. "The Utility and Limitations of Interest Group Theory in Non-American Field Situations," *Journal of Politics*, Vol. XXII (February, 1960), 29–49.

Mackenzie, W. J. M. "Pressure Groups: The 'Conceptual Framework,'" *Political Studies*, Vol. III (October, 1955), 247–55.

Meynaud, Jean. "Les Groupes de Pression sous la Ve Republique," *Revue Française de Science Politique*, Vol. XII (September, 1962), 672–97.

Odegard, Peter H. "A Group Basis of Politics: A New Name for an Ancient Myth," *Western Political Quarterly*, Vol. XI (September, 1958), 689–702.

Pennock, J. Roland, "'Responsible Government,' Separated Powers, and Special Interests: Agricultural Subsidies in Britain and America," *American Political Science Review*, Vol. LVI (September, 1962), 621–33.

Rothman, Stanley. "Systematic Political Theory: Observations on the Group Approach," *American Political Science Review*, Vol. LIV (March, 1960), 15–33.

Wright, Gordon. "Catholics and Peasantry in France," *Political Science Quarterly*, Vol. LXVIII (December, 1953), 526–51.

UNION PUBLICATIONS

Centres d'Apprentissage, FEN-CGT. *Le Travailleur de l'Enseignement Technique.*

Fédération de l'Education Nationale. *L'Ecole Emancipée.* Published at Avignon by the revolutionary syndicalist tendency.

Fédération de l'Education Nationale. *L'Enseignement Public.* Monthly bulletin.

Syndicat National de l'Education Nationale [CFTC]. *Syndicalisme Universitaire.*

Syndicat National de l'Enseignement Secondaire. *L'Université Syndicaliste.* Bimonthly bulletin.

Syndicat National de l'Enseignement Secondaire. *Vade Mécum: Textes Généraux Intéressant Toutes les Catégories du Personnel du Second Degré.* 1er Fascicule. Paris, 1959.

Syndicat National de l'Enseignement Supérieur. *Bulletin du Syndicat National de l'Enseignement Supérieur.*

Syndicat National des Agents de l'Education Nationale. *La Tribune des Agents de l'Education Nationale.*

Syndicat National des Agents des Etablissements de l'Education Nationale [FEN-CGT]. *L'Agent des Lycées et des Etablissements de l'Education Nationale.*

Syndicat National des Chercheurs Scientifiques. *La Vie de la Recherche Scientifique.*

Syndicat National des Instituteurs. *L'Ecole Libératrice.* Weekly bulletin.

Newspapers consulted included primarily *Le Monde,* but also *Combat, L'Express, France-Observateur, L'Observateur d'Aujourd'hui, Le Populaire de Paris,* and *Tribune du Peuple.* Interviews with public and union officials were also utilized.

Index